The Scalpers Playbook

Precision Trading Systems for Fast, Consistent Market Profits

Deepanshu Suman

2025 — First Edition

Copyright

Title: The Scalpers Playbook
Author: Deepanshu Suman

First Edition
ISBN: 978-93-5602-158-7

Disclaimer: This book is intended for educational and informational purposes only. Trading financial markets, including scalping, involves risk of financial loss. The strategies, examples, and frameworks presented are not guarantees of performance and do not constitute financial, investment, tax, or trading advice. Readers should perform their own due diligence and, where appropriate, consult qualified financial professionals before making investment decisions.

The author and publisher assume no responsibility for any loss incurred as a result of applying techniques, strategies, or information contained in this book. Past performance does not guarantee future results. The reader is solely responsible for their own trading and investment decisions.

Dedication

To the traders who show up every day.
To those who keep studying the charts long after others have gone to sleep.
To the ones who are not afraid to lose, not afraid to learn, and not afraid to begin again.
This book is for the relentless — the disciplined minds who choose precision over impulse, patience over noise, and mastery over mediocrity.
May your edge sharpen. May your confidence grow. May your market decisions be clear and profitable.

Trade well. Trade wisely. Trade with purpose.

Acknowledgments

Writing this book has been a journey built on thousands of charts, countless tests, and many lessons from the markets. I am deeply grateful to the people who stood behind me throughout this process.

To the traders and analysts who generously shared their insights, questions, mistakes, and victories — your curiosity and persistence shaped the clarity of this work.

To my friends and family, who supported me with patience, encouragement, and understanding through late nights and early mornings — your belief made this possible.

To the global trading community, the mentors I learned from, and the peers who challenged my thinking — thank you for pushing the boundaries of what scalping can be.

A special acknowledgment to every trader who failed, stood up again, and chose to keep learning. Your resilience inspires me.

Finally, to the markets themselves — the greatest teacher of discipline, humility, and continuous improvement. Every candle, every loss, every breakthrough contributed to this book.

Thank you. May this work help you trade with clarity, confidence, and mastery.

Preface

Scalping is one of the most demanding, misunderstood, and rewarding styles of trading. It requires a blend of speed and patience, clarity and discipline, confidence and humility. Many traders avoid it because it seems too fast, too stressful, or too technical. Yet, those who learn it correctly often discover that it offers one of the most reliable edges in the market.

This book exists because I have seen both sides of that journey. I have watched traders struggle for months with indicators, news, and opinions — only to find consistency when they learned to read price directly. I have also seen traders fail not because they lacked intelligence, but because they lacked structure, risk control, and emotional resilience.

The Scalpers Playbook is written to provide exactly that structure. It is not a collection of tricks. It is a complete system:

- A way of thinking about markets
- A clear method for entering and exiting trades
- A disciplined approach to risk
- A mindset that sustains performance over time

The chapters that follow combine practical trading experience, market theory, and real-world execution. They are designed to give you clarity — not confusion — regardless of whether you are new to trading or have been in the markets for years.

You will find strategies for the 1-minute and 5-minute chart, frameworks for volatile sessions, and playbooks for Forex, Indices, Crypto, and Gold. But beyond techniques, you will find something more important: how to stay calm, focused, and consistent.

Scalping rewards those who treat it as a craft. It punishes those who chase outcomes without process. If you approach this book with curiosity, patience, and an open mind, I believe it will transform the way you see the markets — and yourself.

I invite you to read slowly, experiment carefully, and trade responsibly. Mastery comes not from memorizing a system, but from living it.

May your edge sharpen, and may your confidence grow.

Contents

Part I

Foundations Of Scalping

Chapter 1

What Is Scalping? The True Essence of Fast Trading

Scalping is the practice of capturing small price movements in highly liquid markets through fast, precise execution. It does not depend on large trends or long waiting periods. Instead, it focuses on the continuous flow of orders, volatility, and micro-imbalances that appear throughout the trading day.

In modern electronic markets, tens of thousands of orders are placed, cancelled, filled, and repriced every second. Scalpers learn to read this rhythm. When price moves even slightly away from balance, opportunity appears. When it returns, profit is taken.

Scalping differs from day trading, swing trading, and investing. While others wait for larger market moves, scalpers exploit tiny edges repeatedly. High liquidity, tight spreads, and clear price discovery make this style possible.

Because each edge is small, risk control, execution quality, and cost awareness matter. Spreads, commissions, market makers, and brokers all influence results. Yet when these elements are understood, scalping becomes one of the purest expressions of price behavior: fast, focused, and highly disciplined.

This chapter provides a complete overview of how scalping fits within the market ecosystem, why it thrives where liquidity is deepest, and how consistent micro-profits form a powerful trading approach.

1.1 Real Definition of Scalping in Electronic Markets

Scalping is often described casually as "fast trading on a small timeframe." Such a description is incomplete. It focuses on speed, but ignores structure, logic, and the actual mechanics of the market. To understand scalping correctly, we must look beneath the price chart and into how modern electronic markets function.

Scalping is not primarily about prediction. It is about *price discovery.* Markets are constantly adjusting to new information, new orders, and temporary imbalances. Every second, bids and offers appear, cancel, shift, and fill. Scalping is the art of exploiting these micro-movements — systematic, repeatable, and grounded in the behavior of supply and demand.

Price Discovery, Not Forecasting

Long-term traders ask: *Where will price be tomorrow?* Swing traders ask: *Where will price be this week?* Scalpers ask a different question entirely:

> **Where is price slightly misaligned *right now*, and how will it rebalance?**

This question reflects the true essence of scalping:

- price is never perfectly efficient
- imbalance creates movement
- small movements are enough when repeated

Scalping is the systematic extraction of profit from these small rebalancing events.

A Precise Working Definition

A practical and accurate definition of scalping in electronic markets is:

> **Scalping is the disciplined exploitation of micro-price inefficiencies during continuous order flow and liquidity rebalancing.**

This definition contains five critical components:

1. **Disciplined:** scalping is rule-based, not random.
2. **Exploitation:** opportunity exists when price deviates from equilibrium.
3. **Micro-price:** edges are small, but frequent.
4. **Continuous order flow:** markets never stop adjusting.

5. **Liquidity rebalancing:** price seeks balance, then overshoots, then returns.

Each of these layers contributes to a professional scalper's edge.

Why Scalping Exists

Scalping exists because markets are complex, adaptive, and emotional. There is no perfect equilibrium. Buyers and sellers constantly react to each other. Algorithms compete. Institutional orders create pressure. Retail flow follows too slowly, or too emotionally.

This perpetual imbalance creates opportunity.

When too many orders hit the bid, price drops rapidly. When buyers aggressively lift the offer, price jumps. When both sides pause, price compresses into a narrow range.

These patterns are visible on every timeframe, but they are most abundant on the smallest ones.

Scalpers do not require big moves to make money. They require *micro-edges repeated with discipline.*

Scalping Is Not Gambling

At first glance, scalping may look like gambling. Positions open and close quickly. Losses and wins are small. The trader is active.

Yet the difference between gambling and scalping is simple:

Scalping has positive expectancy.

A positive expectancy system means:

$$(\text{Probability of Win} \times \text{Average Win}) > (\text{Probability of Loss} \times \text{Average Loss}) \tag{1.1}$$

Even a small statistical edge — for example, a win-rate of 55% with a 1:1 risk/reward — can generate exceptional long-term results when repeated thousands of times.

Gambling depends on luck. Scalping depends on:

- structure,
- statistics,
- execution,
- and discipline.

The edge is mathematical, not emotional.

Market Microstructure: The Invisible Layer Beneath the Chart

Most traders see only candles. Price goes up, price goes down.

Scalpers see something else:

- order books,
- bid/ask pressure,
- limit and market orders,
- iceberg activity,
- liquidity pools,
- spread widening and tightening.

The price chart is merely the surface. Beneath it is a constant negotiation between buyers and sellers.

Electronic markets operate like a conversation:

> Every tick is a sentence. Every candle is a paragraph. Every trend is a story.

Scalping listens to this story in real time.

Scalping Is Fast, But Not Reckless

Speed matters because the opportunity window is short. But speed alone is not an edge. Accuracy is the edge.

A professional scalper does not click randomly. A professional scalper observes:

- liquidity appearing,
- liquidity disappearing,
- trapped traders,
- imbalance footprints,
- exhaustion at extremes.

Execution is fast because the decision was made before price arrived. Speed follows analysis, not the other way around.

Why Scalping Works: Liquidity and Rebalancing

Modern electronic markets are liquidity machines. They continuously seek balance.

When balance is lost:

- price moves,
- traders react,
- algorithms follow,
- the spread adjusts.

This movement is often small.

A scalper does not need 100 points. A scalper may only need 5 points, or 10 pips, or a tiny fractional move.

But these small moves happen:

- dozens of times per session,
- hundreds of times per week,
- thousands of times per year.

This frequency is the foundation of the scalper's business model.

Scalping Is the Purest Expression of Price Behavior

Other forms of trading introduce narrative:

- fundamental analysis,
- macroeconomics,
- earnings forecasts,
- sentiment multiples.

Scalping removes narrative.

It observes:

- bid,
- ask,
- volume,
- imbalance,
- reaction.

At this level, price reveals its true nature:

> **Price is simply the negotiation between supply and demand.**

Scalping is not noise. It is *clarity at high resolution.* It is the closest interaction a trader can have with the market.

Summary

The real definition of scalping in electronic markets can be summarized as:

> **Scalping is a structured method of extracting small, consistent profits from temporary price inefficiencies created during continuous order flow.**

It is built on:

- micro-edges,
- high liquidity,
- fast execution,
- tight risk,
- high frequency,
- emotional neutrality.

Scalping is not chaotic. It is systematic. It is not gambling. It is statistical.

It is the purest expression of price behavior available to the modern trader.

1.2 Scalping vs. Day Trading vs. Swing Trading vs. Investing

Trading styles exist on a spectrum defined by time, intention, risk, and psychological needs. From the fastest form of participation — scalping — to the slowest — long-term investing — each approach offers unique strengths and weaknesses. Understanding these differences allows a trader to choose the style that aligns with their personality and financial goals.

Time Horizon: The Core Distinction

The primary difference between the four approaches is the amount of time a position is held.

Style	Typical Holding Time	Objective
Scalping	Seconds to minutes	Micro-movements, fast execution
Day Trading	Minutes to hours	Intraday trends and momentum
Swing Trading	Days to weeks	Multi-day price swings
Investing	Months to years	Long-term value and growth

Time is not merely duration — it is philosophy. Each style sees the market through a different lens.

What Each Style Attempts to Capture

Scalping Scalpers exploit small, temporary inefficiencies in price. They do not need the market to trend strongly. Instead, they take advantage of micro-imbalances caused by order flow, liquidity, and volatility.

> Scalpers trade the *reaction*, not the prediction.

Day Trading Day traders attempt to capture intraday swings. They rely on patterns, momentum, news, and market reactions over a few hours. Positions are almost always closed by the end of the session.

Swing Trading Swing traders look for larger structural moves. They tolerate small fluctuations in exchange for bigger targets. Trend continuation, pullbacks, and breakouts are common tools.

Investing Investors care about value, growth, and fundamentals. They focus on businesses, not candles. The chart is secondary to earnings, innovation, and competitive advantage.

Information Used by Each Approach

Each style relies on a different type of information.

Style	Primary Information
Scalping	Order flow, liquidity, microstructure
Day Trading	Intraday trends, volatility, catalysts
Swing Trading	Market structure, macro themes
Investing	Fundamentals, valuation, long-term outlook

Scalping is closest to raw price behavior. Investing is furthest.

Risk and Position Structure

Risk is structured differently for each style:

Style	Position Size	Stop Size
Scalping	Larger	Very tight
Day Trading	Moderate	Moderate
Swing Trading	Small	Larger
Investing	Varies	Often undefined

Scalpers rely on extremely tight risk because holding time is short and volatility is high. Investors can hold through noise because their thesis is long-term.

Psychological Requirements

Each style demands a different mindset.

Scalping Scalpers need emotional neutrality. They make many decisions quickly, with no attachment to outcomes. Hesitation is costly, but overconfidence is fatal. Speed arises from clarity, not adrenaline.

Day Trading Day traders require patience. They must wait for clear setups, manage intraday swings, and avoid overtrading.

Swing Trading Swing traders need tolerance for short-term discomfort. Positions often move against them before moving in their favor.

Investing Investors need conviction. They must ignore daily noise and stay focused on long-term value.

Frequency of Trades

Style	Number of Trades
Scalping	Many per day
Day Trading	Few per day
Swing Trading	Few per week
Investing	Few per year

A scalper requires more opportunities because each edge is small. An investor requires far fewer because each idea is large.

Why These Differences Matter

Many traders fail not because they lack skill, but because they choose the wrong style. An impatient person who tries swing trading will suffer. A calm and deliberate thinker who attempts scalping may feel overwhelmed.

> Success begins with alignment: your temperament must match your trading style.

Scalping rewards discipline and fast feedback loops. Investing rewards patience and long-term thinking. Neither is superior — each is a tool for a different job.

The Unique Beauty of Scalping

Scalping is the closest interaction a trader can have with price. There are no narratives, no predictions, no stories. Only:

- bid and ask,
- liquidity and imbalance,
- execution and discipline.

Other styles require waiting. Scalping requires *presence.* It offers clarity at the highest resolution.

Summary Comparison Table

Dimension	Scalping	Day Trading	Swing Trading	Investing
Holding Time	Seconds–minutes	Minutes–hours	Days–weeks	Months–years
Focus	Micro-edge	Intraday trend	Multi-day trend	Fundamentals
Frequency	High	Medium	Low	Very low
Risk Size	Very small	Moderate	Large	Variable
Reward Size	Small	Medium	Large	Very large
Psychology	Speed, discipline	Patience, timing	Conviction, tolerance	Belief, time
Goal	Consistent edges	Daily opportunity	Larger swings	Long-term wealth

In short:

> Scalping is not about predicting the future. It is about understanding price behavior now.

Where others see noise, scalpers see opportunity. Where others wait, scalpers act. It is a style built on structure, risk control, and precision.

1.3 Why Scalping Thrives in High-Liquidity Environments

Scalping is a trading style that depends on the availability of rapid execution, tight spreads, and continuous price discovery. These conditions are most reliably found in high-liquidity environments. Liquidity is the oxygen of scalping: without it, the edge suffocates.

Understanding Liquidity

Liquidity refers to how easily an asset can be bought or sold without significantly affecting its price. A market is considered liquid when:

- there are many active buyers and sellers,
- the bid-ask spread is tight,
- large orders can be absorbed quickly,
- price adjusts smoothly to new information.

High-liquidity environments allow scalpers to enter and exit positions efficiently, often in a fraction of a second.

Price Movement and Liquidity

In liquid markets, price changes occur through constant negotiation between buyers and sellers. When demand temporarily overwhelms supply, price rises. When supply overwhelms demand, price falls. These adjustments happen continuously, and often very rapidly.

Scalpers thrive in the space between these micro-adjustments.

> Liquidity creates small but frequent movements. Scalping converts those movements into profit.

Tight Spreads Are Critical

A spread is the difference between the bid (buy price) and the ask (sell price). Tight spreads are a hallmark of liquid markets. They are essential to scalping because:

- every trade begins at a small cost (the spread),
- wide spreads destroy profitability,
- tight spreads allow small targets to make sense.

For example, if the spread is 0.5 points and a scalper aims for 3 points, the spread consumes only a small portion of the trade. In a wide-spread environment, this same target may be impossible.

Fast Order Execution

In high-liquidity environments, orders are filled quickly. This matters because scalping requires:

- fast entries,
- fast exits,
- minimal slippage.

Slippage — the difference between expected and actual fill price — can erode returns. Liquidity reduces slippage and preserves the scalper's edge.

Abundant Opportunity

Highly liquid markets produce constant movement due to:

- institutional flow,
- algorithmic trading,
- retail participation,
- hedging and arbitrage.

Even when the market appears quiet, small imbalances form and resolve. Each rebalancing creates a potential opportunity. A scalper may take dozens of trades in a session, each based on these tiny movements.

> The more liquidity a market has, the more frequently small edges appear.

Examples of High-Liquidity Markets

Scalpers often prefer assets such as:

- Foreign exchange (EURUSD, GBPUSD, USDJPY)
- Index futures (NASDAQ, S&P 500, DAX)
- Commodities with global flow (Gold/XAUUSD)
- Popular cryptocurrencies (BTC, ETH) at peak volume

These instruments provide:

- constant order flow,
- tight spreads,
- deep liquidity pools,
- fast price discovery.

Not all assets are equally suitable. Thinly traded markets create wide spreads, erratic movement, and poor execution.

Institutional Participation

High-liquidity markets attract market makers, hedge funds, and algorithmic systems. These participants provide volume and stabilize the order book.

For scalpers, this is beneficial because:

- the market moves cleanly,
- price responds predictably,
- gaps and illiquidity are rare,
- volatility is controlled.

Ironically, the presence of institutions does not eliminate opportunity — it creates it. When large players rebalance or shift liquidity, small dislocations appear. A skilled scalper can detect and profit from these moments.

Why Low-Liquidity Markets Are Dangerous for Scalpers

In contrast, low-liquidity markets often exhibit:

- wide spreads,
- sudden jumps,
- inconsistent fills,
- poor order depth.

One large order can move price disproportionately. Scalpers cannot rely on consistency in such environments.

> High-liquidity markets offer stability and frequency. Low-liquidity markets offer chaos and uncertainty.

Conclusion

Scalping thrives in high-liquidity environments because they offer:

- tight spreads,
- rapid execution,
- continuous movement,

- stable price discovery,
- abundant micro-imbalances.

These conditions allow scalpers to operate efficiently, repeat small edges, and maintain consistent risk-control.

Ultimately, liquidity is not merely a convenience — it is the foundation of the scalper's craft.

> Without liquidity, there is no scalping. With liquidity, there is opportunity on every candle.

1.4 The "Micro-Edge" Advantage: Exploiting Tiny Movements Consistently

Scalping is built on a simple yet powerful premise: *small edges repeated frequently can create remarkable results.* This principle is known as the micro-edge advantage. It is not based on prediction, opinion, or narrative. It is based on statistical expectancy and disciplined execution.

Small Edges Are Easier to Find Than Big Ones

Large market moves are rare. They require major shifts in sentiment, macro conditions, or institutional flow.

Small movements, however, happen constantly.

- Price tests a level and snaps back.
- Liquidity is consumed and then replaced.
- A trapped participant exits aggressively.
- Market makers create a temporary imbalance.

These are micro-movements.

They appear in every session, every instrument, and every timeframe. Scalping converts these small movements into profit using strict rules.

> The market does not need to go far. It only needs to go slightly in your favor.

Expectancy: The Mathematics Behind the Edge

The foundation of the micro-edge advantage is expectancy. A trading system is profitable when:

$$E = (P_{win} \times Avg_{win}) - (P_{loss} \times Avg_{loss}) > 0 \tag{1.2}$$

Where:

- P_{win} = probability of winning
- Avg_{win} = size of average win
- P_{loss} = probability of losing
- Avg_{loss} = size of average loss

A scalper does not need:

- a large win size
- a high win rate

Even a small edge — for example:

$$P_{win} = 55\%, \quad R : R = 1 : 1$$

produces long-term profitability when repeated across hundreds of trades.

Micro-Edges Are More Stable Than Macro Predictions

Predicting multi-day or multi-week trends is difficult because the market is influenced by many variables:

- geopolitical events,
- central bank decisions,
- earnings releases,
- macroeconomic data,
- sentiment cycles.

Micro-edges, however, arise from local, structural behaviors:

- order flow,
- liquidity distribution,

- short-term imbalance,
- trapped traders,
- stop hunts.

These behaviors are *present in every session.* They do not require prediction of the future. They only require observation of what is happening *right now.*

> It is easier to observe current imbalance than forecast future direction.

Fast Feedback Loops Accelerate Learning

Scalping provides immediate feedback. This makes growth faster than most trading styles.

A swing trader may take:

- 10 trades per month,
- learn slowly,
- endure long uncertainty.

A scalper may take:

- 10 trades per hour,
- learn rapidly,
- reduce emotional burden.

The loop is short:

$$Observe \rightarrow Execute \rightarrow Review \rightarrow Improve$$

This feedback cycle is a core advantage of the micro-edge style.

Precision Risk Management

Micro-movement trading only works with strict risk control. A scalper must cut losses quickly, often in seconds. This is not a weakness — it is a design feature.

> Small losses are part of the system. Large losses destroy the system.

Typical scalping risk:

- very tight stops,
- high accuracy entries,
- small position exposure,
- rapid exits when wrong.

The math works because:

- losses are capped,
- wins are frequent,
- time in the market is small.

Frequency and Compounding

The power of small edges is compounded through repetition.
If a scalper makes:

$$+0.30\% \text{ per trade}$$

and executes:

$$20 \text{ trades per day}$$

the math becomes powerful even with modest capital.

$$Growth \approx (1 + 0.003)^{20\times 20} - 1 \tag{1.3}$$

The result is exponential. Consistency matters more than size.

Do not chase large wins. Chase small edges, repeated often.

Micro-Edges Are Emotionally Easier

Large trades create large emotional swings.
Swing traders and investors face:

- overnight gaps,
- news shocks,
- long uncertainty,

- fear of missing out,
- second-guessing.

Scalpers avoid these burdens.

Positions are small and short-lived. Emotion does not accumulate. Stress is reduced.

Where Micro-Edges Come From

Micro-edges emerge from structural elements:

- liquidity pockets,
- stop hunts,
- mean reversion,
- breakout traps,
- failed auctions,
- VWAP reversions,
- institutional inventory management.

These structures generate:

- high-probability setups,
- short holding time,
- low cost,
- repeatability.

  Scalpers do not need perfect accuracy. They only need a consistent edge.

Conclusion

The micro-edge advantage is built on five principles:

1. Small price movements happen more often than big ones.
2. Micro-imbalances are easier to observe than macro trends.
3. Tight risk makes negative outcomes small.
4. Frequency and discipline convert tiny edges into large results.

5. Fast feedback accelerates learning and mastery.

In a high-liquidity market, micro-edges appear constantly. A scalper's role is to detect these imbalances, execute with precision, and repeat the edge without emotional attachment.

> Scalping is not about prediction. It is about capturing the market's constant attempt to rebalance.

1.5 How Spreads, Commissions, Market Makers, and Brokers Affect Profitability

Scalping profits are small in size but high in frequency. This makes trading costs extremely important. Even a strong strategy can fail if execution costs are not understood. Spreads, commissions, market maker behavior, and broker policies all determine whether the edge is positive or negative.

In this section we examine how these elements influence scalping outcomes, and how a trader can adapt to preserve profitability.

Understanding the Spread

The spread is the difference between the bid (buying price) and the ask (selling price). Every trade begins at a cost equal to the spread. A scalper must overcome this cost before profit can be realized.

$$\text{Spread Cost} = \text{Ask Price} - \text{Bid Price}$$

In tight markets (e.g. EURUSD, NASDAQ futures):

- spreads are small,
- trades begin close to breakeven,
- micro-targets are viable.

In wide-spread markets:

- cost per trade increases,
- required targets become larger,
- profitability declines.

> The spread is the enemy of the scalper. Tight spreads are non-negotiable.

Commissions and Fees

Most brokers charge a cost per trade. In scalping, this cost accumulates quickly because of trade frequency.

Total cost is a combination of:

- spread,
- commissions,
- platform fees,
- exchange fees,
- overnight charges (if applicable).

The formula for a single trade cost becomes:

$$\text{Total Cost} = \text{Spread} + \text{Commission}$$

For frequent trading, even a difference of a few cents per trade can determine whether the strategy is profitable.

Market Makers: The Invisible Counterparty

Market makers provide liquidity by standing ready to buy or sell. They quote both sides of the market, profiting from the spread. Their role is crucial to scalping because:

- they tighten spreads,
- they stabilize price movements,
- they create continuous price flow.

However, market makers are not charitable participants. They protect their interests aggressively.

When they detect:

- one-sided pressure,
- trapped traders,
- stop clusters,

they may widen spreads or move price rapidly.

A scalper must understand that market makers are not adversaries, but they are also not neutral.

> Market makers are not your enemy. They are the environment.

Broker Models and Execution Quality

Brokers can operate under different models:

- ECN (Electronic Communication Network)
- STP (Straight Through Processing)
- Market Maker (Dealing Desk)

Each model influences scalping differently.

ECN Brokers

- direct access to market liquidity,
- tight spreads,
- explicit commissions.

Preferred for scalping because trades fill efficiently.

STP Brokers

- send orders to external liquidity providers,
- moderate spreads,
- variable execution quality.

Market Maker Brokers

- internalize flow,
- may widen spreads during volatility,
- execution can lag.

Not all market maker brokers are bad, but scalpers must test execution.

Slippage: The Hidden Cost

Slippage occurs when the price you receive is different from the price you expected. It is common during:

- news events,
- thin liquidity,
- fast markets.

For scalpers, even small slippage can be fatal. Example:

$$\text{Expect: } +4 \text{ points}, \qquad \text{Receive: } +2 \text{ points}$$

Half the profit disappeared.
Slippage increases during:

- large position size,
- delayed execution,
- wide spreads.

Why Execution Speed Matters

Scalping requires fast entries and exits. Execution delay reduces edge. Milliseconds matter.

Sources of delay:

- platform latency,
- internet latency,
- broker routing time,
- exchange matching speed.

Professional scalpers often use:

- VPS near the exchange,
- direct connection to liquidity pools,
- optimized hardware,
- low-latency platforms.

How Costs Destroy a Weak Strategy

A system may appear profitable before costs. After accounting for spreads and commissions, the edge disappears.

$$Gross\ Profit - Costs = Net\ Profit$$

Even if each trade wins:

$$\text{Small win} - \text{Spread} - \text{Commission} = \text{Loss} \tag{1.4}$$

This is why cost-awareness is a core skill.

In scalping, a strategy is only profitable after costs.

How Costs Strengthen a Good Strategy

A strong scalping system can absorb costs because:

- entries are precise,
- stops are tight,
- targets are realistic,
- frequency is controlled.

Consistency matters more than win-size.

Practical Guidelines for Scalping Costs

To preserve profitability, a scalper should:

1. Choose instruments with tight spreads.
2. Use brokers with transparent cost structure.
3. Avoid thin liquidity periods.
4. Reduce size during volatile news.
5. Measure slippage and execution quality.

A good rule:

> If spread and commissions are larger than your average target, do not scalp that instrument.

Conclusion

Spreads, commissions, market makers, and broker execution collectively determine whether a scalper survives or fails. They influence:

- cost per trade,
- fill quality,
- risk management,
- net profitability.

High-liquidity instruments with tight spreads and fast execution are ideal. Low-liquidity, wide-spread, or slow-execution environments destroy edge.

> Scalping is a game of small edges. Costs must be minimized, or the edge disappears.

1.6 Why Scalping Is the Purest Form of Price Behavior

Scalping removes story, prediction, and interpretation. It focuses on the only thing that truly moves the market: the interaction between buyers and sellers. For this reason, many professionals describe scalping as the purest expression of price behavior. It observes the market at its most fundamental level: *price reacting to supply and demand in real time.*

Price Is Created by Supply and Demand

Price is not created by indicators, forecasts, or opinions. Indicators *display* price. Forecasts *speculate* about price. But price itself is created by only two forces:

- demand (buying pressure)
- supply (selling pressure)

When demand exceeds supply, price rises. When supply exceeds demand, price falls. When both forces balance, price consolidates.

Scalping watches this negotiation directly.

> Every tick is proof of negotiation between buyers and sellers.

Scalping Removes Narrative

Many traders attach stories to the market:

- macroeconomic trends
- central bank policies
- earnings expectations
- sentiment or news flow

These stories can influence price, but scalping does not depend on them. It does not require prediction or opinion.

Instead, scalping asks a simpler question:

> "What is price doing right now?"

The answer is visible in:

- order flow
- liquidity shifts

- micro-trends
- breaks of structure

No story is needed. Only observation.

Scalping Trades Reaction, Not Forecast

Other styles of trading attempt to forecast future movement:

- trend continuation
- mean reversion
- breakout follow-through

Forecasting introduces uncertainty.
Scalping applies a different philosophy:

> Scalpers do not predict. Scalpers react.

When price reaches imbalance, reacts to liquidity, or returns to equilibrium, the scalper takes action. There is no long-term thesis. Only short-term behavior.

Short Holding Time Reduces Noise

The longer a trade is open, the more external variables invade:

- news releases
- sentiment shifts
- overnight risk
- macro events

Swing traders and investors must tolerate noise.
Scalpers avoid it.
Positions are held for seconds or minutes, which means:

- fewer unknowns,
- fewer emotional pressures,
- fewer external influences.

> Short timeframes filter out noise and expose pure price behavior.

Price Action Is the Market's Native Language

Indicators are translations of price:

- moving averages smooth price,
- RSI measures momentum,
- MACD measures trend and velocity.

All translations introduce delay.

Price action is immediate. It is the closest representation of the market's intentions.

Scalping observes:

- wicks,
- absorption,
- break of structure,
- liquidity sweeps,
- exhaustion.

These are not signals from mathematics. They are the market expressing itself.

Microstructure Becomes Visible

Market mechanisms are often invisible on higher timeframes. On the 1-minute chart, they are obvious:

- stop hunts,
- trapped traders,
- market maker inventory,
- spread manipulation,
- aggressive order flow.

Scalping reveals how:

- bids are hit,
- offers are lifted,
- liquidity is consumed,
- price searches for balance.

This is the true behavior of the market. Higher timeframes hide it under smooth lines.

Price Is Always Seeking Balance

Every second, price moves toward balance. When it overshoots, it returns. This cycle is continuous:

$$\text{Imbalance} \rightarrow \text{Movement} \rightarrow \text{Rebalance}$$

Scalping monetizes this natural rhythm.

> Scalping profits from the market's constant attempt to find equilibrium.

Large trends are rare. Micro-adjustments are constant. Scalpers exploit the constant, not the rare.

No Other Style Is Closer to Reality

Other styles involve:

- forecasting,
- narratives,
- opinions,
- predictions.

Scalping strips that away.
It observes:

- bid versus ask,
- buyers versus sellers,
- aggression versus absorption.

There is no abstraction. Only genuine behavior.

Conclusion

Scalping is the purest form of price behavior because it:

1. observes supply and demand directly,
2. removes stories, opinions, and bias,
3. trades reaction rather than prediction,
4. reduces noise by shortening time,

5. reads price action as native market language,
6. reveals microstructure and liquidity dynamics,
7. monetizes the constant search for balance.

> Where others see noise, scalpers see opportunity. Where others predict, scalpers observe. Where others wait, scalpers act.

Scalping does not require belief or narrative. It requires only presence, precision, and discipline.

It is trading at its most elemental level: **price reacting to pressure in real time.**

Chapter 2

The Psychology of a Scalper

Scalping is not only a technical skill. It is a mental discipline. The speed of the market forces the trader to make frequent decisions under pressure, manage risk instantly, and remain emotionally neutral at all times. Winning is often less about strategy and more about mindset.

A scalper must be able to act quickly, but without panic. They must wait patiently, but execute decisively. They must experience losses without emotional reaction, and experience wins without becoming overconfident. This balance is difficult, but it is the foundation of consistent results.

In this chapter we explore the psychological requirements of scalping: emotional control, reaction speed, impulse management, and the ability to perform under stress. We examine how cognitive overload can influence decision-making, how emotional traps such as fear, greed, and FOMO appear in fast markets, and why temperament plays such a crucial role in trading success.

Scalping rewards a stable mind. Building that stability is not optional — it is a core part of the craft. The following sections provide a practical framework for developing the mindset required to trade with clarity, confidence, and consistency.

2.1 Emotional Control, Reaction Speed, and Confidence Under Pressure

Scalping requires a unique psychological profile. The trader must make frequent decisions under uncertainty, respond instantly to changes in price, and manage risk without hesitation or emotional disturbance. This combination of emotional control, reaction speed, and confidence under pressure is essential for consistent performance.

Speed Without Panic

Speed is often misunderstood in scalping. Fast execution is necessary, but it does not mean frantic or impulsive behavior. In reality, the scalper is calm. Speed comes from clarity, not adrenaline.

> Speed is the by-product of preparation, not excitement.

A professional scalper is able to act quickly because:

- setups are known in advance,
- entry criteria are clear,
- risk is predefined,
- nothing is left to improvisation.

When the signal appears, execution is instant. There is no internal debate.

Emotional Neutrality

Every trade must be viewed as one event in a long series. The outcome of a single trade is irrelevant. What matters is the quality of the process.

Emotional neutrality allows the trader to:

- enter without fear,
- exit without regret,
- reduce size when conditions shift,
- continue trading despite short-term losses.

The scalper does not celebrate wins or dwell on losses. Emotions consume mental energy. Energy is needed for execution.

> A scalper's identity is not tied to any trade.

Reaction Speed Through Preparation

The fastest decisions are made before the trade is taken. The scalper recognizes patterns, levels, and conditions in advance. Decision-making is simplified:

1. If market condition A is present,
2. and price reaches zone B,

3. with confirmation C,
4. then enter with risk R.

No improvisation is necessary. No internal negotiation takes place.

> Hesitation is replaced by execution because the decision was made beforehand.

Confidence Under Pressure

Scalping places the trader in a high-intensity environment. Price moves quickly. Opportunities are short-lived. A scalper must act decisively or miss the trade.

Confidence arises from:

- a clear strategy,
- backtested rules,
- experience with losses,
- trust in the system,
- emotional maturity.

Confidence is not arrogance. It is the absence of doubt during execution.

Losses Do Not Create Emotional Disturbance

A scalper will experience many small losses. This is not a sign of failure, but a structural feature of the approach.

$$\text{Small Loss} + \text{Small Loss} + \text{Small Loss} + \text{Small Win} = NetProfit$$

Emotional control allows the trader to continue trading without hesitation after a losing streak. Confidence ensures that the next signal is executed with full clarity.

> Losses are data, not identity.

Physiology and Mental State

The body influences decision-making. A scalper must maintain a relaxed physical state:

- controlled breathing,
- balanced posture,
- unclenched jaw and shoulders,
- clear visual focus.

Stress constricts vision, reduces reaction speed, and increases impulsivity. Calmness expands awareness.

> A calm body produces a calm mind.

Training Emotional Control

Emotional control can be trained. Useful practices include:

- meditation,
- journaling,
- breathing exercises,
- micro-breaks between trades,
- reviewing performance without judgment.

The goal is not to eliminate emotion. The goal is to prevent emotion from influencing execution.

A Practical Operating Rule

A professional scalper follows a simple rule:

> If I feel strong emotion, I do not trade.

Emotion is a signal that clarity has been lost. During such periods, stepping away preserves capital and confidence.

Summary

Scalping requires a combination of:

1. Emotional neutrality,
2. Preparedness for fast execution,
3. Calm confidence under pressure.

Speed is not forced. It flows from intentional practice. Confidence is not loud. It is quiet, stable, and built on repetition.

> The scalper is fast not because they rush, but because they are ready.

2.2 Discipline, Patience, and Impulse Management

Scalping compresses the entire emotional spectrum of trading into short time intervals. Opportunities appear quickly, disappear quickly, and often return in slightly different forms. To navigate this environment successfully, a scalper must cultivate discipline, patience, and the ability to manage impulses with precision.

These qualities are not optional. They form the backbone of consistent execution.

Discipline: Doing What the System Requires

Discipline means following the trading plan even when the mind wants to deviate. It is the ability to act according to rules rather than feelings. A scalper must be willing to:

- enter only when criteria are met,
- exit when the stop is hit, without delay,
- pass on trades that do not match the setup,
- stop trading when the daily limit is reached.

The ritual is simple:

> Plan the trade. Trade the plan. Do nothing else.

Discipline reduces emotional randomness. It makes trading repeatable.

Patience: Waiting for the Right Setup

Scalping may seem fast, but it is built on waiting. The trader may sit for long periods with no action. This is not wasted time. Patience protects capital.

> Most minutes in the market are not suitable for trading.

Patience enables clarity:

- no chasing,
- no forcing trades,
- no reacting to noise.

When the signal arrives, it is obvious. Patience creates this certainty.

Managing Impulses

Impulses arise from emotion:

- fear of missing out (FOMO),
- excitement from a recent win,
- frustration after a loss,
- boredom during quiet markets.

Impulse trading usually appears as:

- entering too early,
- entering too late,
- taking a trade outside the system,
- increasing size impulsively,
- revenge trading.

The scalper must recognize impulses immediately.

> If the decision feels emotional, it is wrong.

The Discipline Loop

Elite scalpers follow a feedback loop:

1. Clear rules
2. Obedient execution
3. Immediate review
4. Small improvement

Each loop strengthens discipline. Over time, habits become automatic.

Creating Friction Against Impulse

The easiest way to stop an impulsive action is to introduce a moment of friction:

- stand up from the desk,
- take three slow breaths,
- drink water,
- write a quick note,
- review the checklist.

These actions interrupt reactivity. They give the brain time to return to clarity.

Impulse thrives in speed. Discipline thrives in stillness.

Rules That Protect the Scalper

Effective scalpers use simple rules that enforce discipline:

- One trade at a time.
- No adding to losers.
- Predetermined daily stop.
- Break after a loss.
- Stop after three losses.

These rules preserve emotional capital.

Patience and Selectivity

A scalper does not trade every movement. They select only clear, high-quality setups.

> Quality over quantity.

A beautiful edge appears only when:

- structure is aligned,
- liquidity is clean,
- confirmation is present.

Patience ensures that the trader acts only in these moments.

Confidence From Consistency

Confidence is not built from wins. Confidence is built from:

- consistent execution,
- disciplined risk,
- adherence to rules,
- emotional neutrality.

When a trader follows the plan, they trust themselves. When they trust themselves, confidence grows.

Summary

Scalping demands a rare combination:

1. **Discipline** to follow the plan,
2. **Patience** to wait for quality setups,
3. **Impulse control** to avoid emotional actions.

The scalper must remain still during uncertainty, calm during opportunity, and neutral during outcome.

> Patience finds the edge. Discipline executes the edge. Impulse destroys the edge.

Consistency emerges when these elements align.

2.3 Cognitive Overload: Managing Decisions at High Speed

Scalping compresses time. Information arrives rapidly, decisions must be made quickly, and consequences are immediate. This creates a unique cognitive challenge: the brain must process complex data under pressure without becoming overloaded, reactive, or chaotic.

Successful scalpers do not think faster. They *think less.* They reduce complexity by simplifying perception, rules, and execution.

Why Overload Happens

Cognitive overload occurs when the brain receives more information than it can process. In scalping, overload is common because the trader is exposed to:

- rapid price movements,
- multiple timeframes,
- indicators and signals,
- emotional reactions,
- risk and uncertainty,
- constant opportunity.

The brain attempts to interpret everything at once. This leads to:

- hesitation,
- confusion,
- impulsive action,
- missed entries,
- late exits.

The Paradox of Speed

Scalping feels fast, but the scalper must feel slow. The paradox is:

> The faster the market moves, the calmer the scalper must be.

Speed comes from:

- pattern recognition,

- preparation,
- automatic execution,
- practiced routines.

Not from forced thinking.

Reducing Cognitive Load

Professional scalpers simplify:

1. Fewer charts. Too many screens increase noise. A clean workspace increases clarity.

2. Clear setups only. A setup is either present or not. There is no debate.

3. One trade at a time. Multiple positions increase complexity, reduce focus, and increase emotional strain.

4. Predefined risk. Risk is calculated before the trade, not during.

All simplification reduces cognitive load.

The Checklist Advantage

A checklist reduces mental strain because each decision is externalized.

A typical scalping checklist:

1. Market condition: trending or ranging?
2. Level: zone of interest?
3. Confirmation: wick, volume, structure?
4. Risk: predefined stop?
5. Execution: enter or skip?

The trader no longer thinks about what to do. They simply verify conditions.

Checklists convert uncertainty into yes/no decisions.

Pattern Recognition Over Analysis

The brain is excellent at recognizing patterns. It is terrible at analyzing too many variables in real time.

Scalpers rely on:

- repeated structures,
- familiar price behaviors,
- known reactions at levels.

Patterns become internalized. When they appear, execution is automatic.

Automation of Decision Making

High performance in scalping does not come from thinking harder. It comes from turning decisions into habits.

$$\text{Signal} \rightarrow \text{Execution}$$

No hesitation. No debate.

Habits reduce cognitive load by:

- freeing mental bandwidth,
- eliminating emotional noise,
- minimizing decision fatigue.

Managing Attention

Attention is a limited resource. Scalpers learn to protect it.

Strategies include:

- removing distractions,
- muting news feeds,
- focusing on one instrument,
- taking breaks during flat markets.

Attention must be conserved for moments that matter.

> It is better to take one clear trade than five distracted ones.

Physiological Control Reduces Overload

Physiology impacts cognition. Stress narrows focus and accelerates thoughts. Calmness expands perception and slows time.

Professional scalpers use:

- steady breathing,
- relaxed posture,
- micro-pauses,
- controlled energy.

These techniques reduce cognitive load and increase reaction speed.

The Recovery Cycle

Scalping is mentally demanding. The brain fatigues quickly. Recovery is essential.

A typical recovery cycle:

1. execute trades,
2. step back,
3. reflect briefly,
4. reset mind and body,
5. return with clarity.

Professional traders use micro-breaks:

- stand up,
- walk,
- drink water,
- stretch.

Every break restores cognitive capacity.

Summary

Cognitive overload is a natural consequence of high-speed trading. The solution is not to think faster, but to think less.

Scalpers manage overload by:

1. simplifying their environment,
2. standardizing decisions,
3. using checklists and routines,
4. automating execution,
5. conserving attention,
6. maintaining physiological calm,
7. taking deliberate breaks.

Speed in scalping arises from clarity, not intensity. When the mind is quiet, execution becomes effortless.

2.4 Correcting Emotional Traps: Fear, Greed, Doubt, and FOMO

Scalping compresses emotion into short time intervals. Price moves quickly, opportunities appear suddenly, and losses can occur in seconds. Under these conditions, emotional traps are common. Fear, greed, doubt, and FOMO distort perception and lead to impulsive decisions. A scalper must learn to identify these traps and correct them before they influence execution.

Fear: The Hesitation Trap

Fear appears in two forms:

1. fear of entering a trade,
2. fear of accepting a loss.

Fear of entering causes hesitation:

- the setup is clear,
- the plan says “enter”,
- but the trader delays,
- the opportunity disappears.

Fear of loss causes avoidance:

- the trader knows the stop should be hit,
- but they hold longer,
- hoping price will reverse.

The antidote is simple:

> Fear disappears when decisions are predefined.

Entry criteria, stop-loss, and exit must be known before the trade. When the plan is clear, fear has no role.

Greed: The Expansion Trap

Greed causes traders to:

- increase size impulsively,
- hold winners too long,
- add to positions without logic,
- chase profits rather than wait for setups.

Greed is disguised as optimism:

> "Just a little more." "It will keep going." "One more trade."

This optimism destroys discipline.
The correction is structural:

- fixed position size,
- fixed targets,
- fixed daily limits.

Rules eliminate the temptation to expand.

Doubt: The Uncertainty Trap

Doubt occurs when the trader does not trust:

- the system,
- their own execution,
- the trading plan.

Doubt causes second-guessing:

- signals appear,
- but the trader hesitates,
- waiting for "confirmation",
- by the time it arrives, the edge is gone.

Doubt is not emotional — it is structural. It is corrected through experience:

1. *backtesting*,
2. *forward testing*,
3. *small real trades*,
4. *journaling results.*

Confidence is built from repetition, not positive thinking.

Certainty grows from data, not emotion.

FOMO: The Chasing Trap

Fear of missing out (FOMO) is one of the most destructive emotions. It appears when price moves rapidly:

- breakout,
- spike,
- large candle.

The trader thinks:

> "Everyone else is making money. I must not miss it."

They enter late, without structure. This is how losses occur.
The solution is discipline:

- if the setup is gone, it is gone,
- the market will provide another one,
- no trade is ever "the last opportunity."

A professional scalper knows:

> Missing a trade is harmless. Chasing a trade is dangerous.

Meta-Emotion: The Trap of Judging Yourself

After a loss, another emotion appears:

> "I should have known." "I made a mistake." "I am not good enough."

This is *meta-emotion* — emotion about emotion. It is damaging because it reduces:

- confidence,
- clarity,
- future performance.

The correction is neutrality:

> A loss is not personal. It is part of the process.

Professional traders do not judge themselves. They evaluate the trade, update the rules, and move forward.

Structural Solutions

Emotional traps are fixed by *structure*, not willpower.
Effective structural solutions include:

- predefined setups,
- fixed position sizing,
- maximum daily loss limit,
- break after losses,
- written checklists,
- trading only in valid conditions.

Structure reduces emotion.

Behavioral Solutions

Emotions are embodied. To reduce emotional activation:

- slow breathing,
- physical relaxation,
- posture adjustment,
- micro-pauses between trades.

These actions lower physiological arousal, improving clarity.

Identity Solutions

Finally, identity shapes behavior. A scalper adopts the identity of a disciplined operator:

> "My job is not to predict. My job is to execute."

Identity reduces ego involvement. Without ego, fear, greed, doubt, and FOMO disappear.

Summary

Emotional traps destroy consistency. The scalper must master:

1. **Fear** through preparation,
2. **Greed** through structure,
3. **Doubt** through experience,
4. **FOMO** through patience.

The solutions are simple:

- predefined rules,
- disciplined execution,
- emotional neutrality,
- identity as a professional.

When rules lead and emotions follow, consistency becomes inevitable.

2.5 How Temperament Shapes Scalping Success

Scalping is not suitable for every personality. It demands a specific temperament — one that blends patience with aggression, calmness with speed, and emotional detachment with precise execution. The right psychological profile accelerates progress, while the wrong temperament creates frustration, inconsistency, and burnout.

Temperament influences how a trader responds to stress, uncertainty, and loss. Understanding one's own personality becomes a central component of success.

Temperament Is More Important Than Technique

Many traders assume that a strategy determines profitability. In scalping, execution quality matters more.

> A perfect strategy in the hands of an unstable temperament fails. An average strategy in the hands of a stable temperament succeeds.

A scalper must possess qualities that support:

- rapid but controlled action,
- emotional neutrality,
- resilience under pressure,
- tolerance for small, frequent losses.

These traits are not purely intellectual — they are psychological.

Key Temperamental Traits of Successful Scalpers

1. Calm Under Pressure The market is fast. Price moves violently. News arrives unpredictably. A successful scalper remains centered.

- heart rate stable,
- breathing smooth,
- no internal panic.

Calmness preserves perception and reaction time.

2. Decisiveness Without Impulsiveness Scalping requires quick decisions, but not impulsive ones. The trader must:

- act instantly when the signal appears,
- wait patiently when nothing is present.

This balance is extremely rare.

> A scalper is both predator and monk.

3. Comfort With Losing A scalper experiences many small losses. This is a structural feature of the strategy, not a failure.

$$\text{Win rate} < \text{profitability}$$

What matters is expectation:

$$(Win \times Average\ Gain) - (Loss \times Average\ Loss) > 0$$

Temperament must allow loss without emotional disturbance. A single trade is meaningless in the context of a career.

4. Patience During Waiting Periods Most market time is not actionable. A strong temperament allows:

- waiting without boredom,
- watching without chasing,
- observing without forcing trades.

Impatience is dangerous:

> Boredom produces the worst trades.

5. Fast Recovery From Mistakes A scalper must recover quickly from:

- a losing trade,
- a missed trade,
- a late entry,
- a small error.

Resilience is essential. Dwelling on mistakes damages the next opportunity.

Recovery speed is a competitive advantage.

6. Low Ego, High Self-Awareness Ego seeks to be right. Scalping requires being correct only long enough to exit profitably.

A successful scalper is willing to:

- change direction instantly,
- admit defeat quickly,
- close losers without hesitation.

Self-awareness supports growth:

- tracking personal weaknesses,
- observing emotional triggers,
- refining behavior.

Temperaments That Struggle With Scalping

Some personality types face significant challenges:

- highly emotional individuals,
- those who seek excitement,
- those who hate losing,
- impulsive personalities,
- people who need certainty before action.

These traits cause:

- overtrading,
- revenge trading,
- hesitation,
- emotional attachment,
- frustration.

Such traders often perform better in:

- swing trading,
- position trading,
- longer-term investing.

Temperament Can Be Trained

Although temperament is partly innate, it can be cultivated.

Methods include:

- emotional journaling,
- mindfulness practice,
- breath and posture control,
- simulation training,
- exposure to small losses,
- strict rule systems.

The objective is not to suppress emotion, but to prevent emotion from influencing execution.

Temperament improves through intentional repetition.

Matching Strategy to Personality

Scalping must fit the trader. The trader should not force themselves to fit scalping.

Questions that help determine compatibility:

- Do I enjoy fast decision-making?
- Can I accept small losses easily?
- Can I remain calm under pressure?
- Can I wait patiently without action?
- Do I prefer reaction over prediction?

If the answer is yes to most, temperament aligns with scalping.

Summary

Temperament shapes scalping success more than any technical factor. The key qualities are:

1. calmness under pressure,
2. decisiveness without impulsiveness,
3. comfort with losing,
4. patience during inactivity,

5. rapid emotional recovery,
6. humility and self-awareness.

A suitable temperament creates clarity and consistency. An unsuitable temperament creates emotional chaos.

> Scalping is not a skill alone — it is a personality. When temperament aligns with method, mastery becomes possible.

2.6 Building a High-Performance Mindset

Scalping demands a unique psychological structure. The trader must remain calm in speed, confident in uncertainty, disciplined in routine, and emotionally neutral under pressure. A high-performance mindset is not a personality trait — it is a system that can be cultivated.

This section outlines the principles and practices that create mental stability and consistency in scalping.

Mindset Is Part of the System

A trading system consists of three elements:

1. method (entries, stops, targets),
2. risk (position sizing and limits),
3. mindset (execution quality).

Most traders focus on the first two. Professionals treat mindset as equal.

> The system does not fail because the rules are bad. It fails because the trader cannot follow the rules.

Mental stability is what enables mechanical execution.

Routine Creates Stability

Stability is built through routine. A professional scalper uses a structured day:

- pre-market preparation,
- focused trading window,
- post-market review,

- daily limits and shutdown rules.

Routine reduces randomness and increases control.
A typical morning sequence:

1. review levels and zones,
2. mark key structures,
3. define risk per trade,
4. visualize execution.

This creates readiness.

The Role of Energy Management

Performance is not only psychological. It is physiological.
A trader must manage:

- sleep,
- nutrition,
- hydration,
- physical posture,
- screen fatigue.

Mental fatigue reduces reaction speed and increases impulsiveness. A high-performance mindset begins with a high-performance body.

Clarity comes from energy, not effort.

Emotional Neutrality as a Habit

Neutrality is not indifference. It is the ability to feel emotion without reacting to it.
Neutrality is built through repetition:

- many small trades,
- many small losses,
- no emotional attachment.

A single trade has no meaning. Sequences matter.

$$\text{Edge} = \text{Repeated Actions} - \text{Randomness}$$

The mindset becomes stable when identity is detached from outcome.

Building Trust Through Data

Confidence does not come from motivational thinking. It comes from evidence.

- backtesting,
- forward testing,
- journaling,
- statistical review.

When the trader sees data that supports the system, doubt disappears.

Data is the antidote to emotion.

Mastery Through Boredom

High performance is not stimulating. It is repetitive.

A professional scalper may take the same setup hundreds of times. Perfection lies in consistency.

Success is found in routine, not excitement.

A stable mindset embraces boredom. It does not seek entertainment from the market.

The Quality of Attention

Attention is the primary resource. A scattered mind produces scattered results.

A stable mindset cultivates:

- deep focus,
- selective attention,
- awareness of internal state.

Distractions are removed. Simplicity is embraced.

Handling Stress and Failure

Stress is inevitable. Losses are unavoidable. The mindset must absorb these without disruption.

Effective strategies include:

- controlled breathing,
- stepping away after a loss,
- micro-breaks,
- daily shutdown rules.

Failure becomes feedback, not identity.

> A losing day does not damage a winning process.

Identity Drives Behavior

A professional identity creates professional behavior.

The scalper adopts a simple identity:

> "I am a disciplined executor of a system."

Identity shapes:

- what actions are acceptable,
- how emotions are processed,
- how rules are followed.

A strong identity protects mindset under pressure.

Summary

A stable, high-performance mindset is built through:

1. routine and structure,
2. physical energy management,
3. emotional neutrality,
4. evidence-based confidence,
5. comfort with repetition,

6. focused attention,
7. resilience under stress,
8. professional identity.

Scalping is a mental craft. The strategy matters. Risk management matters. But mindset determines success.

> The market rewards stability, discipline, and clarity. A high-performance mindset is the scalper's competitive edge.

Chapter 3

High-Probability Scalping Conditions

Scalping is highly dependent on context. A strategy that performs well in trending conditions may fail in a range, and the most precise setup becomes unreliable when liquidity is thin or volatility is unstable. For consistent results, a scalper must understand when the market environment is favorable and when it is hostile.

This chapter explores the conditions that make scalping safe, profitable, and efficient. We will examine how trends, ranges, and consolidations behave at a micro level, and how volatility and liquidity shape opportunity. We will also consider the role of institutional activity, session timing, and news events, all of which influence where and when a scalper should operate.

The goal is simple: identify high-probability periods for execution, avoid "dead markets", and develop situational awareness of when to trade and when to step aside. By mastering market context, a scalper increases consistency and protects capital.

3.1 Ideal Conditions for Scalping

Scalping does not succeed under all market environments. It thrives only when specific conditions are present: liquidity, volatility, structure, and clarity of flow. When these conditions align, the market produces frequent, reliable micro-opportunities. When they are absent, trading becomes random and costly.

This section defines the ideal environment in which scalping becomes safe, efficient, and consistently profitable.

1. Sufficient Liquidity

Liquidity is the foundation of scalping. A market must have:

- deep order books,
- tight bid–ask spreads,
- rapid execution,
- minimal slippage.

High-liquidity instruments include:

- major forex pairs (EURUSD, GBPUSD, USDJPY),
- index futures (NASDAQ, S&P 500, DAX),
- gold (XAUUSD) during active hours,
- top cryptocurrencies during peak volume.

Without liquidity, spreads widen and fill quality declines. Small targets become unprofitable.

> Liquidity makes scalping possible. Tight spreads make scalping profitable.

2. Stable Micro-Volatility

The market must move, but not unpredictably. Ideal scalping conditions show:

- frequent small movements,
- clean oscillations,
- minimal gaps,
- no violent spikes.

Micro-volatility provides continuous opportunity. Each fluctuation becomes a trade.

$$\text{Small Movement} \rightarrow \text{Small Profit}$$

Chaotic volatility is dangerous: it increases slippage and invalidates stop placement.

3. Clear Structure

Price should respect structure:

- swing highs and lows,
- demand and supply zones,
- micro-trends,
- break of structure,
- liquidity pools.

When structure is present, price behavior is predictable. Entries and exits become mechanical.

In contrast, when structure is broken or absent, scalping becomes guesswork.

4. Directional Bias

Scalping works best with a clear directional bias:

- strong micro-trend,
- higher time-frame alignment,
- institutional footprint,
- VWAP orientation.

Trading in the direction of bias reduces friction. Counter-trend scalping is possible, but riskier.

> Trade with the current, not against it.

5. Frequent Price Interaction With Levels

The best opportunities arise when price interacts repeatedly with:

- previous highs and lows,
- order blocks,
- liquidity pockets,
- imbalances and fair value gaps,
- VWAP bands.

Each interaction is a decision point. The market reveals intention at the level.

Levels create behavior. Behavior creates trade signals.

6. Active Trading Session

Scalping thrives when volume and volatility are highest. Optimal sessions include:

- London open,
- New York open,
- London–New York overlap.

These periods generate:

- increased order flow,
- clean movement,
- frequent setups.

Thin sessions (late Asian, post-New York) often produce "dead markets".

7. Predictable Rhythm

Ideal conditions exhibit rhythm. The price moves in sequences that repeat:

- impulse,
- pullback,
- continuation,
- exhaustion,
- reversal.

This rhythm creates clarity. Scalpers do not need to predict the future — only respond to patterns.

8. Clean Order Flow

Order flow should be smooth:

- no erratic jumps,
- no drying liquidity,
- no sudden spreads,
- no random spikes.

Clean flow means the market is balanced. Trades fill reliably.

9. No Major News Releases

High-impact news introduces chaos:

- spreads widen,
- orders slip,
- price whipsaws,
- liquidity disappears.

A professional scalper will:

- avoid trading minutes before news,
- avoid trading during news,
- wait for structure to return after news.

10. Emotional Neutrality

Ideal conditions are not only external. The trader must be internally calm:

- alert but relaxed,
- no urgency,
- no panic,
- no impatience.

The market offers opportunities constantly. There is no need to chase.

Calm perception is part of the environment.

Summary

Ideal conditions for scalping include:

1. deep liquidity,
2. tight spreads,
3. stable micro-volatility,
4. clear structure,
5. directional bias,
6. price interaction with key levels,
7. active trading sessions,
8. predictable rhythm,
9. clean order flow,
10. avoidance of major news.

When these align, scalping becomes efficient and consistent. When they are absent, the probability of success declines.

> Scalping is not about trading all the time. It is about trading when conditions are optimal.

3.2 Trend, Range, Consolidation, and Volatility Regimes

Scalping performance depends heavily on market regime. Price behaves differently when trending, ranging, or consolidating, and volatility expands or contracts in response to liquidity and order flow. A scalper must recognize these regimes quickly and adjust expectations, setups, and risk accordingly.

This section explains how each regime functions and how scalpers interact with them.

Trends: The Path of Least Resistance

A trend occurs when price moves directionally with higher highs and higher lows (uptrend) or lower highs and lower lows (downtrend). Trends are ideal for continuation scalping.

Characteristics of a good trend:

- clear directional bias,

- shallow pullbacks,
- strong impulsive legs,
- volume aligned with direction,
- price respecting moving averages.

In trends, the scalper focuses on:

- pullback entries,
- continuation signals,
- breakout traps against counter-trend traders.

The goal is simple:

> Enter with the trend and exit on the next burst of momentum.

Scalping against the trend requires precision and often lower expectations.

Ranges: Repeated Opportunity at Boundaries

A range forms when price oscillates between support and resistance. The market is balanced: buyers absorb lows, sellers absorb highs.

Range conditions offer:

- mean reversion trades,
- rapid entries and exits,
- clearly defined boundaries.

Key principles:

- long at demand (bottom),
- short at supply (top),
- avoid trading in the center,
- expect multiple rotations.

Ranges provide frequent opportunities:

$$\text{Support} \rightarrow \text{Resistance} \rightarrow \text{Support}$$

Scalpers profit from repeated oscillation, not breakout expectations.

> In ranges, the edge lives at the edges.

Consolidation: Energy Preparation

Consolidation is a period of compression. Price becomes narrow, volatility contracts, and order flow slows. This regime precedes expansion.

During consolidation:

- price trades in a tight box,
- volume decreases,
- breakouts often fail,
- patience is required.

Professional scalpers do not force trades inside consolidation. They prepare for the breakout.

$$\text{Compression} \rightarrow \text{Expansion}$$

The breakout reveals direction. The first pullback after breakout provides the high-probability entry.

Consolidation is the spring. The breakout is the release.

Volatility Regimes

Volatility is the range of price movement over a period. Scalping requires volatility — but not chaos.

There are two critical volatility regimes:

1. Stable Volatility Ideal for scalping:

- small frequent moves,
- predictable swings,
- low slippage,
- clean interaction with levels.

Stable volatility exists during active sessions in liquid markets.

2. Chaotic Volatility Dangerous for scalping:

- random spikes,
- wide spreads,
- violent candles,
- large slippage.

Chaotic volatility occurs:

- during news events,
- in thin liquidity periods,
- at session transitions,
- after sudden shocks.

Scalpers step aside during chaos and wait for structure to return.

Switching Between Regimes

Price moves between regimes throughout the day:

1. trending,
2. consolidating,
3. ranging,
4. expanding volatility,
5. contracting volatility.

A scalper must recognize transitions:

- trend losing momentum,
- fake breakout near range boundary,
- compression before expansion,
- volatility spike during news,
- return to rhythm afterward.

Profit comes from adapting to the regime, not from forcing the market to match your preference.

Practical Guidelines

1. **In trends:** trade pullbacks and continuation.
2. **In ranges:** trade reversals at boundaries.
3. **In consolidation:** wait for breakout, then enter pullback.
4. **In chaotic volatility:** stand aside.

Risk adjusts with regime:

- smaller size in volatility,
- larger size in stable trends,
- minimal activity in consolidation.

Summary

Market regimes determine scalping opportunity. The scalper must identify:

- trend strength,
- range boundaries,
- consolidation zones,
- volatility expansion and contraction.

Matching tactics to conditions creates consistency.

> Scalping does not control the market. It follows the rhythm of its regime.

3.3 Liquidity Pockets and Institutional Activity

Scalping is not random. It is a response to liquidity. Large participants — market makers, hedge funds, banks, and algorithms — create zones where orders accumulate. These zones act as magnets for price. Understanding liquidity pockets and institutional behavior allows the scalper to anticipate movement before it happens.

This section explains where liquidity forms, how institutions interact with it, and why these dynamics create consistent scalping opportunities.

What Is a Liquidity Pocket?

A liquidity pocket is a price zone where a large amount of resting orders exists. These orders may include:

- stop-losses,
- take-profit orders,
- pending buy/sell orders,
- algorithmic execution orders.

When price approaches such a zone, it accelerates:

1. orders are triggered,
2. volume increases,
3. volatility expands,
4. price moves rapidly.

This is where scalpers operate.

> Liquidity is fuel. Price moves fastest when fuel is consumed.

Sources of Liquidity Pockets

Liquidity clusters around predictable locations:

1. Previous highs and lows Human behavior creates patterns:

- traders place stops below swing lows,
- profit targets sit above swing highs.

These levels become liquidity magnets.

2. Breakout Levels When price breaks a level:

- breakout traders enter,
- stops accumulate on the other side,
- market makers exploit both groups.

3. Imbalance and Fair Value Gaps Institutions often leave price imbalances behind. Price later returns to fill them, generating movement.

4. VWAP and Institutional Anchors Institutions monitor:

- VWAP (Volume-Weighted Average Price),
- session volume,
- monthly/weekly anchors.

Liquidity pools form near these references.

Institutional Activity: The True Engine of Price

Retail traders do not move markets. Institutions do.

Institutional actions include:

- inventory hedging,
- liquidity provision,
- stop hunting,
- algorithmic execution.

Their behavior is predictable:

- they seek liquidity,
- they avoid moving price unnecessarily,
- they disguise intentions,
- they accumulate before expansion.

Price often moves against retail expectation because institutions must fill orders efficiently.

> Institutions move price where liquidity exists, not where logic suggests.

Liquidity as Magnetism

Liquidity attracts price.

1. stops are clustered below a low,
2. price dips into the cluster,
3. liquidity fills,

4. price reverses sharply.

Retail traders call this manipulation. Professionals call it execution.

Price goes where orders are, not where traders want it to go.

The Scalping Opportunity

When liquidity is harvested:

- price becomes fast,
- spreads often tighten,
- volatility expands briefly,
- reaction becomes predictable.

A scalper watches:

- the approach to liquidity,
- the moment of sweep,
- the immediate response.

Typical sequence:

$$\text{Sweep} \rightarrow \text{Absorption} \rightarrow \text{Reversal}$$

The scalper enters on the reversal, not on the sweep.

Absorption and Exhaustion

Absorption occurs when large buyers or sellers absorb market orders without allowing price to move further. This signals intent.

Signs of absorption:

- repeated rejection at level,
- high volume but shallow movement,
- long wicks,
- footprint imbalance.

Exhaustion is the opposite:

- order flow dries up,

- price cannot continue,
- trend weakens,
- reversal likely.

These moments are ideal for scalping.

Institutional Footprints

Institutions leave footprints:

- rapid absorption,
- sudden expansion,
- block trades,
- fair value gaps,
- iceberg orders.

A scalper learns to read these footprints instead of predicting narratives.

Price behavior reveals the presence of large players.

Practical Scalping Techniques Around Liquidity

Effective methods include:

1. wait for sweep of liquidity,
2. confirm with wick rejection or imbalance,
3. enter with tight stop,
4. exit quickly upon momentum burst.

Never enter before liquidity sweep. Patient traders are rewarded.

Summary

Liquidity pockets and institutional activity create:

- predictable areas of movement,
- rapid execution opportunities,
- consistent reversal patterns,
- strong continuation setups.

A scalper must learn to see liquidity as:

- target,
- magnet,
- fuel.

> Institutions seek liquidity. Price follows institutions. Scalpers follow price.

3.4 Best Trading Sessions (Asian → London → New York)

Scalping performance varies dramatically based on the trading session. Each global session has distinct characteristics in terms of volume, volatility, liquidity, and institutional participation. Understanding these differences enables a scalper to focus on the most profitable periods and avoid unproductive, "dead" market hours.

This section explains how the Asian, London, and New York sessions operate, how they overlap, and which periods offer the highest probability setups.

Session Overview and Characteristics

The global trading day can be divided into three major sessions:

1. Asian Session (Tokyo, Sydney)
2. London Session (Europe)
3. New York Session (United States)

Volume and price action change as capital moves from one region to another.

Asian Session: Calm and Controlled

The Asian session is generally the slowest of the three. It is characterized by:

- reduced liquidity,
- narrower ranges,
- slower market movement,
- fewer institutional orders.

Price behavior is typically:

- range-bound,
- mean-reverting,
- clean and controlled.

Asian session is suitable for:

- range scalping,
- fading extremes,
- small targets.

It is *not* ideal for breakout trading or large momentum moves.

Trade small, trade slow, and focus on clear boundaries.

London Session: The Engine of Volatility

London is the most active session for forex and index markets. Characteristics include:

- sharp increases in volume,
- institutional orders from Europe,
- frequent directional moves,
- strong breakouts and trend formation.

Price often transitions from Asian range into London trend:

$$\text{Range (Asia)} \rightarrow \text{Expansion (London)}$$

London session is ideal for:

- trend continuation scalping,
- breakout and pullback setups,
- volatility-based strategies.

Risks include:

- false breakouts at open,
- initial stop hunting,
- wide spreads during transition.

London provides movement. Patience finds direction.

New York Session: Maximum Participation

The New York session introduces additional volatility and liquidity:

- U.S. equities open,
- futures volume increases,
- economic news releases,
- institutional hedging.

New York produces:

- very fast price swings,
- strong trends,
- sharp reversals,
- frequent two-sided action.

It is the best session for experienced scalpers.

New York offers the highest reward — and the highest risk.

Session Overlap: Prime Scalping Period

The most active time of day occurs during overlap:

$$\text{London} + \text{New York} \approx \text{Maximum Liquidity}$$

During this period:

- spreads are tightest,
- order flow is deepest,
- volatility is cleanest,
- trends are strongest.

This window creates the best scalping conditions:

London Open → New York Open → Overlap

Scalpers focus heavily on these hours.

Good Times Become Bad Times

Not all activity is beneficial. There are moments to avoid:

- session transition (opens/closes),
- lunch hours,
- low-liquidity gaps,
- major news spikes.

These periods often produce:

- wide spreads,
- unpredictable movement,
- false price signals.

Patience protects capital.

Practical Time-of-Day Rules

Professional scalpers use simple rules:

- **Trade London Open for expansion.**
- **Trade New York Open for volatility.**
- **Trade overlap for premium opportunity.**
- **Avoid low-volume hours.**
- **Stand aside during major news.**

One of the most effective principles:

> Trade when the market is active. Rest when it is quiet.

Summary

Each global session offers distinct characteristics:

- Asian: range-bound, patient scalping.
- London: breakout, trend, expansion.
- New York: volatility, reversals, strong flow.
- Overlap: maximum liquidity and opportunity.

A scalper improves performance by aligning activity with session quality.

> The best trades happen when liquidity, volatility, and flow converge. Timing is part of the edge.

3.5 Identifying "Dead Markets" and Avoiding No-Trade Zones

One of the most important skills in scalping is knowing when *not* to trade. A dead market is a period where price movement is slow, liquidity is thin, and opportunities are scarce. Attempting to force trades in such environments leads to frustration, overtrading, and cumulative loss. The professional scalper learns to recognize no-trade zones quickly and step aside with discipline.

What Is a Dead Market?

A dead market is an environment where:

- spreads widen,
- candles shrink,
- volume declines,
- price oscillates without direction,
- movement becomes unpredictable.

In such conditions, every trade has a low expectancy:

$$\text{Risk} > \text{Reward}$$

The scalper's edge disappears.

Visual Characteristics of Dead Markets

Dead markets have clear visual patterns:

- many small candles,
- flat EMAs,
- overlapping price bars,
- no break of structure,
- no strong highs or lows.

Charts look *crowded but inert.* There is motion, but no progress.

When price looks busy but goes nowhere, it is a dead market.

Behavioral Characteristics

Price behavior provides clues:

- every breakout fails,
- every pullback stalls,
- every direction reverses immediately.

It becomes impossible to secure follow-through.

There is no "edge" to exploit.

Common Causes of Dead Markets

Dead markets often occur during:

1. low volume sessions (late Asian, post-New York),
2. lunch hours,
3. before major news releases,
4. after strong directional moves,
5. during holiday periods,
6. around session transitions.

Institutions are inactive during these times. Without institutional flow, price lacks energy.

Indicators of No-Trade Zones

A scalper must learn to detect no-trade conditions quickly. Warning signs include:

- spread widening without reason,
- liquidity dropping from order book,
- price hovering around VWAP with no reaction,
- collapsing volume,
- flat EMA clusters.

Any one of these may indicate a pause; several together confirm a dead market.

Why Most Losses Come From Dead Markets

In active markets, the scalper is aligned with flow. In dead markets, the scalper is fighting randomness. This leads to:

- overtrading,
- revenge trading,
- emotional exhaustion,
- cumulative small losses.

The market is not hostile; it is simply inactive.

Trading without flow is gambling.

How Professionals Avoid Dead Markets

Experienced scalpers use strict filters:

1. Trade only during active sessions.
2. Trade only when volatility is stable.
3. Avoid trading before major news.
4. Stop when spreads widen.
5. Stop when volume drops.

They understand that capital is preserved through selective participation.

The Power of Not Trading

There is enormous psychological power in stepping aside. No-trade periods allow:

- emotional reset,
- cognitive clarity,
- energy recovery,
- avoidance of frustration.

A professional scalper sees inactivity not as loss, but as protection.

Waiting is part of strategy. Not trading is a trading decision.

The "Hourly Shutdown Rule"

A simple rule prevents overtrading:

> If no valid setup appears within one hour, stop trading.

Dead markets often last longer than expected. Stepping away reduces damage.

When to Resume Trading

Trading resumes when:

- volume increases,
- spreads normalize,
- structure returns,
- direction is visible.

Look for:

1. break of structure,
2. shift of momentum,
3. strong rejection or imbalance,
4. clear trend or range formation.

This signals the market has awakened.

Summary

Dead markets are dangerous because they offer:

- low volatility,
- random movement,
- poor follow-through,
- declining liquidity.

By recognizing no-trade conditions, the scalper avoids unnecessary losses and protects mental energy.

> The most profitable action in a dead market is no action.

3.6 News Volatility: When to Scalp and When NOT to Scalp

News events introduce sudden influxes of information into the market. They generate rapid changes in order flow, liquidity, and volatility. For scalpers, this environment can produce either extraordinary opportunity or extreme risk. Understanding when to trade and when to step aside is critical for longevity.

This section explains how news affects price behavior and provides rules for navigating high-volatility periods.

Why News Matters

Major news events create three immediate effects:

1. Spreads widen.
2. Liquidity disappears.
3. Price becomes unstable.

This creates conditions where:

- stops may slip,
- fills may occur far from expected price,
- candles may spike violently in both directions.

Predicting direction becomes nearly impossible.

> During news, the market is not trading price. It is trading information.

Types of News That Impact Scalping

High-impact news includes:

- interest rate decisions,
- non-farm payrolls (NFP),
- inflation reports (CPI/PPI),
- GDP announcements,
- unemployment reports,
- central bank press conferences,
- geopolitical shocks.

Markets react strongly to these events.
Medium-impact news can also influence volatility:

- manufacturing PMI,
- housing data,
- consumer confidence.

Low-impact news rarely matters for scalping.

The Three Phases of News Movement

News volatility follows a recognizable sequence:

1. Pre-Event Phase (No-Trade Zone) Minutes before the release:

- spreads widen,
- price becomes erratic,
- liquidity thins.

Scalpers should avoid trading.

2. Release Phase (Extreme Volatility) The moment of release produces:

- violent spikes,
- multiple whipsaws,
- random direction.

This is the most dangerous period. Even tight stops can slip significantly.

3. Post-Event Phase (Opportunity Window) After price absorbs the news:

- structure returns,
- spreads normalize,
- directional bias becomes visible.

This is where reliable scalping opportunities appear.

The opportunity is after the news, not during it.

Why Scalpers Should Avoid Trading During News

During the release, the market is driven by:

- algorithms,
- institutional hedging,
- high-frequency trading (HFT),

- inventory adjustments.

Retail traders cannot compete in this environment.
Risks include:

- stop slippage,
- failed execution,
- platform freezes,
- emotional shock.

Even correct direction may not be profitable.

When Scalping Is Possible After News

After the spike, price often reveals:

- trend continuation,
- reversal,
- liquidity sweep,
- break of structure.

Ideal conditions include:

- spread tightening,
- volume stabilizing,
- clean retest of levels.

The first structured pullback after the spike provides a high-probability entry.

> Wait for structure. Trade the reaction, not the release.

A Practical Rule for News Trading

Professional scalpers use a simple guideline:

> Stop trading five minutes before a major news event, and do not resume until structure returns.

This avoids the most chaotic period.
Sometimes the waiting period is:

- five minutes,
- fifteen minutes,
- one hour,
- or the rest of the day.

Patience protects capital.

Exceptions: When Scalping the Spike Makes Sense

Experienced traders may scalp during news if:

- spreads remain stable,
- execution is reliable,
- volatility is orderly,
- they are using micro-size,
- risk is predetermined.

Such scalping is advanced and not recommended for beginners. It is easy to confuse luck with edge.

Danger Signals: Stop Immediately

Do not scalp when:

- spreads are unusually wide,
- candles are extremely large,
- fills are delayed,
- slippage increases,
- price has no direction.

This environment destroys expectancy.

Summary

News volatility creates both risk and opportunity. The key principles are:

1. Avoid trading *before and during* the release.
2. Wait for structure to return.
3. Scalping opportunities appear *after* the spike.
4. Manage risk carefully and reduce size.

    The best trade during news is often no trade. The best scalping opportunity is the first structured pullback after chaos.

Part II

Technical Foundations

Chapter 4

Timeframes & Chart Selection

Successful scalping depends on seeing the market from the correct perspective. Timeframe selection influences how structure forms, how signals are interpreted, and how trades are executed in real time. The scalper must combine speed with clarity: fast enough to capture opportunity, but structured enough to avoid noise.

This chapter explores the unique role of the 1-minute chart as the core execution timeframe, the 5-minute chart as the primary structure layer, and the use of tick and ultra-fast charts for precision entries. We will also examine how to stack timeframes for higher accuracy and how different instruments — indices, forex, gold, and cryptocurrencies — respond to timeframe selection.

The objective is not to predict price, but to observe it correctly. By mastering the right views of the market, a scalper increases precision, consistency, and confidence in every decision.

4.1 1-Minute Chart: The Core Scalping Battlefield

The 1-minute chart (1M) is the primary execution environment for scalping. It captures the immediate behavior of price, revealing micro-structure, order flow, and momentum in real time. No other timeframe provides the same combination of speed, clarity, and opportunity.

This section explains why the 1-minute chart is central to high performance scalping, how to read it effectively, and how professionals operate within it.

Why the 1-Minute Chart Matters

Scalping is the art of exploiting small, frequent movements. These movements are easiest to observe on the 1M chart, where:

- candles complete rapidly,
- trends evolve visibly,
- pullbacks form quickly,
- entries and exits become precise.

Every decision must be supported by clear price action. The 1M chart provides this clarity.

> The 1-minute chart is where scalping happens. Higher timeframes explain why; lower timeframes explain how.

Micro-Structure and Flow

The 1M chart shows *micro-structure*:

- swings,
- break of structure (BOS),
- continuation patterns,
- liquidity sweeps,
- exhaustion wicks.

Patterns form quickly:

$$\text{Impulse} \rightarrow \text{Pullback} \rightarrow \text{Continuation}$$

The scalper does not need large moves. A small burst of momentum is enough to capture profit.

Entry Precision

The 1M chart enables highly accurate entries:

- tight stop-loss placement,
- minimal drawdown,
- high R-multiples,

- controlled risk.

A typical scalping entry may target:

- 5–20 pips in forex,
- 5–50 points in indices,
- micro-moves in gold or crypto.

The stop-loss is often smaller than the target. This creates a favorable expectancy.

Small loss, frequent gain

Signal Density

The 1M chart offers a high frequency of setups. Each swing, pullback, or level interaction becomes a potential trade.

Examples:

- EMA pullbacks,
- liquidity sweeps,
- VWAP reversion,
- order block reactions.

However, this abundance can be dangerous. The trader must learn to filter noise.

> High frequency of signals does not mean high frequency of trades.

Fast Feedback Loop

The 1M chart accelerates learning:

- patterns repeat quickly,
- mistakes become obvious,
- adjustments are immediate.

A beginner may take hundreds of samples in a short time. This builds confidence and intuition.

> The 1-minute chart is a teaching machine.

Emotional Control on the 1M Chart

The rapid pace of the 1M chart can trigger emotions:

- fear of missing out (FOMO),
- impulsive entries,
- revenge trading,
- hesitation.

To succeed, the scalper must remain calm:

- enter only on valid setups,
- ignore noise,
- accept frequent small losses.

A professional scalper has no emotional attachment to any trade.

Trade Management

Trade duration on the 1M chart is short:

- seconds to minutes,
- not hours.

Profits are taken quickly:

- 1:1, 1:2, or 1:3 reward,
- partials on momentum bursts,
- exit before reversal.

The focus is on execution, not prediction.

Take the move, not the market.

Context from Higher Timeframes

The 1M chart operates within a larger structure:

- 5M provides alignment,
- 15M sets zones,
- 1H shows trend,
- daily provides bias.

The hierarchy is simple:

1. use higher timeframes for direction,
2. use 1M for execution.

Top-down analysis → Bottom-up execution

Summary

The 1-minute chart is the core scalping battlefield because it provides:

- precise entries,
- fast pattern recognition,
- high signal density,
- tight stops and fast profits,
- immediate feedback,
- micro-structure clarity.

Higher timeframes guide bias; the 1-minute chart delivers execution.

> Scalping is played on the 1-minute chart. Master this battlefield, and the market becomes readable.

4.2 5-Minute Chart: Structure, Alignment, and Confirmation

The 5-minute chart (5M) is the structural backbone of scalping. While the 1-minute chart provides execution and precision, the 5M creates context, direction, and alignment. It filters noise, clarifies trend, and defines the zones in which a scalper can act confidently.

This section explains how the 5M chart is used to confirm bias, identify structure, and avoid low-probability trades.

Why the 5-Minute Chart Matters

The 5M chart offers a balance between speed and stability:

- fast enough to adapt quickly,
- slow enough to avoid emotional noise.

It reveals patterns that are often invisible on the 1M chart:

- trend direction,
- swing structure,
- higher-timeframe levels,
- break of structure (BOS),
- liquidity zones.

> The 1-minute chart shows the battle. The 5-minute chart shows the battlefield.

Structure Identification

On the 5M chart, structure becomes obvious:

1. higher highs and higher lows (uptrend),
2. lower highs and lower lows (downtrend),
3. equal highs/lows (range),
4. compression and expansion cycles.

Swing points are clearer. This helps the scalper avoid trading against larger momentum.

Structure → Bias → Entries

Alignment With the 1-Minute Chart

Alignment between 5M and 1M increases probability. A basic rule used by professionals:

> Trade the 1-minute chart only in the direction of the 5-minute trend.

Alignment means:

- 5M trend up, 1M entries long,
- 5M trend down, 1M entries short,
- avoid counter-trend impulses unless clear evidence exists.

Misalignment is dangerous:

- reduced follow-through,
- frequent reversals,
- lower expectancy.

Confirmation of Trade Setups

The 5M chart confirms:

- direction,
- structure,
- levels,
- zones of interest.

Typical confirmations include:

1. break of structure (BOS),
2. rejection from supply/demand,
3. liquidity sweep,
4. FVG or imbalance creation,
5. VWAP interaction.

After confirmation, the scalper waits for the 1M entry trigger.

> 5-minute chart gives permission. 1-minute chart gives precision.

Zone and Level Creation

The 5M chart defines actionable zones:

- supply and demand blocks,
- fair value gaps,
- previous highs/lows,
- VWAP deviations,
- institutional liquidity.

These zones become:

- targets,
- entry locations,
- stop-loss boundaries.

The scalper marks zones on 5M and executes on 1M.

Filtering Noise

The 1M chart can generate excessive signals. Without the 5M filter, traders may:

- overtrade,
- chase entries,
- misinterpret micro-movement.

The 5M chart filters:

- false breakouts,
- random wicks,
- meaningless pullbacks.

If 5M shows no structure, stand aside.

No structure means no trade.

Trade Duration and Targets

The 5M chart also influences target size:

- micro targets on 1M,
- structural targets on 5M.

Targets often align with:

- swing highs/lows,
- VWAP bands,
- liquidity clusters.

Trade duration increases slightly — still minutes, not hours.

Psychological Stability

The 5M chart reduces emotional noise:

- slower candle formation,
- less whipsaw,
- clearer rhythm.

It protects the trader from:

- impulsive entries,
- reactionary behavior,
- panic in micro-volatility.

Summary

The 5-minute chart is essential for scalping because it provides:

1. structural clarity,
2. directional alignment,
3. confirmation of setups,
4. zone and level creation,
5. noise filtering,
6. psychological stability.

The operational formula is simple:

5M determines direction and structure → 1M executes entries and exits

> The 1-minute chart wins the battle. The 5-minute chart wins the war.

4.3 Tick Charts & Ultra-Fast 15-Second Charts

While the 1-minute and 5-minute charts provide structure and execution, certain scalping environments require even greater precision. Tick charts and ultra-fast 15-second charts reveal price behavior on a micro scale. They allow the scalper to see what candles hide: order flow, momentum bursts, and the exact moment a trade becomes valid.

These charts are not for prediction. They are for *timing*.

Tick Charts: Price Moves Only When Orders Arrive

A tick chart creates a new candle after a fixed number of transactions, not after a fixed period of time. For example:

- a 100-tick chart prints a candle every 100 trades,
- a 200-tick chart prints every 200 trades.

This creates several advantages:

- candles form faster during high activity,
- candles form slower during calm periods,
- chart speed reflects market activity,
- false signals are reduced when volume is low.

> Time is replaced by **market activity**.

Tick charts expose:

- absorption,
- exhaustion,
- hidden momentum,
- micro pullbacks,
- liquidity taps.

These details enable razor-sharp entries.

Ultra-Fast 15-Second Charts

A 15-second chart shows the flow of price movement more dynamically than the 1-minute chart. It is ideal during:

- fast trends,
- breakout continuation,
- news reaction after stabilization,
- active session opens.

Benefits include:

- early signal detection,
- precise entry on pullback,
- smaller stop-loss,
- granular view of momentum.

The 15-second chart reveals:

- lower timeframe structure,
- micro liquidity sweeps,
- acceleration before breakout.

> If the 1-minute chart shows the heartbeat, the 15-second chart shows the pulse.

Execution Precision

Tick and micro-timeframe charts allow scalpers to:

1. enter at the edge of pullbacks,
2. reduce drawdown,
3. tighten stops,
4. scale in with confidence.

Typical execution pattern:

$$\text{5M structure} \rightarrow \text{1M setup} \rightarrow \text{15S entry trigger}$$

The 15-second or tick chart confirms entry:

- wick rejection,
- engulfing candle,
- micro break of structure,
- momentum surge.

This stacking produces consistency.

Avoiding Noise and Overtrading

Ultra-fast charts carry a risk: *excessive noise.* A scalper must avoid:

- chasing every candle,
- reacting emotionally,
- entering without higher-timeframe context.

To control noise:

- trade only in direction of 5M trend,
- use 1M for setup,
- use tick/15S only for entry timing.

Micro charts are for precision, not prediction.

When to Use Tick and 15-Second Charts

Ideal conditions include:

- breakouts from consolidation,
- trend continuation after pullback,
- active session opens (London, New York),
- liquidity sweeps at highs/lows,
- post-news micro structure.

Avoid using micro charts when:

- volatility is extremely low,
- spreads are wide,
- market is dead or slow.

These charts must enhance, not replace, higher-timeframe structure.

Scalping Workflow Using Micro Charts

A consistent workflow:

1. Identify bias on 15M and 5M.
2. Confirm setup on 1M.
3. Refine entry on tick or 15S:
    - micro pullback,
    - wick rejection,
    - momentum shift.
4. Execute with tight stop.
5. Take profit quickly.

This creates:

- high accuracy,
- minimal risk,
- fast cycle time.

Summary

Tick charts and 15-second charts enhance scalping by providing:

- faster feedback,
- clearer order flow,
- earlier signal detection,
- precise entry timing,
- tighter stop losses.

But they must be used correctly:

> The structure comes from higher timeframes. The entry comes from micro-timeframes.

$$\text{Macro structure} \rightarrow \text{Micro precision}$$

When integrated properly, tick charts and ultra-fast 15-second charts turn the scalper into a surgical operator, capturing opportunity with accuracy and control.

4.4 Multi-Timeframe Stacking for Higher Accuracy

Scalping requires both speed and context. No single timeframe provides all necessary information. Multi-timeframe stacking is the process of combining multiple charts to form a unified understanding of structure, momentum, and execution.

The principle is simple:

> Higher timeframes provide direction. Lower timeframes provide entries.

When all layers align, probability increases significantly. When they conflict, trades are avoided.

The Hierarchy of Timeframes

A typical scalping stack:

15M	Macro bias and levels
5M	Structure and confirmation
1M	Execution and entry triggers
Tick/15S	Precision timing

Each layer serves a purpose:

- 15M identifies key zones,
- 5M defines trend and structure,
- 1M reveals pullbacks and signals,
- micro charts refine entry.

Top-down analysis → Bottom-up execution

Top-Down Bias Creation

The process begins on higher timeframes:

1. Identify trend direction.
2. Mark supply/demand zones.
3. Observe VWAP, highs, lows.

Bias is determined:

$$\text{Long bias} \quad \text{or} \quad \text{Short bias}$$

No entries are taken against the established bias unless clear reversal evidence appears.

Structural Confirmation on the 5-Minute Chart

The 5M chart confirms trend structure:

- higher highs / higher lows (bullish),
- lower highs / lower lows (bearish),
- compression before expansion,
- range boundaries.

The scalper identifies potential zones where price may react:

- FVG,
- order blocks,
- previous highs/lows,
- VWAP bands.

$$\text{Zone confirmed} \Rightarrow \text{Wait for 1M trigger}$$

Execution on the 1-Minute Chart

The 1M chart is used to enter the trade. Signals include:

- micro pullback,
- break of structure (BOS),
- liquidity sweep,
- wick rejection,
- momentum continuation.

Stops are placed beyond:

- swing high/low,
- micro zone boundary.

The entry is tight. Risk is minimal.

Precision Timing With Micro-Charts

Tick and 15-second charts enhance timing:

- confirmation of rejection,
- footprint of order flow,
- early momentum detection.

This reduces drawdown and increases R-multiple.
A typical workflow:

$$15M \to 5M \to 1M \to 15S$$

The last chart is not used to predict, only to refine.

When Timeframes Agree

High-probability situations occur when:

1. 15M support/resistance is clear,
2. 5M trend aligns with bias,
3. 1M shows clean setup,
4. micro-chart confirms entry.

These conditions produce:

- natural flow,
- strong follow-through,
- reduced risk.

Alignment creates expectancy.

When Timeframes Conflict

If timeframes do not align:

- skip the trade,
- reduce size,
- wait for clarity.

Examples of conflict:

- 15M bullish, 5M range, 1M bearish,
- trending on 1M, but structure broken on 5M,
- micro entries against macro zones.

Trading during conflict causes:

- random outcomes,
- emotional stress,
- overtrading.

If the story does not align, the trade does not exist.

Benefit: More Accuracy, Less Stress

Multi-timeframe stacking provides:

- fewer, higher-quality setups,
- increased confidence,
- reduced hesitation,
- less emotional involvement.

The trader waits for confluence:

- level,
- signal,
- timing.

Then executes mechanically.

Summary

Multi-timeframe stacking is the core of precision scalping. It combines:

1. macro bias (15M),
2. structural confirmation (5M),
3. execution (1M),
4. timing (tick/15S).

$$\text{Confluence} = \text{Bias} + \text{Structure} + \text{Trigger} + \text{Timing}$$

When all timeframes speak the same language, execution becomes effortless.

4.5 Choosing the Right Instruments (Indices, Forex, Gold, Crypto)

Scalping success depends not only on skill or strategy, but on the choice of instrument. Some markets are smooth and liquid, offering tight spreads and reliable movement. Others are chaotic, illiquid, or expensive to trade. Selecting the correct instruments increases profitability, reduces risk, and improves execution quality.

This section explores the four major categories used by scalpers — indices, forex pairs, gold, and cryptocurrencies — and explains their unique characteristics.

Selection Criteria

A scalper evaluates instruments using clear criteria:

- **liquidity**,
- **spread**,
- **volatility**,
- **cost of trading**,
- **predictability of flow**,
- **availability of clean structure**.

The ideal instrument has:

$$\text{High Liquidity} + \text{Tight Spread} + \text{Stable Volatility}$$

Dead or illiquid instruments are avoided.

Indices: Fast, Clean, and Highly Tradable

Index futures and CFDs (NASDAQ, S&P 500, DAX, NIFTY, US30) are among the best scalping instruments due to:

- high liquidity,
- institutional participation,
- predictable sessions,
- strong volatility bursts.

Typical characteristics:

- clean trends during active hours,
- strong reactions to levels,
- fast follow-through after breakouts.

Ideal strategies include:

- micro pullbacks,
- VWAP reversions,
- momentum continuation on session opens.

Indices produce opportunities daily.

Indices are the scalper's playground.

Forex: Liquidity and Consistency

Major forex pairs provide exceptional liquidity:

- EURUSD,
- GBPUSD,
- USDJPY.

Advantages:

- spreads are extremely tight,
- 24-hour market continuity,
- smooth price flow,
- frequent micro-structures.

Forex works especially well for:

- range scalping in Asian session,
- trend continuation during London,
- reaction trading near news events (post-structure).

Because of deep liquidity, risk is easier to control.

Gold (XAUUSD): High Volatility, High Reward

Gold is a favorite instrument for experienced scalpers. It offers:

- explosive movement,
- deep liquidity during London and New York,
- strong reaction to levels,
- high R-multiple potential.

However, gold is dangerous for beginners due to:

- fast spikes,
- sudden reversals,
- large wicks,
- wide spread during news.

Professionals treat gold with respect:

- trade only during active sessions,
- avoid pre-news,
- use tight stops,
- exit quickly.

Gold rewards skill but punishes hesitation.

Gold magnifies both talent and error.

Cryptocurrency: 24/7 Volatility

Crypto markets operate without closing hours. This creates a unique environment:

- constant movement,
- variable liquidity,
- periodic chaos,
- large opportunities.

Major instruments include:

- BTCUSDT,
- ETHUSDT,
- high-volume altcoins.

Crypto scalping is effective during:

- high-volume periods,
- funding rate extremes,
- clear trend days,
- breakouts from consolidation.

Risks include:

- thin order books on smaller assets,
- overnight traps,
- liquidation cascades.

Use leverage cautiously.

Instruments to Avoid

Scalpers should avoid:

- illiquid small caps,
- exotic forex pairs,
- low-volume crypto tokens,
- instruments with wide spreads,
- dead markets.

These destroy edge.

$$\text{Wide Spread} + \text{Slow Movement} = \text{Loss}$$

How to Choose Your Primary Market

A scalper should specialize. Choose one instrument first:

- master its rhythm,
- understand its sessions,
- observe typical behavior,
- learn how it reacts at levels.

Once fluent, expand to a second instrument.

Depth beats variety. Expertise beats diversification.

Summary

Choosing the right instruments increases accuracy, safety, and profitability. The key principles:

1. prioritize liquidity,
2. prefer tight spreads,
3. avoid low-volume assets,
4. focus on one instrument at a time.

Best categories:

- indices: clean, volatile, reliable,
- forex: liquid and stable,
- gold: high reward for skilled traders,
- crypto: volatile, 24/7 opportunity.

The right market makes scalping easier. Choose instruments that support your edge.

Chapter 5

Indicators That Actually Work

Scalping is primarily a price-action discipline. Indicators do not replace skill, structure, or judgment. They serve a simpler purpose: to improve clarity, filter noise, and confirm what price already suggests. The right tools enhance execution without slowing the trader's reaction time.

This chapter focuses only on indicators that are practical, reliable, and proven in fast markets. We will examine how EMA clusters shape trend and pullback entries, how VWAP provides institutional bias, and how RSI and MACD assist in identifying micro-reversals and momentum shifts. Finally, we will explore ATR as a foundation for stop-loss precision and how to combine indicators without overcomplicating the chart.

The objective is to use indicators with intention: fewer tools, deeper understanding, and cleaner execution.

5.1 EMA Clusters (5/8/13, 9/20, 20/200) and Their Roles

Exponential Moving Averages (EMAs) are among the most useful tools for scalpers when used correctly. They are not prediction devices. They are *dynamic structure guides* that help define trend, momentum, and high-probability pullback zones.

Instead of relying on a single EMA, professional scalpers use **EMA clusters**: groups of EMAs that work together as a visual framework. In this section, we focus on three powerful clusters:

- 5/8/13 EMA — micro-trend and scalper flow,
- 9/20 EMA — short-term trend and pullback zone,
- 20/200 EMA — macro alignment and regime filter.

Why Use EMA Clusters Instead of Single Lines

A single moving average gives only one point of reference. Clusters create *zones* and *layers* of structure.

Benefits of EMA clusters:

- define trend strength (tight vs. wide spacing),
- show momentum shifts (crossovers and flattening),
- provide pullback entry zones,
- act as dynamic support and resistance,
- help prevent counter-trend trading in noise.

EMA clusters are not signals. They are the skeleton of the market's short-term structure.

The 5/8/13 EMA Cluster: Micro-Trend and Scalper Flow

The 5, 8, and 13 EMAs respond quickly to price. They are ideal for:

- identifying micro-trends,
- timing scalping entries,
- judging momentum strength.

On the 1-minute chart, the 5/8/13 cluster shows:

- **Strong uptrend:** EMAs stacked (5 above 8, above 13), all sloping upward, with price riding above.
- **Strong downtrend:** EMAs stacked in reverse (5 below 8, below 13), all sloping downward, with price staying below.
- **Weak or choppy:** EMAs tangled, flat, or frequently crossing.

Practical uses:

1. **Pullback Entries:** In a strong trend, price pulling back into the 8 or 13 EMA often provides a high-probability continuation zone.
2. **Momentum Gauge:** The tighter the EMAs and the steeper the slope, the stronger the micro-trend.
3. **No-Trade Filter:** When EMAs are flat and twisted, step aside — the market is likely ranging or dead.

Micro-EMAs (5/8/13) $\Rightarrow$ Immediate flow and momentum

The 9/20 EMA Cluster: Short-Term Trend and Pullback Zone

The 9 and 20 EMAs are slightly slower and smoother than 5/8/13. They function as:

- short-term trend filter,
- primary pullback zone,
- confirmation layer for 1M entries.

On the 5-minute chart (and sometimes 1-minute):

- when price is above both 9 and 20 EMA and they are aligned upward, the short-term trend is bullish,
- when price is below both and they are aligned downward, the short-term trend is bearish,
- when price is repeatedly oscillating through both, conditions are choppy.

Key roles:

1. **Trend Filter:** Only take long scalps when price is above the 20 EMA and EMAs slope up; only take shorts when price is below and slope down.
2. **Pullback Zone:** Price often pulls back into the 9/20 EMA cluster before continuing; this becomes a "reload" area for scalpers.
3. **Structure Confirmation:** A break and hold above/below the 20 EMA often signals a micro shift in control between buyers and sellers.

9/20 EMA $\Rightarrow$ Short-term bias + pullback map

The 20/200 EMA Cluster: Macro Alignment and Regime Filter

The 20 and 200 EMAs define a larger structural context:

- 20 EMA: short-term equilibrium.
- 200 EMA: macro trend anchor.

On 5M or 15M charts:

- when price is consistently above the 200 EMA, the macro bias is bullish,
- when price is consistently below, macro bias is bearish,
- when price is chopping around the 200 EMA, the market is in transition or range.

Roles of 20/200 EMA:

1. **Regime Filter:** Only trade in the direction of the 200 EMA on higher timeframes to avoid counter-trend scalping in weak phases.
2. **Mean Reversion Levels:** The 20 EMA often acts as a "snapback" level after quick moves away from it.
3. **Avoiding Bad Areas:** When price is very close to the 200 EMA with no clear direction, conditions are often messy.

$$20/200 \text{ EMA} \Rightarrow \text{Market regime and macro bias}$$

How the Clusters Work Together

The three clusters form a layered view:

5/8/13	micro-trend and immediate scalping flow
9/20	short-term trend and pullback zone
20/200	macro context and regime filter

A high-probability environment looks like:

1. On higher timeframe (5M/15M): price is above the 200 EMA and the 20 EMA is sloping upward.
2. On 5M: 9 and 20 EMAs are aligned and trending; clear swings are visible.

3. On 1M: 5/8/13 EMAs are stacked in the direction of bias; price pulls back into the cluster, then continues.

This creates confluence:

$$\text{Macro Bias} + \text{Short-Term Structure}$$
$$+\text{Micro Flow} \Rightarrow \text{High-Probability Scalping Setup}$$

Common Mistakes When Using EMAs

Traders often misuse EMAs by:

- treating them as magical reversal lines,
- entering simply because price "touched" an EMA,
- ignoring context and regime,
- using too many moving averages, creating visual clutter.

Correct usage:

- EMAs support a setup; they are not the setup by themselves,
- price action at the EMA (wicks, rejection, structure) matters more than the line itself,
- the slope and spacing of EMAs are often more important than the exact value.

> The edge does not come from the EMA. It comes from how you read price *around* the EMA.

Summary

EMA clusters help a scalper:

- define micro and macro trend,
- locate high-probability pullback zones,
- filter out low-quality trades,
- align entries with structure and bias.

In short:

- 5/8/13 EMA: **immediate flow and micro-trend**,
- 9/20 EMA: **short-term trend and pullback zone**,
- 20/200 EMA: **market regime and directional filter**.

> EMAs do not predict the future. They organize the present so your decisions become cleaner and faster.

5.2 VWAP as Institutional Bias Anchor

The Volume-Weighted Average Price (VWAP) is one of the most powerful institutional indicators. It represents the average price at which the asset has traded throughout the session, weighted by volume. For scalpers, VWAP is not simply a line. It is a dynamic equilibrium point around which institutional sentiment and execution revolve.

VWAP is used by banks, hedge funds, and algorithmic execution engines to manage inventory and assess fair value. When price interacts with VWAP, it often reveals the intentions of large participants. For this reason, VWAP becomes an anchor of bias for intraday scalping.

Why VWAP Matters

VWAP captures three critical components of market behavior:

1. **Price**
2. **Volume**
3. **Time**

It reflects where the bulk of trading has occurred. Above VWAP, buyers have control. Below VWAP, sellers have control.

$$\text{Price above VWAP} \Rightarrow \text{Bullish bias}$$

$$\text{Price below VWAP} \Rightarrow \text{Bearish bias}$$

VWAP is not a signal to trade. It is a framework that establishes directional preference.

> Institutions use VWAP to judge whether they are getting a "good deal." Scalpers use VWAP to align with institutions.

VWAP as Dynamic Support and Resistance

VWAP acts like a gravity center. Price frequently returns to it throughout the session. This creates recurring opportunities:

- reversions to VWAP,
- continuation from VWAP,
- rejection from VWAP,
- break-and-hold moves.

Typical behaviors:

1. If price is above VWAP and pulls back into it, the level often becomes support.
2. If price is below VWAP and rallies into it, the level often becomes resistance.

This forms a structural map for scalpers.

$$\text{VWAP} = \text{fair value zone}$$

When VWAP Is Most Useful

VWAP is most effective in liquid markets during active sessions:

- futures (indices),
- forex,
- gold,
- high-volume cryptocurrencies.

Best time windows:

- London session,
- New York session,
- session overlaps.

During dead markets, VWAP loses significance because volume is low.

VWAP as Trend Filter

VWAP provides directional bias:

- long above VWAP,
- short below VWAP,
- avoid trading across VWAP when choppy.

A simple rule:

If price is tangled with VWAP, step aside.

When VWAP is flat and price oscillates around it, conditions are unstable. This is often a no-trade zone.

VWAP flattening = no direction = no edge.

VWAP Bands and Standard Deviations

Many traders use VWAP with standard deviation bands (similar to Bollinger Bands):

- VWAP $\pm 1\sigma$ (first deviation),
- VWAP $\pm 2\sigma$ (extended move),
- VWAP $\pm 3\sigma$ (extreme).

These bands represent zones of institutional imbalance:

- price stretched away from VWAP often reverts,
- extreme deviations create scalping opportunities.

Typical workflow:

1. price stretches to $\pm 2\sigma$,
2. exhaustion appears,
3. reversal or mean reversion setup becomes likely.

$$\text{Stretch} \rightarrow \text{Exhaustion} \rightarrow \text{Reversion}$$

VWAP as Execution Trigger

VWAP is also used as an execution reference:

- enter on pullback to VWAP,
- exit on burst away from VWAP,
- scale partials near bands.

A high-probability pattern:

$$\text{Higher timeframe trend} + \text{VWAP pullback} + \text{1M entry}$$

Stops are tight:

- below VWAP for longs,
- above VWAP for shorts.

Profit target: the next structural burst.

Common Pitfalls With VWAP

Incorrect usage includes:

- entering only because price "touched" VWAP,
- ignoring volatility spikes,
- trading when VWAP is flat inside chop,
- treating VWAP as a magic reversal line.

Correct usage:

- VWAP provides context, not signals,
- price action at VWAP matters more than the line itself,
- directional bias must be confirmed by structure.

> Price interacting with VWAP is information. Price reacting from VWAP is opportunity.

Summary

VWAP is an institutional anchor. It helps a scalper:

- define directional bias,
- locate fair value zones,
- identify dynamic support and resistance,
- manage entries and exits with precision.

Core principles:

1. Above VWAP = bullish bias.
2. Below VWAP = bearish bias.
3. Flat VWAP = stand aside.

VWAP shows where institutions perceive value. Trade with that perception, and scalping becomes easier.

5.3 RSI for Micro-Reversals

The Relative Strength Index (RSI) is one of the most widely used momentum oscillators. For scalpers, it has a very specific and powerful role: **spotting short-term exhaustion and micro-reversals** in fast markets.

Used correctly, RSI does not predict tops and bottoms. Instead, it highlights moments when momentum is stretched, sentiment is one-sided, and a short-term snapback is likely.

What RSI Actually Measures

RSI measures the strength of recent price moves by comparing average gains to average losses over a lookback period (commonly 14). The classic formula is:

$$RSI = 100 - \left(\frac{100}{1 + RS}\right)$$

where

$$RS = \frac{\text{Average Gain}}{\text{Average Loss}}$$

Values range from 0 to 100:

- RSI above 70 is traditionally considered "overbought",
- RSI below 30 is traditionally considered "oversold".

For scalpers, these thresholds are not rigid rules. They are *zones* of potential exhaustion.

> RSI does not say "price must reverse." It says "momentum is stretched; be alert for a reaction."

RSI in the Context of Scalping

In scalping, timing is critical. RSI helps identify:

- when a strong move is likely to stall,
- when a mini-pullback may begin,
- when a local high/low might form,
- when chasing momentum is dangerous.

Typical use cases:

- fading micro-exhaustion at extremes (counter-trend scalps),
- aligning with trend by waiting for RSI to cool off before re-entering,
- confirming divergence between price and momentum.

RSI should always be read *with* price action, not alone.

Micro Overbought and Oversold Zones

On lower timeframes (1-minute, 5-minute), classic RSI levels (70/30) can be too conservative. For aggressive scalpers, micro-reversal zones might be:

- 80–90 for overbought,
- 10–20 for oversold.

Interpretation:

- RSI above 80 on a strong spike suggests buyers are temporarily exhausted,
- RSI below 20 suggests sellers are temporarily exhausted.

However, in strong trends, RSI can stay extended for a long time. Therefore:

- do not short *only* because RSI is above 80,
- do not long *only* because RSI is below 20.

Price action confirmation is required.

RSI Divergence: A Powerful Micro-Reversal Signal

Divergence occurs when:

- price makes a new high, but RSI makes a lower high (bearish divergence),
- price makes a new low, but RSI makes a higher low (bullish divergence).

This suggests that:

- momentum is weakening,
- the current move is losing strength,
- a micro-reversal or consolidation is likely.

In scalping:

1. identify divergence on 1M or 5M RSI,
2. confirm with wick rejection or structure at a key level,
3. execute with tight stops and small targets.

$$\text{Divergence} + \text{Key Level} + \text{Rejection} \Rightarrow \text{Micro-Reversal Setup}$$

RSI as a Trend Filter: Avoiding Counter-Trend Traps

RSI can also help avoid bad trades:

- in a strong uptrend, repeated RSI readings above 60 suggest persistent buying pressure,
- in a strong downtrend, repeated RSI readings below 40 suggest persistent selling pressure.

This means:

- avoid aggressive shorts when RSI keeps resetting from 40 to 80 in an uptrend,
- avoid aggressive longs when RSI keeps moving from 60 down to 20 in a downtrend.

Instead, use RSI to:

- wait for pullbacks (RSI cooling off),
- re-enter in the direction of the trend.

In a trend, RSI is more useful for timing entries *with* the trend than for picking tops and bottoms.

Combining RSI With Price Action

RSI works best when paired with:

- support and resistance,
- order blocks,
- EMA clusters,
- VWAP.

Example long setup:

1. price is in an uptrend (above VWAP and 20 EMA),
2. price pulls back into EMA cluster or demand zone,
3. RSI dips into oversold or shows bullish divergence,
4. 1M candle prints a strong rejection wick,
5. enter long with stop below swing low.

Example short setup:

1. price is in a downtrend,
2. price rallies into resistance or supply,
3. RSI enters overbought or shows bearish divergence,
4. rejection appears (engulfing, pin bar),
5. enter short with stop above swing high.

Context (Trend) + Level + RSI Signal + Candle Confirmation

RSI Settings for Scalping

Common settings:

- Period: 14 (default, smoother, better for context),
- Period: 7–9 (faster, more sensitive, better for micro-signals).

For scalping:

- use 14-period RSI on 5M for context,
- use 7–9 period RSI on 1M for micro-reversals.

Shorter RSI reacts faster, but produces more noise. Use it only with strong filtering (trend, levels, structure).

Common Mistakes With RSI

Mistakes include:

- treating overbought as an automatic sell signal,
- treating oversold as an automatic buy signal,
- ignoring trend direction,
- using RSI in isolation,
- forcing trades just because RSI hit an extreme.

Correct mindset:

- RSI is a *warning*, not a command,
- price action and context always come first,
- divergence and levels matter more than raw numbers.

> RSI does not tell you what to do. It tells you where to pay attention.

Summary

For scalpers, RSI is a valuable tool for:

- detecting short-term exhaustion,
- spotting micro-reversals,
- avoiding chasing extended moves,
- refining entries at key levels.

The key principles:

1. use RSI to support price action, not to replace it,
2. focus on divergence and extremes at important levels,
3. align RSI usage with trend and structure,
4. avoid trading *only* because RSI is overbought/oversold.

> RSI is most powerful when it whispers "something is changing" just before price confirms it.

5.4 MACD for Momentum Confirmation

The Moving Average Convergence Divergence (MACD) is one of the most effective tools for confirming momentum in intraday trading. For scalpers, MACD is not a primary signal generator. Instead, it acts as a **confirmation engine** that validates the strength and direction of a move already identified through price action, EMAs, and VWAP.

Used correctly, MACD helps answer a critical scalping question:

> "Is this move gaining momentum or losing it?"

What MACD Measures

MACD is built from moving averages of price:

- a fast EMA (e.g. 12-period),
- a slow EMA (e.g. 26-period),
- a signal line (EMA of the MACD line, e.g. 9-period).

The classic components:

- **MACD line** = fast EMA − slow EMA,
- **Signal line** = EMA of MACD line,

- **Histogram** = MACD line − Signal line.

Interpretation:

- MACD above zero: bullish momentum (fast EMA above slow),
- MACD below zero: bearish momentum (fast EMA below slow),
- histogram growing: momentum increasing,
- histogram shrinking: momentum fading.

For scalpers, the histogram is especially useful as a visual map of momentum bursts.

MACD on Scalping Timeframes

For intraday scalping, MACD is typically used on:

- the 5-minute chart (for structure and context),
- sometimes the 1-minute chart (for fine confirmation).

Because MACD is a slower indicator, it is more meaningful on slightly higher intraday timeframes than on ultra-fast charts.

Effective use:

- 5M MACD: confirms trend direction and momentum environment,
- 1M MACD (optional): confirms local continuation or fading.

> Price gives the signal. MACD confirms whether the move has fuel.

Momentum Confirmation in Trend Trades

In trend-following scalps, MACD helps confirm that you are trading with active momentum rather than fading a dying move.

Example long scenario:

1. Price is above VWAP and 20 EMA on 5M.
2. EMAs are stacked bullishly; structure shows higher highs and higher lows.
3. MACD line is above zero, histogram positive and expanding.
4. Price pulls back on 1M to EMA cluster or demand zone.

5. MACD histogram on 1M turns back up, or MACD line crosses back above signal line.

This sequence suggests:

- macro bias bullish,
- short-term pullback completed,
- momentum resuming upward.

The scalper takes a long with confidence that momentum supports continuation.

Similarly, for short trades:

- MACD below zero,
- histogram negative and expanding,
- price below VWAP and 20 EMA,
- pullback into resistance,
- MACD turns back down.

$$\text{Trend} + \text{Pullback} + \text{MACD Resumption} \Rightarrow \text{Momentum-Backed Scalping Entry}$$

MACD as a "Do Not Chase" Filter

One of MACD's most powerful roles in scalping is preventing traders from chasing moves that are already exhausted.

Warning signs:

- price makes a new high, but MACD histogram fails to make a new high,
- price accelerates, but the histogram starts shrinking,
- price is extended far from EMAs, while MACD begins to flatten.

These conditions suggest:

- momentum is weakening,
- late entries are dangerous,
- risk of sharp pullback or reversal is high.

If MACD is fading while price is breaking out, the move is likely tired.

MACD therefore acts as a brake, preventing impulsive entries at the end of a move.

MACD Divergence and Micro-Reversals

Like RSI, MACD can form divergence:

- **Bearish divergence:** price makes a higher high, but MACD makes a lower high.
- **Bullish divergence:** price makes a lower low, but MACD makes a higher low.

Divergence does not guarantee reversal, but it warns that existing momentum is losing strength.

For scalpers, MACD divergence can be used to:

- tighten stops,
- take profits earlier,
- prepare for reversal scalps at key levels.

Ideal pattern:

1. price reaches a major intraday level (previous high/low, VWAP band, order block),
2. MACD shows clear divergence,
3. strong rejection candle forms on 1M,
4. volume confirms reaction.

$$\text{Level} + \text{MACD Divergence} + \text{Rejection} \Rightarrow \text{Micro-Reversal Opportunity}$$

MACD and Volatility Bursts

MACD histogram expansion often precedes or confirms volatility bursts. When the histogram:

- crosses from negative to positive and expands strongly, it signals a fresh surge of bullish momentum,
- crosses from positive to negative with expansion, it signals a fresh bearish wave.

This is useful for:

- breakouts from consolidation zones,
- session opens (London, New York),
- post-news continuation setups.

The scalper can time entries to coincide with the early part of a momentum surge rather than its end.

Recommended MACD Settings for Scalping

Common intraday settings:

- Standard: 12, 26, 9 (fast EMA, slow EMA, signal line),

This is usually sufficient for 5M and 1M scalping charts.

Some advanced scalpers may experiment with slightly faster parameters (e.g. 8, 21, 5), but the key is consistency:

- choose one setting,
- study its behavior deeply,
- avoid constant tweaking.

> Edge comes from understanding one configuration deeply, not from constantly changing it.

Common Mistakes With MACD

Traders misuse MACD when they:

- treat MACD crossovers as standalone buy/sell signals,
- ignore price action, levels, and structure,
- use MACD on too many timeframes at once,
- chase late-stage moves because MACD turned moments ago.

Correct approach:

- use MACD to confirm an existing idea based on price,
- rely on levels (VWAP, EMAs, structure) first,
- interpret MACD behavior in context of the broader regime (trend, range, volatility).

MACD is a supporting witness, not the judge.

Summary

For scalpers, MACD is a powerful tool for:

- confirming trend direction and momentum,
- filtering out late or exhausted entries,
- spotting weakening moves through divergence,
- aligning with volatility bursts.

Core principles:

1. let price, structure, and levels define the setup,
2. use MACD to confirm that momentum agrees,
3. avoid chasing moves when MACD is fading,
4. treat divergence as a warning, not an automatic reversal.

In scalping, MACD's job is simple: to tell you whether the move you want to trade still has energy.

5.5 ATR for Stop-Loss Engineering

The Average True Range (ATR) is one of the most practical tools for scalpers when it comes to risk management. While most indicators try to describe direction, ATR describes **volatility**. It answers a critical question:

> "How far can price reasonably move against me before my idea is invalid — not just before noise stops me out?"

Used correctly, ATR helps a scalper set stop-losses that are:

- logically tied to market behavior,
- adaptive to volatility,
- neither too tight nor too wide.

What ATR Measures

ATR measures the average range of price movement over a defined period. It is based on the "true range" of each candle, which incorporates gaps and wicks:

$$TR_t = \max \begin{cases} H_t - L_t, \\ |H_t - C_{t-1}|, \\ |L_t - C_{t-1}| \end{cases}$$

Where:

- H_t = current high,
- L_t = current low,
- C_{t-1} = previous close.

ATR is then the moving average (often 14 periods) of the true range:

$$ATR = MA(TR_t)$$

Interpretation:

- higher ATR = more volatility,
- lower ATR = quieter market.

For scalpers, ATR defines the *normal breathing space* of price.

The Problem With Arbitrary Stop-Losses

Many beginners set stops using:

- fixed pip/point distances (e.g. 5 pips, 10 points),
- random numbers (e.g. "this feels safe"),
- emotional thresholds ("I don't want to lose more than this").

These stops ignore volatility.
If the market is highly volatile:

- fixed stops are too tight,
- normal fluctuations trigger losses,
- trader gets stopped out before the move develops.

If the market is quiet:

- fixed stops are too wide,
- risk is larger than necessary,
- R:R (reward-to-risk) becomes inefficient.

ATR solves this by aligning stop distance with current volatility.

ATR-Based Stop Placement

A simple and effective rule:

$$\text{Stop Distance} = k \times ATR$$

Where k is a multiplier based on your scalping style (e.g. 0.5, 1.0, 1.5).
Examples:

- If ATR on 1M is 5 points and you use $k = 1.0$, stop distance = 5 points.
- If ATR on 1M is 10 points and you use $k = 0.7$, stop distance = 7 points.

This ensures:

- stops expand during volatile markets,
- stops contract during calm markets,
- risk per trade is structurally consistent.

  ATR does not tell you *where* to place the stop. It tells you *how far* it should logically be from your entry.

Combining ATR With Structure

ATR is most powerful when combined with technical structure:

- swing highs/lows,
- order blocks,
- support and resistance,
- VWAP or EMA zones.

Typical stop engineering process:

1. Identify the structural invalidation point (e.g. below a prior low for a long).
2. Measure distance between entry and that structure.
3. Compare it to ATR.
4. Adjust position size so that:

$$\text{Monetary Risk} = \text{Stop Distance (in points)} \times \text{Position Size}$$

If the structural stop is within a reasonable multiple of ATR (e.g. 0.5–1.5 ATR), the trade is valid. If it requires 3–4 ATR, the trade may be too expensive for a scalper.

ATR and Position Sizing

ATR helps answer:

> "How large can I size this trade while keeping risk per trade constant?"

Let:

- R = fixed risk per trade (e.g. 1% of account),
- D = stop distance in points or pips,
- V = value per point/pip.

Then:

$$\text{Position Size} = \frac{R}{D \times V}$$

Because D is linked to ATR, your position size will:

- decrease in high volatility,
- increase in low volatility.

This keeps **risk constant** even as market conditions change.

Filtering Bad Trades With ATR

ATR can also help you avoid low-quality setups:

- If ATR is extremely low, the market is too quiet; there may not be enough range to justify scalping.
- If ATR is extremely high, conditions may be chaotic; stops must be wide, and risk may be too large.

Practical filters:

- avoid scalping when ATR collapses to unusually low levels,
- reduce size or stand aside when ATR spikes to extreme highs (post-news, panic, liquidations).

ATR tells you whether the current environment is *worth* trading.

ATR on Different Timeframes

For scalping, ATR may be used on:

- 1M chart: for precise stop engineering on the execution timeframe,
- 5M chart: for broader volatility context and expected range.

Example usage:

- Use 5M ATR to gauge typical move size for the current session.
- Use 1M ATR to fine-tune stop placement at the micro level.

$$\text{Macro ATR (5M)} \Rightarrow \text{Session volatility context}$$
$$\text{Micro ATR (1M)} \Rightarrow \text{Exact stop engineering}$$

Common Mistakes Using ATR

Mistakes include:

- using ATR as a directional indicator (it is not),
- blindly using a fixed multiplier without checking structure,
- ignoring news and regime shifts,

- applying ATR from a higher timeframe that is too slow for scalping decisions.

Correct principles:

- ATR defines risk distance, not trade direction,
- structure decides where the stop must go, ATR decides if it is reasonable,
- always cross-check ATR with market context (trend, news, session).

Summary

ATR is an essential tool for stop-loss engineering in scalping. It allows the trader to:

- size stops according to real volatility,
- maintain consistent risk across changing conditions,
- filter out dead or hyper-chaotic environments,
- combine structure and volatility into a rational risk model.

Key rules:

1. Use ATR as a volatility yardstick, not a signal.
2. Align stops with both structure and ATR multiples.
3. Adjust position size so that monetary risk stays constant.
4. Avoid markets where ATR is too low (no range) or too high (chaos).

> In scalping, your edge is small but repeatable. ATR ensures that noise does not steal it and that volatility does not destroy it.

5.6 Indicator Combinations That Reduce False Signals

Indicators are most dangerous when used alone. A single signal — an RSI cross, a MACD flip, a VWAP touch, or an EMA tag — can easily mislead a trader, especially on fast intraday charts. Scalping requires a framework where indicators *confirm* each other and sit inside a larger context of price action and structure.

The goal is not to stack many indicators. The goal is to create a **minimal, coherent combination** that:

- filters out low-quality trades,
- reduces noise and fake signals,
- increases confidence in execution,
- keeps charts clean and readable.

Principle: Price First, Indicators Second

Before combining indicators, one core rule must be established:

> Price action and structure come first. Indicators only confirm or filter.

That means:

- identify trend, range, levels (highs/lows, supply/demand, VWAP, previous session levels),
- define the context and bias (bullish, bearish, neutral),
- then ask: *do my indicators agree with what price is already telling me?*

Indicators should not create trades that price does not justify.

A Clean Core Stack for Scalping

A simple but powerful indicator stack for scalping might include:

- EMA clusters (5/8/13 and 9/20) for trend and pullback zones,
- VWAP for institutional bias and fair value,
- RSI for micro-reversal and exhaustion,
- MACD for momentum confirmation,
- ATR for stop-loss engineering (risk, not entry).

Each plays a different role:

EMA clusters	structure + dynamic S/R
VWAP	directional bias + equilibrium
RSI	micro-exhaustion + divergence
MACD	momentum confirmation
ATR	volatility + logical stop distance

No indicator overlaps another's function. This reduces redundancy and confusion.

Combination 1: Trend + Pullback + Momentum

This is a classic continuation scalping template.

Components:

- 5/8/13 and 9/20 EMA clusters,
- MACD (trend and momentum),
- optional: RSI for micro timing.

Bullish example:

1. Price is above 20 EMA and 200 EMA on 5M; EMAs aligned upward.
2. MACD on 5M is above zero; histogram positive or expanding.
3. On 1M:
    - EMAs (5/8/13) are stacked bullishly,
    - price pulls back into 9/20 EMA or micro demand,
    - RSI cools down from overbought towards mid-levels (40–60), not collapsing.
4. A bullish rejection or engulfing candle forms on 1M.

Only when **all** conditions align:

- trend confirmed (EMAs, MACD),
- pullback confirmed (price into EMA cluster),
- momentum resuming (MACD or RSI turning),

does the scalper enter.
This combination filters:

- counter-trend trades,
- pullbacks that are actually reversals,
- entries during momentum exhaustion.

Combination 2: VWAP + EMA Cluster + RSI Exhaustion

This is effective for intraday mean reversion and continuation around fair value.

Components:

- VWAP (session anchor),
- 9/20 EMA (short-term trend),
- RSI (overbought/oversold and divergence).

Short example (rejection from VWAP in downtrend):

1. Price is below VWAP and 20 EMA on 5M — bearish bias.
2. On 1M:
    - price rallies back up towards VWAP and 9/20 EMA cluster,
    - RSI moves toward overbought (70–80 zone),
    - micro structure shows rejection wicks near VWAP.
3. A bearish rejection candle forms, and RSI begins to turn down.

Here VWAP gives:

- institutional fair value,
- a likely resistance zone in a downtrend.

EMAs show:

- pullback against short-term trend.

RSI shows:

- temporary exhaustion of buyers.

The combination reduces the chance of shorting too early or too late. You short when:

$$\text{Bias (VWAP)} + \text{Structure (EMA)} + \text{Exhaustion (RSI)} + \text{Rejection (Candle)}$$

Combination 3: Breakout Filter — MACD + RSI + ATR

Scalpers often get trapped in fake breakouts. Indicators can help filter which ones are worth taking.

Components:

- MACD (momentum expansion),
- RSI (avoid extreme overextension),
- ATR (ensure volatility justifies trade).

Long breakout example:

1. Price is approaching an intraday resistance level with established trend behind it.
2. MACD on 5M:
   - above zero,
   - histogram expanding.
3. RSI:
   - rising, but not yet at extreme (e.g. between 55 and 70),
   - no clear bearish divergence.
4. ATR:
   - at a healthy level (not extremely low),
   - suggests sufficient volatility for a breakout to run.
5. Breakout occurs with strong candle and increased volume.

If instead:

- MACD is flattening,
- RSI is already extremely overbought and diverging,
- ATR has collapsed,

the trader may skip the breakout, expecting a fake or short-lived move.

> The combination helps you distinguish a breakout with fuel from a breakout running on fumes.

Combination 4: Divergence + Level + EMA Alignment

Divergence alone (on RSI or MACD) is not enough to trade. However, when combined with key levels and EMA structure, it becomes a powerful reversal filter.

Components:

- RSI or MACD (divergence),
- horizontal level (high/low, prior session, supply/demand),
- EMA clusters (trend shift or flattening).

Bullish reversal example:

1. Price makes a lower low into a key demand level.
2. RSI or MACD makes a higher low (bullish divergence).
3. EMAs on 1M:
    - flatten or begin to curl upward.
4. A strong bullish engulfing candle prints from the level.

Here:

- the level provides location,
- divergence provides early warning,
- EMAs show that momentum is shifting.

All three together dramatically reduce the probability of fading a move too early or in the middle of a trend.

Best Practices for Combining Indicators

To reduce false signals:

1. **Limit the number of indicators.** 3–5 well-understood tools are better than 10 cluttered signals.
2. **Assign each indicator a role.** Do not use multiple indicators for the same function (e.g. three momentum oscillators).
3. **Demand confluence.** A single indicator signal is not enough; require agreement between:
    - context (trend, session, volatility),
    - structure (levels, EMAs, VWAP),
    - confirmation (RSI/MACD/price reaction).
4. **Use ATR for risk, not entries.** ATR should shape stop distances and position size, not tell you when to trade.
5. **Always let price lead.** Indicator alignment without clear price action is still low probability.

Common Mistakes When Combining Indicators

Typical errors include:

- indicator overload (too many tools, conflicting signals),
- searching for "perfect" confluence and missing valid trades,
- overfitting: forcing indicator rules onto every chart,
- ignoring time-of-day, news, and regime while trusting indicators blindly.

The correction is philosophical:

> Indicators should simplify decisions, not complicate them.

If the combination makes your choices harder, remove something.

Summary

The purpose of combining indicators is to:

- filter out bad trades,
- increase the quality of good trades,
- reduce emotional doubt at the moment of execution.

Effective combinations usually include:

- one tool for structure and trend (EMAs, VWAP),
- one tool for momentum (MACD),
- one tool for exhaustion or reversals (RSI),
- one tool for volatility and risk (ATR).

> Price is the story. Indicators are supporting characters. When they agree with the story, you have a higher-probability trade. When they disagree, you wait.

Chapter 6

Price Action Mastery for Scalpers

Scalping is built on a single foundation: the movement of price. Indicators can assist, but they follow price. Price action is always first.

This chapter focuses on how price behaves on fast timeframes, how structure forms and breaks, and how volatility and liquidity shape opportunity. By learning to read price directly, a scalper can execute with speed, accuracy, and confidence, even in rapidly changing conditions.

6.1 Market Structure (HH, LL, BOS, CHOCH) Simplified

Market structure is the foundation of price action. It describes how price moves, where it is likely to continue, and where it is likely to reverse. For scalpers, structure must be understood in the simplest possible terms, because decisions are made quickly.

At the core of all structure are four elements:

- Higher High (HH)
- Lower Low (LL)
- Break of Structure (BOS)
- Change of Character (CHOCH)

Even without indicators, these concepts reveal the direction of flow and the intention of the market.

Higher Highs (HH) and Higher Lows (HL)

An uptrend is defined by:

$$HH \to HL \to HH \to HL$$

- A **Higher High** means buyers pushed price beyond the previous high.
- A **Higher Low** means sellers attempted to push down, but failed to reach the prior low.

When scalping:

- do not short when the market is consistently making HH/HL,
- look to buy pullbacks into structure or dynamic support (EMA cluster, VWAP, demand).

In an uptrend:

> Pullbacks are opportunities, not threats.

Lower Lows (LL) and Lower Highs (LH)

A downtrend is the reverse pattern:

$$LL \to LH \to LL \to LH$$

- A **Lower Low** shows sellers have control.
- A **Lower High** shows buyers cannot push back with strength.

In a downtrend:

- avoid buying aggressively,
- look for short entries when price pulls back into resistance or supply zones.

> Trade in the direction of structure, not against it.

Break of Structure (BOS)

A Break of Structure occurs when price breaks the previous high or low in the direction of the existing trend.

- In an uptrend, BOS means price breaks a previous high.
- In a downtrend, BOS means price breaks a previous low.

BOS confirms:

- trend continuation,
- liquidity taken above/ below prior swing,
- new impulse leg has begun.

For scalpers, BOS is a critical confirmation:

> BOS = permission to look for continuation entries.

Typically, entries are taken on:

- the next pullback,
- retest of structure,
- or micro-demand/supply around the break.

$$BOS \Rightarrow Pullback \Rightarrow Entry$$

Change of Character (CHOCH)

CHOCH signifies the first clue of a potential reversal. It occurs when price breaks a structural swing in the *opposite* direction of the existing trend.

- In an uptrend, CHOCH is the first break below a significant higher low.
- In a downtrend, CHOCH is the first break above a significant lower high.

CHOCH does not guarantee a trend change. It simply signals:

- momentum may be shifting,
- trend may be weakening,
- caution is required.

For scalpers:

> CHOCH means stop trading continuation until price confirms the new direction.

Structure Drives Entry Logic

Structure provides the directional map:

- HH/HL = only look for longs,
- LL/LH = only look for shorts,
- BOS = continuation entries,
- CHOCH = prepare for potential reversal.

This prevents emotional trading:

- no guessing,
- no chasing,
- no counter-trend temptation.

Practical Scalping Workflow

A simple real-time process:

1. Identify the current structure:
    - HH/HL or LL/LH?
2. Mark the last BOS.
3. Wait for pullback into:
    - EMA clusters,
    - VWAP,
    - supply/demand,
    - liquidity zone.
4. Confirm with:
    - candle rejection,
    - momentum resumption.
5. Execute with tight stop.

$$\text{Structure} \rightarrow \text{Location} \rightarrow \text{Trigger}$$

Summary

Market structure is the simplest and most reliable roadmap for scalpers. The core elements:

- Higher Highs and Higher Lows = uptrend and long setups,
- Lower Lows and Lower Highs = downtrend and short setups,
- BOS confirms continuation,
- CHOCH signals the first shift in character.

Price structure reveals the path of least resistance. Trade with it, not against it.

6.2 Micro Pullbacks and Impulse Legs

Markets do not move in straight lines. Even the strongest trend consists of two alternating phases:

1. an **impulse leg** — fast directional movement,
2. a **pullback** — temporary pause or retracement.

For scalpers, mastering the relationship between impulse and pullback is essential. It determines where to enter, where to avoid entries, and when momentum is likely to resume.

Impulse Legs: The Engine of Trend

An impulse leg is a strong, directional move with:

- large candles,
- minimal wicks,
- strong momentum,
- clear market intent.

Impulse behavior shows that:

- imbalance exists between buyers and sellers,
- liquidity has been consumed,
- price is traveling toward the next target.

In an uptrend:

$$Impulse = HigherHigh(HH)$$

In a downtrend:

$$Impulse = LowerLow(LL)$$

Impulses reveal the active side:

- if impulse candles are long and clean, the trend is healthy,
- if they shrink or stall, momentum is fading.

Pullbacks: The Opportunity Zone

A pullback is a controlled retracement against the trend. It represents:

- profit taking,
- rebalancing of orders,
- a chance for new participants to enter.

For scalpers, pullbacks are the **entry point** into a trend. Characteristics of healthy pullbacks:

- smaller candles than the impulse,
- shallow retracement,
- declining momentum,
- occurs into structure or dynamic support (EMAs, VWAP).

In an uptrend, a pullback ends when buyers resume control, typically at:

- the EMA cluster (5/8/13 or 9/20),
- previous structure (prior HL),
- demand or liquidity zone.

A good entry location often occurs at the end of a pullback, when momentum resumes.

$$Impulse \Rightarrow Pullback \Rightarrow Impulse$$

This rhythmic sequence is the heartbeat of trending markets.

Micro Pullbacks on Fast Timeframes

On 1-minute and tick charts, pullbacks are often very small:

- 2–6 candles,
- sharp but controlled,
- often end with a wick rejection.

Micro pullbacks allow scalpers to:

- enter close to structure,
- use tight stop-losses,
- capture a large reward relative to risk.

Signals that a micro pullback is ending:

- momentum slows,
- wicks form against the pullback direction,
- EMAs flatten then curl back with trend,
- small inside bars or doji clusters appear,
- a strong candle prints in trend direction.

Weak Pullbacks vs Reversals

Not every pullback is an entry. Some pullbacks are the beginning of a reversal. We distinguish these by structure:

- **Healthy pullback:** higher low in an uptrend, lower high in a downtrend.
- **Reversal:** break of structure (BOS) or change of character (CHOCH).

Rules of thumb:

- If the pullback forms a **higher low** after an impulse up, bias remains long.
- If the pullback breaks below the most recent swing low, momentum has changed.

Structure tells the truth faster than indicators.

Impulse-Pullback Symmetry

The size of a pullback often mirrors the size of the previous impulse. A strong impulse usually leads to a shallow pullback:

$$\text{Strong impulse} \Rightarrow \text{Small pullback}$$

A weak impulse often leads to a deeper pullback:

$$\text{Weak impulse} \Rightarrow \text{Deep pullback or reversal}$$

Scalpers should measure impulse strength by:

- candle size,
- length of move,
- volume expansion,
- clean structure.

Where Scalpers Enter

The optimal entry is rarely at the breakout of the impulse. Instead, entries occur when the pullback ends and the next impulse begins.

Locations:

- EMA clusters,
- VWAP,
- prior swing high/low,
- imbalance or FVG fill,
- demand/supply zones.

Triggers:

- rejection wick,
- engulfing candle,
- break of minor micro-structure,
- momentum resumption.

$$Pullback \rightarrow Rejection \rightarrow Momentum \rightarrow Entry$$

This keeps stops tight and targets clean.

Why Impulse-Pullback Patterns Matter to Scalpers

Scalpers do not need to predict the market. They need to **react to structure**:

- identify the impulse direction,
- wait for the pullback,
- enter as momentum resumes.

This eliminates:

- chasing,
- emotional entries,
- random trading.

> Scalping is waiting, not chasing. The waiting happens during the pullback. The profit happens during the impulse.

Summary

- Markets move in cycles of impulse and pullback.
- Impulse shows direction and momentum.
- Pullback provides entry location.
- Micro pullbacks on fast timeframes are ideal for tight stops.
- Structure determines whether a pullback is healthy or reversing.

$$Impulse \rightarrow Pullback \rightarrow Impulse \rightarrow Pullback$$

This sequence is the backbone of trending markets. Scalpers who understand it trade with rhythm, patience, and precision.

6.3 Liquidity Sweeps and Stop-Hunt Behaviors

Financial markets do not move randomly. Before price travels in one direction, it often moves in the opposite direction briefly. This is not noise or manipulation; it is the natural process of harvesting liquidity before continuation.

> Price seeks liquidity first, then makes the real move.

For scalpers, understanding this pattern is critical. It prevents premature entries, explains failed trades, and reveals high-probability opportunities.

What Is Liquidity?

Liquidity represents stop orders, pending orders, and trapped traders. These orders are fuel for movement.

Common liquidity zones:

- above swing highs,
- below swing lows,
- near round numbers (00, 50),
- at previous session highs/lows,
- near obvious support/resistance.

Markets move toward these zones because:

- stop-losses are buy/sell orders,
- breakout traders place entries there,
- market makers use that volume to build positions.

Liquidity Sweep (Stop-Hunt)

A liquidity sweep is a fast move that takes out stops, triggers breakout traders, and then reverses.

It looks like:

1. price approaches a swing high,
2. wicks spike above the high,
3. stops are taken,
4. price quickly reverses.

This move is intentional: it clears liquidity to fuel the next impulse.

$$\text{Sweep} \Rightarrow \text{Reverse} \Rightarrow \text{Impulse}$$

The same applies below swing lows.

Why Sweeps Happen

Most traders place stops:

- just above a high,
- just below a low.

Large participants know this. To accumulate positions:

- they push price into those areas,
- trigger stop-losses,
- fill large orders against the crowd.

> Sweeps are not manipulation. They are the natural mechanics of order flow.

Recognizing Sweeps in Real Time

Sweeps often show the same characteristics:

- long wick through a level,
- fast reversal,
- trapped breakout traders,
- momentum shifts immediately after.

Common locations:

- Asian highs and lows (common targets during London open),
- previous session highs/lows,
- high-volume nodes on volume profile,
- VWAP deviations,
- key supply/demand zones.

A scalper does not enter *during* the sweep. They wait for the sweep to complete and then enter the reversal or continuation.

Continuation Sweeps

Not every sweep causes reversal. Many sweeps are continuation setups:

- price sweeps a low in an uptrend,
- takes liquidity,
- then continues upward.

Example in uptrend:

1. uptrend with higher highs and higher lows,
2. price pulls back,
3. sweeps below a previous higher low,
4. immediate rejection,
5. trend continues upward.

This is not trend change. It is trend **maintenance through liquidity capture**.

The best continuation trades occur right after a sweep.

Reversal Sweeps

Sweeps at the end of a trend often mark exhaustion:

- price makes a final push,
- liquidity above highs is consumed,
- volume dries up,
- momentum collapses,
- reversal begins.

These appear as:

- double top with a sweep,
- long upper wick,
- engulfing reversal candle,
- divergence (RSI/MACD).

Scalpers capitalize by:

- entering after the reversal signal,
- placing stops beyond the sweep.

How to Trade Sweeps Safely

A practical workflow:

1. Identify a clear liquidity zone (swing high/low).
2. Wait for price to sweep the level.
3. Watch for:
    - wick rejection,
    - engulfing candle,
    - micro BOS in the new direction.
4. Enter with stop beyond the sweep.

$$\text{Sweep} \rightarrow \text{Rejection} \rightarrow \text{Micro BOS} \rightarrow \text{Entry}$$

Common Mistakes

Traders fail around sweeps by:

- entering too early,
- chasing breakouts,
- placing stops too close to obvious levels,
- ignoring structure.

Two dangers:

1. Buying the high of the sweep.
2. Shorting the low of the sweep.

The correct entry is always **after** confirmation.

Why This Matters to Scalpers

Scalping lives in microstructure. Sweeps explain:

- why stop-losses are hit before the real move,
- why breakouts fail,
- why reversals begin abruptly,
- where high-probability trades occur.

Sweeps are not accidents. They are invitations.

Price sweeps liquidity to fuel direction. A scalper who waits for the sweep gains:

- better entries,
- tighter stops,
- cleaner targets.

Summary

- Liquidity hides above highs and below lows.
- Price often sweeps those levels before moving in the real direction.
- Sweeps create stop-hunts, trap traders, and build fuel.
- Continuation sweeps maintain the trend.
- Reversal sweeps mark exhaustion.
- The best trades occur **after** the sweep, not during it.

Understand liquidity, and the market becomes predictable.

6.4 Breaker Blocks, Imbalance, and Fair Value Gaps (FVG)

Price does not move in a smooth, even rhythm. It accelerates, pauses, reverses, and often leaves behind areas of inefficiency. These inefficiencies contain valuable information about order flow and institutional activity.

Three related concepts help scalpers understand this behavior:

- breaker blocks,
- imbalance,
- fair value gaps (FVG).

These are not theoretical tools. They are practical areas where price repeatedly reacts, pauses, or reverses, especially on intraday charts.

Imbalance: When Price Moves Too Fast

An imbalance occurs when price moves so quickly in one direction that the opposite side has little chance to trade.

For example:

- a large bullish candle with almost no wick,
- a sudden sell-off with minimal pullback.

Imbalances show where:

- aggressive order flow entered,
- liquidity was consumed,
- resting orders may exist.

Because price moved too quickly, it may return later to "rebalance". This return is often the scalper's entry.

Visual signature:

- clean directional candles,
- little or no overlap,
- space between highs and lows.

Fair Value Gaps (FVG)

A Fair Value Gap (FVG) is a specific form of imbalance. It is typically defined using a three-candle pattern:

$$\text{Candle 1 High} < \text{Candle 3 Low}$$

for bearish FVG, or:

$$\text{Candle 1 Low} > \text{Candle 3 High}$$

for bullish FVG.

This creates a "gap" where little trading happened. Price often returns to this zone later.

Why FVG matters:

- markets seek fair value,
- price fills inefficient zones,
- fills often align with continuation setups.

Example workflow:

1. Identify a strong impulse creating an FVG.
2. Wait for price to return to the FVG.
3. Look for:
   - rejection,
   - continuation,
   - resumption of trend.

This combines:

$$\text{Efficiency} + \text{Trend} = \text{High-probability scalping entry}$$

Breaker Blocks: Failed Breakouts That Reverse

A breaker block is a candle or zone that was an attempt to continue trend, but failed.

Typical sequence:

1. price forms a swing high (or low),
2. market attempts a breakout,
3. breakout fails,
4. price reverses aggressively,
5. that breakout area becomes a key zone.

In other words:

> A breaker block is a failed attack that becomes a defensive wall.

Bullish breaker block:

- price takes out a swing low (stop sweep),
- reverses strongly upward,
- the candle that caused the sweep becomes a demand zone.

Bearish breaker block:

- price takes out a swing high,
- reverses downward,
- the candle responsible becomes resistance.

Scalpers use breaker blocks to enter with tight stops:

- price returns to breaker block,
- prints rejection wick or engulfing candle,
- trend resumes.

How Imbalance, FVG, and Breaker Blocks Interact

These concepts are often found together:

- a sweep occurs,
- a strong impulse creates imbalance and FVG,
- price returns to fill the FVG,
- breaker block holds structure,
- the next impulse begins.

A full sequence looks like:

$$\text{Sweep} \rightarrow \text{Impulse} \rightarrow \text{FVG} \rightarrow \text{Retrace} \rightarrow \text{Breaker Block} \rightarrow \text{Continuation}$$

This pattern is extremely common in fast markets.

How Scalpers Trade These Zones

A practical workflow:

1. Identify a strong impulse creating imbalance or FVG.
2. Mark the FVG zone.
3. Mark the breaker block within or around it.
4. Wait for price to return.
5. Look for:
    - wick rejection,

  - micro BOS in trend direction,
  - volume confirmation.

6. Enter with stop beyond the breaker block.

Targets:

- previous highs/lows,
- next liquidity pocket,
- VWAP or EMA target,
- session range extremes.

Why These Tools Matter for Scalpers

On fast timeframes, price behavior is fast and noisy. Imbalance, FVG, and breaker blocks provide:

- structure,
- logic,
- repeatable behavior,
- precision locations.

They reveal:

- where large orders entered,
- where trapped traders exist,
- where price is likely to react.

Scalpers do not predict direction. They locate where the next battle will happen.

Common Mistakes

Avoid:

- assuming every gap must fill immediately,
- forcing trades on weak impulses,
- ignoring broader trend or session context,
- entering before confirmation.

Correct approach:

- the impulse must be strong,
- the zone must align with trend or structure,
- entry requires reaction, not prediction.

Summary

- Imbalance occurs when price moves too fast, creating inefficiency.
- Fair Value Gaps (FVG) are three-candle gaps that price often returns to fill.
- Breaker blocks form from failed breakouts and become key zones.
- These concepts frequently occur together and drive continuation.

$$\text{Imbalance} \Rightarrow \text{FVG} \Rightarrow \text{Return} \Rightarrow \text{Breaker Block} \Rightarrow \text{Continuation}$$

> Price always returns to efficiency. This return creates scalping opportunities.

6.5 Candle Behavior on Micro Timeframes

On fast charts (1-minute, 30-second, 15-second, tick), price moves quickly and patterns form rapidly. To scalp effectively, the trader must read the language of candles with clarity. Candles reveal intention, pressure, rejection, absorption, and exhaustion long before indicators respond.

> When speed increases, patterns become simpler, not more complicated.

Micro timeframes do not require complex formations. They require sharp observation of:

- bodies,
- wicks,
- sequences,
- momentum,
- location.

Bodies: Strength and Commitment

The candle body shows how far price traveled between open and close.

- large bodies = strong commitment,
- small bodies = lack of conviction.

Rules of thumb:

- A series of large bodies in one direction is an impulse.
- A series of small bodies is consolidation or indecision.

In trending conditions:

- look for large bodies in the direction of the trend,
- avoid fading strong bodies directly.

Wicks: Rejection and Absorption

Wicks reveal where price was rejected. Long wicks show that price attempted to move into an area but failed.

- upper wicks = seller aggression,
- lower wicks = buyer aggression.

On micro timeframes, wick behavior often signals:

- end of pullback,
- sweep of liquidity,
- exhaustion before reversal.

A high-quality signal:

- multiple wicks into the same level,
- followed by strong body in the opposite direction.

$$\text{Wicks} = \text{Warning}, \quad \text{Strong Body} = \text{Confirmation}$$

Sequences: Patterns Without Names

Micro timeframes move fast. Classic patterns (head and shoulders, triangles) often do not complete. Instead, observe simple sequences:

- strong candle, pause, continuation,
- two or three small candles, then breakout,
- rejection wick, engulfing candle.

Names are irrelevant. Behavior matters:

$$\text{Energy} \rightarrow \text{Pause} \rightarrow \text{Energy}$$

This pattern is the heartbeat of continuation.

Momentum and Speed

Momentum can be seen without indicators:

- candles increase in size = momentum building,
- candles decrease in size = momentum fading.

Add wick analysis:

- large bodies, small wicks = clean movement,
- small bodies, long wicks = indecision or reversal pressure.

For scalpers, momentum is often more important than direction. A slow trend is dangerous. A fast trend is profitable.

Location: Context Gives Meaning

Micro candle behavior only matters in context:

- rejection wicks at random locations are meaningless,
- rejection wicks at levels are powerful.

Key locations:

- previous highs and lows,
- VWAP bands,
- EMA clusters,
- breaker blocks,
- fair value gaps.

Always ask:

> Is this candle rejecting something meaningful?

Engulfing Candles: Micro Reversal Triggers

Engulfing candles are simple and reliable on fast charts.
They show:

- a complete shift in control,
- from buyers to sellers or vice versa.

High-probability reversal entries occur when:

1. there is a sweep of a level,
2. wick rejection is visible,
3. engulfing candle forms,
4. momentum returns.

This sequence happens repeatedly around liquidity zones.

Inside Bars: Compression Before Expansion

Inside bars (small candle inside previous candle) represent compression.

Compression leads to expansion:

$$\text{Small Range} \rightarrow \text{Large Range}$$

Inside bars near structure:

- signal pause,
- prepare for breakout,
- reduce noise.

Three or more inside bars in a row:

$$\text{Coil} \rightarrow \text{Release}$$

The breakout direction is often aligned with trend.

Exhaustion: When the Move Is Done

Exhaustion is visible before reversal:

- candles lose size,
- wicks increase,
- momentum slows,
- range compresses.

Classic exhaustion pattern:

- strong impulse,
- weak continuation,
- tiny candles,
- large opposite candle.

This is where many scalpers enter:

$$\text{Strong} \rightarrow \text{Weak} \rightarrow \text{Opposite} = \text{Reversal}$$

Trap Zones

Micro timeframes reveal places where traders get trapped:

- chasing breakouts after a long candle,
- entering on the last push before exhaustion,
- fading strong trends too early.

Often:

- price sweeps a level,
- traps traders,
- reverses sharply.

Avoid entering inside the trap zone. Wait for:

- confirmation candle,
- micro BOS,
- structure shift.

Why Candle Behavior Matters for Scalpers

Scalping is fast. Price action must be read in seconds.
Candles provide:

- instant feedback,
- real-time sentiment,
- momentum clues.

> Candles are the most honest indicator. They cannot lag because they are price itself.

Summary

On micro timeframes, candle reading is:

- simple,
- fast,
- contextual.

Key lessons:

- large bodies = strength,
- small bodies = indecision,
- wicks = rejection and absorption,
- engulfing = control shift,
- inside bars = compression before expansion,
- exhaustion = fading momentum and reversal potential.

Always combine candle behavior with location:

$$\text{Signal} + \text{Location} = \text{Trade}$$

> On fast charts, candles tell the story. Indicators only confirm it.

6.6 Recognizing Trap Zones and Exhaustion

Scalping requires precision. Many losses do not come from bad strategy, but from trading in the wrong location at the wrong moment. Trap zones and exhaustion patterns are two of the most common causes of failed trades. Learning to recognize them prevents impulsive entries and protects capital.

> A trap is where most traders enter. Exhaustion is where the move is already finished.

What Is a Trap Zone?

A trap zone is a price area where market participants enter with strong conviction, only to be reversed immediately.

Signs of a trap:

- strong breakout candle,
- price crosses a key level,
- traders chase the breakout,
- price instantly snaps back.

Trap zones form around obvious locations:

- prior swing highs and lows,
- round numbers (00, 50),

- session highs/lows,
- breakout levels,
- trendline touches.

If a level is obvious to everyone, it is bait.

Micro Structure of a Trap

The sequence usually looks like:

1. price approaches a level,
2. breakout candle forms,
3. volume spikes,
4. traders enter on fear of missing out,
5. price reverses violently.

This reversal is not random. It is the result of liquidity collection:

- stop losses are triggered,
- breakout traders are trapped,
- large players take the opposite side.

$$\text{Trap} = \text{Liquidity Collected}$$

After the trap, the real move begins.

How to Avoid Getting Trapped

Rules for avoiding traps:

1. Do not enter at the exact breakout level.
2. Wait for pullback or retest.
3. Look for reaction before entry.
4. Confirm with structure (HH/HL or LL/LH).

The safest approach:

$$\text{Breakout} \rightarrow \text{Retest} \rightarrow \text{Entry}$$

Not:

$$\text{Breakout} \rightarrow \text{Chase} \rightarrow \text{Loss}$$

Exhaustion: When the Move Is Over

Exhaustion happens when price has traveled too far, too fast, and buyers or sellers begin to lose strength. It precedes reversal or deeper pullback.

Characteristics:

- candles shrink,
- wicks become larger,
- volume drops,
- momentum indicators flatten,
- divergences form.

Visual signature:

- strong impulse,
- weak continuation,
- tiny candles,
- large opposite candle.

This is a classic exhaustion model.

> When price loses energy, reversal is imminent.

Location of Exhaustion

Exhaustion often appears at key levels:

- supply/demand zones,
- previous high/low,
- VWAP deviations,
- imbalance edges,
- FVG boundaries.

The most dangerous place to enter is at the end of an exhausted move. This is where inexperienced traders chase price.

> The best trades are made at the beginning of energy, not at the end of it.

Trap Before Reversal

Many reversals begin with traps:

1. price sweeps the high,
2. breakout traders enter,
3. early shorts get stopped out,
4. strong rejection candle forms,
5. reversal follows.

Trap + Exhaustion = High-probability reversal.

$$\text{Sweep} + \text{Exhaustion} \Rightarrow \text{Reversal}$$

Trap Zones in Ranges

Trap zones are especially common in range-bound markets:

- price touches range high,
- breakout candle triggers traders,
- reversal sweeps back to range low,
- reverse sequence occurs at range low.

The range becomes a trap machine.

Scalpers should avoid breakout trades at range edges. Better trades occur at:

- midpoint,
- VWAP,
- imbalances within the range.

How a Scalper Uses Traps to Their Advantage

Instead of avoiding traps entirely, scalpers can trade **from** them.

Setup:

1. identify obvious level (high/low),
2. wait for sweep and rejection wick,
3. look for micro BOS in opposite direction,
4. enter with tight stop beyond sweep.

This provides:

- asymmetric reward-to-risk,
- minimal drawdown,
- strong directional follow-through.

Macro vs Micro Exhaustion

Exhaustion appears on multiple timeframes:

- macro exhaustion = end of trend,
- micro exhaustion = pullback opportunity.

Scalper cares about both:

- micro exhaustion = continuation setup,
- macro exhaustion = reversal setup.

Clues to macro exhaustion:

- divergence across timeframes,
- failing structure (CHOCH),
- large wicks at major levels.

Summary

- Trap zones form where breakout traders enter aggressively.
- Exhaustion occurs when the movement is out of energy.
- Both are visible through candle size, wick behavior, volume, and location.
- Sweeps collect liquidity, then the real move begins.
- Avoid chasing breakouts into obvious levels.
- Enter after confirmation from:
  - rejection,
  - micro BOS,
  - structure alignment.

The losing trader trades inside the trap. The winning trader waits outside the trap and enters after the breakout fails.

Chapter 7

Order Flow & Tape Reading

Price moves because orders are executed. Behind every candle lies a stream of bids and offers, filled and unfilled, visible and hidden. Order flow analysis makes these forces visible. It shows how liquidity enters the market, where traders are trapped, and when reversals or continuations are likely.

This chapter introduces the essential concepts of order flow for scalpers: bid/ask dynamics, footprint charts, imbalance, absorption, iceberg orders, and tape reading. The goal is not to predict price, but to understand the pressure behind each movement and to recognize how real-time liquidity shifts create opportunity.

7.1 Bid/Ask Dynamics

Every price on a chart is the result of an agreement between buyers and sellers. To understand this process at a granular level, a scalper must look beneath the candles and observe the constant interaction between bid and ask prices.

> Price does not move because of lines or indicators. Price moves because someone hit the bid or lifted the offer.

Bid/ask dynamics are therefore the most direct expression of order flow.

The Bid and Ask Explained

The market always displays two key prices:

- **Bid** — the highest price a buyer is willing to pay.
- **Ask** (or **Offer**) — the lowest price a seller is willing to accept.

The difference between them is the **spread**:

$$\text{Spread} = \text{Ask} - \text{Bid}$$

Movements in the spread represent the dance of liquidity:

- when spreads widen, uncertainty increases,
- when spreads tighten, execution becomes easier.

For scalpers, a tight spread is essential. Wide spreads make fast trading expensive and unpredictable.

How Trades Actually Execute

There are only two ways price can move:

1. Someone **hits the bid** by selling into waiting buyers.
2. Someone **lifts the offer** by buying from waiting sellers.

In microstructure:

$$\text{Aggressive orders move price.}$$

Passive orders (limit orders) sit and wait. Aggressive orders (market orders) take liquidity.

Trend strength is a function of aggression.

Buy Pressure vs. Sell Pressure

If aggressive buyers are stronger:

- offers get lifted,
- price moves upward.

If aggressive sellers dominate:

- bids get hit,
- price moves downward.

A scalper does not need to see every order, but must recognize the **pattern of aggression**:

$$\text{Lift} \rightarrow \text{Lift} \rightarrow \text{Lift} \Rightarrow \text{Uptrend intent}$$

$$\text{Hit} \rightarrow \text{Hit} \rightarrow \text{Hit} \Rightarrow \text{Downtrend intent}$$

Bid/Ask Walls

Large clusters of limit orders at bid or ask represent "walls" of liquidity.

- A wall of bids can act as temporary support.
- A wall of offers can act as temporary resistance.

However, walls can be:

- real (true supply/demand),
- fake (liquidity bait that disappears),
- absorptive (soaking aggressive orders without moving price).

Observation:

- If a bid wall absorbs repeated selling, price often rallies.
- If an offer wall absorbs repeated buying, price often drops.

Absorption vs. Exhaustion

Two opposing forces shape short-term price:

Absorption

When one side absorbs the other's aggression:

- repeated hits on the bid,
- but price does not go down,

then buyers are absorbing sell pressure.
This often precedes a rally.

Exhaustion

When aggressive orders run out:

- offer lifting slows,
- wicks form at highs,
- price cannot move further.

This often precedes reversal or pullback.

Absorption stops the move. Exhaustion ends the move.

Speed and Sequence

On micro timeframes, the **speed of transactions** matters:

- fast prints = high participation,
- slow prints = uncertainty or lack of interest.

Watch for:

- clusters of fast trades at one price level,
- immediate continuation or rejection.

A useful mental model:

$$Speed = Commitment$$

If price moves slowly, commitment is low. If price moves aggressively, commitment is high.

Bid/Ask Dynamics and Trend

Trends form when one side dominates:

$$\text{Buyers lift offers faster than sellers hit bids} \Rightarrow \text{Uptrend}$$

$$\text{Sellers hit bids faster than buyers lift offers} \Rightarrow \text{Downtrend}$$

Reversals often begin when aggression changes sides:

- buyers stop lifting offers,
- sellers begin hitting bids aggressively.

A micro-break in aggression is often the first signal of CHOCH or BOS.

Scalper's Practical Interpretation

A scalper reads bid/ask dynamics to answer:

1. Who is aggressive right now?
2. Is aggression continuing or slowing?
3. Is liquidity absorbing or yielding?
4. Is exhaustion forming?

If aggression is clear and increasing:

- continuation setups are favored.

If aggression fades at a key level:

- reversal or pullback becomes likely.

Summary

- Bids are buyers waiting; asks are sellers waiting.
- Aggressive orders (market orders) move price.
- If buyers lift offers, price rises; if sellers hit bids, price falls.
- Bid/ask walls show potential support/resistance, but can be real or fake.
- Absorption means price holds despite aggression; exhaustion means the move ends.
- Speed and sequence of trades reveal commitment.

Price is the visible result of invisible order flow. Bid/ask dynamics show who is in control.

7.2 Footprint Charts and Volume Imbalance

Candles show where price moved. Footprint charts show *why* price moved.

A footprint chart displays executed volume at each price level, separated into:

- bid volume (aggressive sellers),
- ask volume (aggressive buyers).

This gives a detailed view of order flow inside each candle.

Footprint charts reveal the pressure behind every tick.

What Footprint Charts Display

Unlike regular candles, where we only see open, high, low, close, footprint charts show:

- how many contracts traded at each price,
- whether they traded on the bid or ask,
- where absorption occurred,
- where imbalance appeared.

The result is a "volume map" inside the candle.

Understanding Bid/Ask Volume

Each price level contains two numbers:

- left side = volume executed at the bid,
- right side = volume executed at the ask.

Example:

$$120\times340$$

means:

- 120 contracts hit the bid (sellers aggressive),
- 340 contracts lifted the offer (buyers aggressive).

If the right side dominates, buyers are more aggressive. If the left side dominates, sellers are more aggressive.

Volume Imbalance

Volume imbalance is a key footprint concept.

An imbalance occurs when:

$$\text{Ask Volume} \geq \alpha \times \text{Bid Volume}$$

or vice versa.

Common ratio:

$$\alpha = 2$$

Meaning:

$$\text{Ask Volume} > 2 \times \text{Bid Volume}$$

This indicates aggressive buying pressure.

- Bullish imbalance = upward continuation likely.
- Bearish imbalance = downward continuation likely.

Stacked Imbalances

One imbalance is informative. Multiple imbalances stacked vertically are powerful.

$$\text{Price Level 1: Ask} \gg \text{Bid}$$

$$\text{Price Level 2: Ask} \gg \text{Bid}$$

$$\text{Price Level 3: Ask} \gg \text{Bid}$$

This forms a "wall of aggression":

- buyers are lifting offers across several ticks,
- sellers cannot absorb,
- price is likely to continue upward.

Similarly for stacked bid imbalance.

Absorption on Footprint

Absorption occurs when:

- volume is large,
- but price does not move.

Example:

$$800 \times 300$$

but price barely ticks down.
This means:

- buyers are absorbing sell pressure,
- hidden limit orders are supporting price.

Absorption is nearly always followed by a move **away** from the absorbed side.

Absorption stops the move. Imbalance drives the move.

Footprint Clues for Entry

Scalpers look for:

- stacked ask imbalance in an uptrend,
- stacked bid imbalance in a downtrend,
- absorption at pullback lows/highs,
- failed attempts to break a level.

A strong setup:

1. trend is established,
2. price pulls back into structure (VWAP, EMA, demand/supply),
3. footprint shows absorption at the pullback,
4. imbalance prints in trend direction,
5. entry with tight stop.

Footprint Clues for Reversal

At exhaustion zones:

- aggressive buying hits a wall,
- large ask volume, but no price movement,
- wick forms on chart,
- sellers take control.

The opposite at lows.
This combination is one of the most reliable reversal signals.

Delta: Net Aggression

Many footprint platforms compute **delta**:

$$\text{Delta} = \text{Ask Volume} - \text{Bid Volume}$$

- positive delta = buyer aggression,
- negative delta = seller aggression.

Delta helps confirm:

- trend strength,
- breakout continuation,
- exhaustion during reversal.

When to Ignore Footprint

Scalpers should avoid footprint-based decisions when:

- liquidity is extremely thin,
- pre-market or post-market sessions,
- during violent news spikes,
- extreme volatility with no structure.

In these conditions, footprints are chaotic and unreliable.

Practical Scalping Workflow

A clean process:

1. Identify context (trend, session, levels).
2. Wait for price at a location of interest.
3. Observe footprint:
   - imbalance direction,
   - absorption,
   - speed of prints.
4. Enter only when aggression aligns with structure.

Summary

- Footprint charts show executed bid and ask volume at each price.
- Volume imbalance reveals directional aggression.
- Stacked imbalances indicate strong continuation.
- Absorption stops moves and often precedes reversals.
- Delta summarizes net buying or selling pressure.
- Scalpers combine footprint with structure, not as a standalone signal.

Footprint charts turn candles into conversations. Imbalance and absorption show which side is speaking louder.

7.3 Absorption & Exhaustion Zones

In modern electronic markets, price does not move simply because someone buys or sells. Price moves when one side overwhelms the other. Absorption and exhaustion describe the two most critical moments in this battle: the moment when effort stops working, and when one side runs out of energy.

Absorption blocks movement. Exhaustion ends movement.

Understanding these phenomena allows a scalper to anticipate reversals, avoid chasing late trends, and identify high-probability entries with minimal risk.

What Is Absorption?

Absorption occurs when aggressive orders come into the market, yet price does not move in their direction.

Example:

- sellers hit the bid repeatedly,
- but price refuses to go down.

This means:

- buyers are absorbing sell pressure,
- hidden limit orders are sitting at that level,
- a potential reversal or continuation is brewing.

Absorption is most visible through:

- footprint charts,
- cumulative delta,
- tape reading.

Visual Clues of Absorption:

1. large volume,
2. small candle bodies,
3. multiple wick taps at the same level,
4. no follow-through despite aggression.

$$\text{Effort} > \text{Result} \Rightarrow \text{Absorption}$$

Absorption in Uptrends and Downtrends

In an uptrend:

- sellers attack support,
- price holds,
- buyers defend levels.

This often leads to continuation.
In a downtrend:

- buyers lift offers repeatedly,
- price does not rise,
- sellers are absorbing.

Continuation downward becomes likely.

Exhaustion: When Energy Runs Out

Exhaustion is different. It is not defense against aggression, but the **failure of aggression**.
Example:

- buyers lift offers aggressively,
- candles shrink,
- wicks appear,
- volume fades,
- price stops advancing.

This is the end of the move.

$$\text{Effort} < \text{Result} \Rightarrow \text{Exhaustion}$$

Distinguishing Absorption vs Exhaustion

Clear distinction:

- Absorption = energy blocked (opposing force strong),
- Exhaustion = energy exhausted (no more force available).

Absorption Example:

- sellers attack support,
- price holds,
- buyers are strong.

Exhaustion Example:

- buyers attack resistance,
- price fails,
- buyers are out of energy.

Where Absorption Occurs

Most common locations:

- demand or supply zones,
- VWAP bands,
- fair value gaps,
- previous high/low,
- round numbers (00, 50).

Absorption at structure is a powerful continuation signal. Absorption without structure is meaningless.

Where Exhaustion Occurs

Exhaustion appears at extremes:

- end of a swing,
- top of a strong trend,
- bottom of a sell-off,
- after stop-hunt sweeps.

Classic exhaustion pattern:

1. strong trend candle,
2. smaller candle,
3. wick at the extreme,
4. opposite direction candle.

This pattern often precedes a sharp reversal.

Absorption + Imbalance

When absorption is followed by imbalance in the opposite direction, a strong trade setup emerges.

Sequence:

1. absorption at level,
2. price stops moving,
3. first imbalance prints,
4. continuation begins.

This is the footprint model of reversal.

$$\text{Absorption} \rightarrow \text{Imbalance} \rightarrow \text{Move}$$

Exhaustion After a Sweep

Many exhaustion events follow liquidity sweeps:

- price spikes above a high,
- traps breakout traders,
- wicks long,
- volume collapses,
- reversal begins.

This is a high-probability scalping setup.

How Scalpers Use These Concepts

Practical trading workflow:

1. Identify a key level or structure zone.
2. Watch for absorption:
    - multiple taps,
    - strong volume,
    - price holds.
3. Look for exhaustion:
    - candles weaken,
    - momentum fades.

4. Enter on first strong shift (micro BOS).

Stops are placed:

- just beyond the absorbed zone,
- ensuring minimal risk.

Targets:

- next liquidity pocket,
- VWAP,
- recent swing high/low.

Common Mistakes

Avoid:

- chasing momentum at exhaustion,
- trading absorption at random levels,
- ignoring volume,
- entering before confirmation.

Correct approach:

- absorption must happen at structure,
- exhaustion must be visible,
- entry only after clear shift.

Summary

- Absorption occurs when one side defends a level against aggression.
- Exhaustion occurs when the attacking side runs out of energy.
- Absorption is visible through volume, wicks, and footprints.
- Exhaustion is visible through shrinking candles, falling volume, and failed continuation.
- A powerful setup is:

$$\text{Absorption} + \text{Exhaustion} + \text{Imbalance}$$

$$= \text{High-Probability Reversal or Continuation}$$

A scalper thrives by entering where others are trapped, not by chasing where they are attacking.

7.4 Iceberg Orders and Hidden Liquidity

Not every order in the market is visible. Large participants often need to buy or sell massive size without revealing their intentions. They do this through **iceberg orders** and other forms of hidden liquidity.

> Price does not move because someone wants to buy. Price moves when they finish buying.

Understanding this behavior allows a scalper to recognize where the real battle is happening—even when it is invisible on the surface.

What Is an Iceberg Order?

An iceberg order is a large order that is broken into smaller visible parts.

- Only a small portion is displayed on the order book.
- When that portion fills, another appears.

Like the name suggests:

Most of the order is hidden beneath the surface.

Example:

- Visible offer: 50 contracts.
- Hidden quantity: 500 contracts.

As traders lift the offer, the 50 reappears repeatedly, absorbing volume.

Why Iceberg Orders Exist

Large traders cannot show their full size. If they revealed everything:

- price would run ahead,
- liquidity would disappear,
- execution cost would spike.

They need to:

- buy quietly in a down move,
- sell quietly in an up move.

How Iceberg Orders Affect Price

Iceberg orders create the illusion that:

- size is small,
- yet price does not move through the level.

Clues:

- repeated fills at the same price,
- constant refresh of visible quantity,
- slow grind into a level without breakout,
- large delta but no price movement.

This is not random.
It is accumulation or distribution.

Absorption From Icebergs

Iceberg orders are often the cause of **absorption**:

- sellers keep hitting the bid,
- price does not go down,
- hidden buyers absorb the flow.

This is a precursor to upside reversal.
Conversely:

- buyers lift offers aggressively,
- price does not go up,
- hidden sellers absorb.

This is a precursor to downside reversal.

Detecting Iceberg Orders

There are several ways to spot hidden liquidity.

1. Time & Sales (Tape)

Look for:

- repeated prints at the same price,
- large cumulative volume,
- small displayed size.

2. Footprint Charts

Look for:

- big volume at one tick,
- but no directional movement.

3. Order Book Behavior

Look for:

- bid/ask size that keeps refreshing,
- even after repeated hits.

This is the classic "iceberg signature":

$$\text{Hit} \rightarrow \text{Fill} \rightarrow \text{Refresh} \rightarrow \text{Repeat}$$

Hidden Liquidity at Key Levels

Icebergs are most common at:

- previous highs/lows,
- round numbers (00, 50),
- VWAP bands,
- supply/demand zones,
- session open/close.

This is where large participants want to enter or exit size.

Iceberg Orders and Traps

Icebergs often create trap behavior:

1. price spikes into a level,
2. retail traders chase breakout,
3. iceberg absorbs volume,
4. price reverses aggressively.

This is how many stop-hunts are built.

Large players use the crowd's aggression as liquidity.

Icebergs During Trends

In trends, iceberg orders help maintain direction:

- hidden bids support pullbacks in uptrend,
- hidden offers cap retracements in downtrend.

This creates:

- shallow pullbacks,
- strong continuation,
- minimal retracement.

Trend traders often ride behind iceberg activity.

Why Icebergs Matter for Scalpers

For scalpers, the presence of iceberg orders provides:

- confidence in direction,
- clear entry at defended levels,
- tight stop placement.

The best entries often occur:

- just above an iceberg bid (long),
- just below an iceberg offer (short).

The iceberg acts as a protective barrier.

Common Mistakes

Avoid:

- assuming every stalled move is an iceberg,
- entering without confirmation,
- ignoring context (session, trend, levels).

Correct interpretation requires:

- evidence from tape,
- footprint volume,
- structural location.

Summary

- Iceberg orders hide large size to avoid price impact.
- They cause absorption: large aggressive orders, no movement.
- Hidden liquidity supports reversals and continuation.
- Detection comes from:
  - tape,
  - footprint,
  - order book refresh behavior.
- Key insight:

  $$\text{Absorption} \Rightarrow \text{Continuation or Reversal}$$

  Scalpers win not by seeing everything, but by knowing what to look for.

7.5 Tape Reading for Early Reversal Detection

Tape reading is the oldest market skill. Before charts existed, traders watched nothing but price, time, and volume. Today the tools are more advanced, but the core idea remains the same:

> Price movement reveals intention before direction changes.

Tape reading allows scalpers to see reversals seconds before they appear on candles.

What Is the Tape?

The "tape" is the real-time stream of executed trades showing:

- price,
- size,
- direction (bid/ask),
- speed of transactions.

Tape reading focuses on:

- aggression,

- effort,
- absorption,
- exhaustion.

It answers the question:

Who is pushing the market right now?

Why Tape Reading Predicts Reversals

Reversals do not begin with candles. They begin with behavior:

- aggression shifts from one side to the other,
- orders stop consuming levels,
- absorption appears,
- exhaustion rises,
- then price finally turns.

Tape reveals these shifts before they show on charts.

Key Reversal Clues on Tape

Several patterns consistently show up before reversals.

1. Sudden Drop in Aggression

If buyers were lifting offers aggressively, then suddenly stop:

- prints slow down,
- size of prints shrinks,
- momentum fades.

This is early exhaustion.

2. Shift in Control

You may see:

- sellers begin hitting bids,
- buyers stop lifting offers,
- pace reverses.

This is control transfer.

3. Absorption at Extremes

At highs:

- large ask volume executes,
- price does not go up.

At lows:

- large bid volume executes,
- price does not go down.

4. Three Consecutive Fail Attempts

Repeated attempts to break a level that fail:

1. **1st attempt:** minor rejection.
2. **2nd attempt:** trapped traders.
3. **3rd attempt:** exhaustion.

The third failure often signals reversal.

Speed and Rhythm

Tape is rhythm. Reversals have a distinct sound even without visuals:

- fast, fast, fast, slow.

Price decelerates before turning.
This is mechanical:

$$Loss\ of\ aggression = Loss\ of\ trend.$$

Micro Pauses

Before reversal, the tape shows:

- small pauses,
- fairness checks,
- hesitant prints,
- lack of interest.

Then:

- opposite direction prints accelerate,
- reversal begins.

Combining Tape With Levels

Tape signals are powerful when aligned with structure:

- supply/demand,
- previous highs/lows,
- VWAP,
- FVG boundaries,
- breaker blocks,
- round numbers.

A signal without location is noise. A signal at location is opportunity.

Classic Reversal Workflow

A scalper watches the following sequence:

1. Price approaches a known level.
2. Prints accelerate (excited traders).
3. Absorption appears (hidden liquidity).
4. Aggression slows.
5. Opposite aggression begins.
6. Reversal confirms with micro BOS.

Entry is taken after confirmation, not anticipation.

False Signals

Tape alone can mislead. Common mistakes:

- interpreting thin liquidity as exhaustion,
- reading noise during news spikes,
- ignoring broader trend.

To avoid this:

- always frame tape inside context,
- only act at meaningful levels,
- wait for shift, not guess.

Tape + Candles = Precision

Tape reading does not replace charts. It supplements them.

Ideal combination:

1. structure (trend, level),
2. candlestick rejection (wick, engulfing),
3. tape shift (speed/volume),
4. micro BOS.

$$\text{Structure} + \text{Tape} = \text{Early and Precise Entry}$$

Scalper Advantage

Tape provides:

- earlier detection of reversals,
- tighter stop-loss,
- optimal timing,
- reduced drawdown.

A scalper often enters:

- while candles still look strong in the old direction,
- because tape shows the shift first.

  The crowd sees reversal late. The tape reader sees reversal early.

Summary

- Tape is the stream of executed trades showing size, price, and intensity.
- Reversals begin with behavior, then appear on charts.
- Key clues:
  - drop in aggression,
  - control shift,
  - absorption at extremes,
  - failure attempts,
  - speed changes.
- Combine tape with structure for high accuracy.

  Tape reading is not prediction. It is observation of intent.

7.6 How Scalpers Interpret Real-Time Liquidity Shifts

Liquidity is not static. It moves, hides, appears, disappears, and constantly reorganizes around price. Scalpers who learn to interpret these shifts gain a decisive advantage: they can anticipate movement before it becomes visible on candles.

> The market is not moved by price. The market is moved by liquidity.

The Nature of Liquidity

Liquidity consists of:

- limit orders waiting to be filled,
- stop losses resting above and below swings,
- market orders consuming available depth.

When liquidity concentrates, price slows. When liquidity is thin, price jumps.

Scalpers read these behaviors in real time.

Shifts in Liquidity Are Signals

Liquidity shifts reveal clues such as:

- who is defending a level,
- who is trapped,
- where price is likely to go next.

Key observations:

- Liquidity appearing = barrier.
- Liquidity disappearing = opportunity.

If a large bid suddenly vanishes, downside becomes easier. If a large offer disappears, upside becomes easier.

Three Types of Liquidity

Liquidity takes three forms:

1. **Visible liquidity** — what you see on the order book.
2. **Hidden liquidity** — iceberg and undisclosed orders.
3. **Resting liquidity** — stop losses and pending orders.

Price often moves toward resting stops first.

Liquidity is both target and fuel.

Watching the Order Book

A scalper monitors the order book for:

- large clusters of bids or offers,
- sudden additions or removals,
- walls that hold or collapse.

Signals:

- if a wall holds = continuation or reversal,
- if a wall collapses = breakout is likely.

But the order book alone is incomplete. It must be confirmed with tape and footprint.

Resting Liquidity as Target

Price seeks liquidity. This is why markets often move toward:

- swing highs,
- swing lows,
- round numbers,
- previous session levels.

These areas are full of:

- stop losses,
- breakout orders,
- trapped traders.

A liquidity sweep often occurs at these points before the real move begins.

Liquidity Displacement

Liquidity displacement occurs when price quickly:

- runs through one side of the book,
- prints aggressively in one direction,
- then lands at the next pool.

This feels like a "vacuum" on fast charts.

Example:

- bids are thin below price,
- sell orders hit the bid,
- price drops fast until new bids appear.

This shows:

- movement was caused by lack of liquidity,
- not necessarily overwhelming aggression.

Liquidity Appearing Suddenly

When new liquidity appears at a level, it often signals intention:

- institutions step in,
- limit orders defend the zone,
- aggressive orders fail to break through.

This is absorption.
It often precedes:

- continuation in trend direction,
- reversal if at extremes.

Liquidity Disappearing Suddenly

When liquidity vanishes:

- a breakout is likely,
- price jumps through the empty space.

Indicators of this:

- a wall disappears in the book,
- tape prints accelerate,
- price slices through with ease.

This is liquidity evacuation.

How Scalpers Read Shifts in Real Time

A practical process:

1. Define key levels in advance.
2. Watch order book, tape, footprint at those levels.
3. Ask:
    - Is liquidity defending?
    - Is liquidity fleeing?
    - Is liquidity waiting above or below?
4. Combine with:
    - candle behavior,
    - market structure,
    - session context.
5. Execute when alignment appears.

Structure + Liquidity = Edge

Liquidity alone is insufficient. Structure alone is incomplete. Together they create edge.

$$\text{Location} + \text{Liquidity Shift} = \text{Scalping Opportunity}$$

Classic Examples

1. Breakout Through Thin Liquidity

- price approaches resistance,
- offers vanish,
- price explodes upward.

2. Trap at Heavy Liquidity

- breakout candle into heavy offers,
- trapped buyers,
- reversal begins.

3. Pullback Continuation

- trend established,
- pullback to defended bid zone,
- absorption,
- continuation.

The Scalper's Mindset

A scalper does not predict:

> A scalper waits for confirmation of liquidity behavior.

They ask:

1. Who is aggressive?
2. Who is absorbing?
3. Where is liquidity hiding?
4. Where is liquidity fleeing?
5. Is this level meaningful?

Only when answers align, they act.

Summary

- Liquidity shifts reveal intent before price moves.
- Visible, hidden, and resting liquidity all matter.
- Price seeks liquidity, then reacts.
- Liquidity appearing means defense; disappearing means breakout.
- Scalpers combine:
  - structure,
  - order book,
  - tape,
  - footprint.

Scalping is not chasing price. It is following liquidity.

Part III

Scalping Strategies

Chapter 8

Core Scalping Strategies

Scalping success does not come from hundreds of random patterns. It comes from mastering a small set of reliable, repeatable setups that appear every day in liquid markets. Each strategy in this chapter includes clear rules for entry, stop placement, targets, and optimal market conditions. These are the ten foundational setups used by professional intraday traders:

- EMA Pullback Scalping
- VWAP Reversal
- Micro Trend Continuation
- Liquidity Sweep Reversal
- Breaker Block Scalping
- FVG (Imbalance) Scalping
- Range Bound Fade
- Trendline Trap Reversal
- Volume Burst Scalping
- News Spike Reaction Scalping

The purpose is not to predict the market, but to recognize specific conditions where probabilities tilt in your favor. One setup, executed consistently with discipline, can produce stable results. Ten setups give you flexibility across sessions, instruments, and volatility regimes while maintaining simplicity and precision.

8.1 EMA Pullback Scalping

EMA pullback scalping is one of the most reliable and repeatable intraday setups. It exploits the natural rhythm of trends: price expands, pulls back into value, and then continues. The trader enters *with* momentum, not against it, using exponential moving averages (EMA) as dynamic support and resistance.

> Trends breathe. An impulse is followed by a pullback. Scalpers trade the breath, not the lungs.

Why EMAs Work in Scalping

EMAs weight recent price more heavily than older price, making them fast and responsive—ideal for low timeframe trading. They reflect the **average location where transactions are happening right now**.

Key benefits:

- track short-term momentum,
- define structure,
- create "value zones" for pullback entries,
- act as dynamic support and resistance.

EMAs do not predict direction. They reveal how price behaves during trend continuation.

Recommended EMA Sets

Scalpers commonly use layered clusters:

- **5/8/13** EMA — micro momentum
- **9/20** EMA — structural pullbacks
- **20/200** EMA — trend vs mean

Interpretation:

- when fast EMAs are above slow EMAs = uptrend,
- when fast EMAs are below slow EMAs = downtrend.

Spacing matters:

$$\text{Wide spacing} = \text{strong trend}$$

$$\text{Tight spacing or crossover} = \text{chop and caution}$$

Market Conditions for EMA Pullback Trades

Ideal environments:

- strong trend with clear impulse legs,
- high-liquidity instruments (gold, indices, forex),
- London or New York session,
- smooth and directional movement.

Avoid:

- tight ranges,
- overlapping candles,
- news spikes,
- session closes.

Entry Logic

The core idea:

1. An impulse pushes price away from EMAs.
2. Price pulls back into the EMAs.
3. A rejection candle or engulfing pattern forms.
4. The trend resumes.

Typical sequence:

$$\text{Impulse} \rightarrow \text{Pullback to EMAs} \rightarrow \text{Rejection} \rightarrow \text{Continuation}$$

Confirmation Rules

Look for:

- wick rejection at the EMAs,
- strong body in trend direction,
- volume pickup,
- no immediate opposite aggression on tape.

Stop Placement

Stops are tight because structure is clear.

Recommendations:

- below the wick of the rejection candle (for longs),
- above the wick of the rejection candle (for shorts),
- or beyond the EMA cluster if volatility is high.

Risk is minimal because pullback failures are obvious.

Targets

Targets depend on session context:

- recent swing high/low,
- next liquidity pool,
- VWAP bands,
- ADR/ATR projections.

Scalpers often scale out:

$$50\% at 1R, \quad remainder at structure.$$

Examples of Price Behavior

During an uptrend:

- EMAs are stacked upward,
- pullback touches 9/20 EMA,
- wick forms,
- strong green candle follows,
- entry with stop below wick.

During a downtrend:

- EMAs stacked downward,
- pullback touches cluster,
- bearish engulfing candle,
- entry short with stop above wick.

Common Mistakes

Avoid these errors:

- entering during consolidation,
- entering before pullback completes,
- trading against higher timeframe trend,
- placing stops too tight inside wick,
- trading tiny impulses lacking momentum.

The pullback must return to *value*. Not far, not shallow. Just right.

Checklist Before Entry

1. Is the trend clear? (HH/HL or LL/LH)
2. Are EMAs stacked cleanly in trend direction?
3. Has price pulled back into the EMA zone?
4. Is there a rejection signal?
5. Is volume or tape confirming?
6. Is session/time appropriate?

If all answers are yes, enter.

Why This Setup Works

This setup works because:

- trends require rebalancing,
- pullbacks represent profit-taking and new entry,
- EMAs define value during pullbacks,
- continuation begins once imbalance returns.

It captures the path of least resistance.

Summary

EMA pullback scalping provides:

- frequent opportunities,
- simple rules,
- tight stops,
- strong reward-to-risk.

Core pattern:

$$\text{Impulse} \rightarrow \text{Pullback to EMAs} \rightarrow \text{Rejection} \rightarrow \text{Continuation}$$

> The trend is your ally. The EMA is your guide. Pullback is your entry.

8.2 VWAP Reversal

VWAP (Volume-Weighted Average Price) is a core intraday reference for institutions. It represents the average traded price of the session, weighted by volume. For scalpers, VWAP acts as a dynamic equilibrium line where price often:

- reverts after extended moves,
- rejects violently in trending days,
- rotates around during balanced sessions.

The VWAP Reversal setup focuses on **fading stretched moves back toward VWAP** or **reversing from VWAP after an aggressive, failed attempt to cross it**.

> VWAP is where the market checks: "Are we trading too high or too low for today?"

Why VWAP Is Powerful for Reversals

Institutions use VWAP as a benchmark:

- to measure execution quality,
- to manage intraday inventory,
- to determine whether price is rich (above) or cheap (below).

Price behavior around VWAP reveals:

- mean reversion conditions,
- trend continuation or failure,
- exhaustion after emotional moves.

For scalpers, VWAP provides:

- a clear, objective reference line,
- a high-probability magnet for stretched moves,
- a rejection zone when the market rejects fair value.

Two Types of VWAP Reversal Setups

There are two main VWAP-based reversal concepts for scalpers:

1. **Reversion to VWAP** Fading an extended move back toward VWAP when price is stretched far away.
2. **Rejection From VWAP** Trading a reversal when price attempts to cross VWAP and fails.

Both require:

- clear extension or clear rejection,
- exhaustion or absorption signals,
- structure and candle confirmation.

Setup 1: Reversion to VWAP

This is a mean-reversion play.

Context:

- price has moved far away from VWAP,
- move is sharp and emotional (multiple long candles),
- ATR is elevated (strong intraday volatility),
- the move is extended relative to typical session range.

Logic:

- price is temporarily inefficient,
- traders who chased late are vulnerable,
- VWAP acts as a gravity center.

Entry Conditions (for a short reversion):

1. Price is significantly above VWAP (preferably after strong impulse).
2. Candle structure shows exhaustion:
    - shrinking bodies,
    - long upper wicks,
    - failed pushes higher.
3. Momentum indicators (e.g. RSI, MACD) show divergence or loss of strength (optional but supportive).
4. A strong bearish confirmation candle prints (engulfing or strong rejection).

Entry trigger:

- enter short on close of confirmation candle,
- or on small retrace into its body.

Stops and Targets:

- stop above the swing high or above the confirming candle wick,
- primary target = VWAP line,
- optional: partial take-profit earlier (e.g. structure level or 1R).

Long trades are symmetric when price is extended *below* VWAP.

Setup 2: Rejection From VWAP

This is a directional reversal or continuation from VWAP itself.

Context:

- prevailing intraday trend exists (bullish or bearish),
- price pulls back to VWAP from above or below,
- VWAP acts as fair value in a trending environment.

Logic:

- in a strong downtrend, VWAP often acts as resistance,
- in a strong uptrend, VWAP often acts as support,
- when price fails to cross VWAP, it shows that the opposing side is not strong enough.

Entry Conditions (bearish rejection example):

1. Overall trend is down (lower highs, lower lows, EMAs aligned bearish).
2. Price rallies up into VWAP from below.
3. At VWAP:
    - footprint or tape shows absorption at the offer,
    - candles show upper wicks and rejection,
    - price fails to hold above VWAP.
4. A bearish reversal structure forms on 1M:
    - micro BOS to the downside,
    - bearish engulfing or strong red candle.

Entry trigger:

- enter short after confirmation candle closes below VWAP,
- optionally refine entry on a tiny pullback.

Stops and Targets:

- stop just above the VWAP rejection high,
- target = next intraday low, liquidity pool, or measured R multiple.

Long setups are symmetric in bull trends with VWAP acting as support.

Key Filters for VWAP Reversals

To avoid bad trades, apply these filters:

- **Session Filter:** Prefer London and New York active hours. Avoid low-liquidity times.
- **Trend Filter:** Know if you are counter-trend (reversion to VWAP) or with-trend (VWAP rejection in direction of the trend).

- **Extension Filter:** For reversion trades, ensure price is truly stretched away from VWAP—not just slightly extended.
- **Structure Filter:** Do not trade VWAP in the middle of a tight range where it is flat and choppy.

  Flat VWAP with sideways chop = no trade zone.

Common Mistakes

Avoid:

- trading every VWAP touch as a reversal,
- ignoring broader market context (trend vs range),
- entering before confirmation candle,
- using stops that are too tight inside noise near VWAP,
- fading strong trends too early just because price is away from VWAP.

Remember:

$$VWAPisareference, notamagicreversalline.$$

Checklist: VWAP Reversion Trade

1. Is price far from VWAP?
2. Was the move to this extreme impulsive and emotional?
3. Is there exhaustion (wicks, smaller candles, divergence)?
4. Has a clear reversal candle printed?
5. Is there enough room back to VWAP for a clean R:R?

Checklist: VWAP Rejection Trade

1. Is there a clear intraday trend?
2. Is VWAP aligned as dynamic support (uptrend) or resistance (downtrend)?
3. Is price pulling back into VWAP (not chopping around it)?
4. Do you see rejection and failure to cross or hold above/below VWAP?
5. Is there a micro BOS or strong reversal candle to confirm?

Why the VWAP Reversal Setup Works

This setup works because:

- intraday participants track VWAP as a fairness benchmark,
- price becomes inefficient when too far away from VWAP,
- emotional moves (overextensions) often revert,
- VWAP acts as a decision point for institutions (defend or release).

VWAP reversals capture:

- the collapse of emotional late entries,
- the snapback toward fair value,
- or the rejection of a failed attempt to change bias.

Summary

VWAP Reversal scalping provides two core opportunities:

- fading extreme moves back toward VWAP,
- trading rejections off VWAP in the direction of the trend.

Key principles:

- VWAP is a bias anchor and fairness line,
- extremes away from VWAP often revert,
- failed attempts to reclaim VWAP often reverse,
- structure, session, and confirmation are mandatory.

> VWAP is where intraday memory lives. Trade the moments when price disrespects it—or snaps back to it.

8.3 Micro Trend Continuation

Micro Trend Continuation is a high-frequency setup built on a very simple idea: trends continue more often than they reverse. Instead of trying to find tops or bottoms, the scalper focuses on entering during short pauses inside an existing trend, and riding the next impulse.

> Reversals are rare and emotional. Continuations are frequent and mechanical.

This setup is especially effective on 1-minute charts, 15-second charts, and tick charts, where price action is fast and structure is visible.

Why Micro Trend Continuation Works

Trends do not move in straight lines. They expand and contract:

$$\text{Impulse} \rightarrow \text{Pullback} \rightarrow \text{Impulse}$$

The pullback is caused by:

- profit-taking,
- temporary absorption,
- short-term counter-trend orders.

But if the trend is strong, these pullbacks fail quickly, and continuation resumes.

The scalper enters during the pullback, not at the start of the trend.

Identifying Micro Trends

A micro trend has clear structure:

- uptrend: Higher Highs (HH), Higher Lows (HL)
- downtrend: Lower Highs (LH), Lower Lows (LL)

EMAs help confirm:

- uptrend: fast EMAs above slow EMAs
- downtrend: fast EMAs below slow EMAs

Spacing between EMAs shows trend strength:

$$\text{Wide spacing} = \text{strong trend}$$

If EMAs compress, the trend may be slowing.

The Ideal Pullback

The best pullbacks are shallow and quick:

- 2–5 small candles against the trend,
- low volume,
- minimal overlap,
- wicks showing rejection.

Avoid:

- deep pullbacks,
- slow and grinding reversals,
- pullbacks with strong opposite candles.

Entry Logic

Entry occurs when the pullback ends and the trend resumes.

Checklist before entry:

1. Trend is clear.
2. EMAs aligned and clean.
3. Pullback touches:
    - EMA zone,
    - VWAP band,
    - prior structure.
4. Candle rejection or engulfing forms.
5. Momentum returns (body size increases).

$$\text{Pullback} \rightarrow \text{Rejection} \rightarrow \text{Continuation}$$

Stop Placement

Stops are tight:

- below pullback low in an uptrend,
- above pullback high in a downtrend,
- or outside EMA zone for safety.

Risk is small because failure is obvious.

Targets

Targets are logical:

- previous swing high/low,
- next liquidity pool,
- session high/low,
- fixed R-multiple (2R, 3R).

Micro continuation trades often produce:

$$2R - 5R \text{ quickly}$$

Trend continuation is fast. Reversals are slow and messy.

Multiple Entries Within Same Trend

One trend can produce multiple entries:

- impulse,
- pullback,
- continuation,
- repeat.

The scalper harvests each impulse:

$$\text{Slice} \rightarrow \text{Slice} \rightarrow \text{Slice}$$

The goal is not to capture the entire trend, but the high-probability slices.

Session Timing

Micro trends perform best during active sessions:

- London open,
- New York open,
- News reaction periods,
- High-liquidity futures or indices.

Avoid:

- lunch hours,
- pre-market chop,
- low-liquidity environments.

Confirmation Through Order Flow

On footprint or tape:

- during pullback = low aggression opposite trend,
- at continuation = aggression resumes.

Clues:

- stacked imbalances,
- acceleration in tape speed,
- absorption at the pullback low/high.

Common Mistakes

Avoid:

- entering too early before pullback completes,
- trading inside chop without trend,
- chasing candles after they break structure,
- ignoring higher timeframe levels.

High-Probability Filters

Enhance performance by adding filters:

- direction aligned with session bias,
- location near VWAP or EMA zone,
- clear impulse leg before pullback,
- shallow retracement,
- strong rejection candle.

Why This Setup Works

Micro trend continuation works because it aligns with market mechanics:

- trends contain multiple impulses,
- pullbacks are profit-taking, not reversal,
- new participants enter during pullbacks,
- continuation resumes when imbalance returns.

Scalpers do not need to predict tops or bottoms. They ride the path of least resistance.

Summary

- Trends expand, pull back, and expand again.
- Micro continuation trades capture the second expansion.
- EMAs and structure help identify pullback zones.
- Stops are tight and failures are obvious.

Core pattern:

$$\text{Impulse} \rightarrow \text{Pullback} \rightarrow \text{Rejection} \rightarrow \text{Continuation}$$

> The easiest money is made going with the flow. Not fighting it.

8.4 Liquidity Sweep Reversal

Markets do not reverse without reason. Before large moves change direction, the market often performs a liquidity sweep: a quick, sharp move beyond a key level to trigger stop orders and fill hidden institutional positions. Once liquidity is collected, price often snaps back violently. This pattern is called the **Liquidity Sweep Reversal**.

> The market hunts stops, fills inventory, and then reveals the real direction.

This setup exploits that behavior.

Why Sweeps Happen

Stops and pending orders accumulate in predictable locations:

- previous highs and lows,
- round numbers (00, 50),
- session highs/lows,
- supply/demand boundaries,
- the edges of ranges.

When price approaches these levels, traders expect breakout. Institutions, however, expect liquidity.

- Breakout traders enter late.
- Stop-loss orders from opposite traders get triggered.
- Institutional orders fill quietly.

Once executed, price often snaps back.

> The breakout is bait. The reversal is the trade.

Structure of a Liquidity Sweep

A typical sweep has three parts:

1. **Approach:** price grinds toward an obvious level.
2. **Break:** price spikes beyond that level.
3. **Rejection:** price fails to hold and reverses.

On chart:

$$\text{Level} \rightarrow \text{Sweep} \rightarrow \text{Reversal}$$

Visual Characteristics

Key signs on candles:

- long wicks beyond the level,
- strong rejection candle (engulfing or pin bar),
- high volume at the sweep,
- lack of follow-through.

On footprint or tape:

- aggressive buying into highs fails,
- or aggressive selling into lows fails,
- absorption at the extreme.

Where Sweeps Occur Most Frequently

High-probability zones:

- Yesterday high / low,
- London or New York session extremes,
- Prior swing highs/lows,
- Range boundaries,
- Supply/demand,
- Round numbers (psychological barriers).

If a level is obvious, it is a candidate for a sweep.

Entry Logic

Entry occurs only after confirmation.
General workflow:

1. Price takes out a known level.
2. Candle quickly rejects (wick or engulfing).
3. There is a **Break of Structure** (BOS) in opposite direction on the micro timeframe.
4. A small pullback offers the entry.

$$\text{Sweep} \rightarrow \text{Rejection} \rightarrow \text{BOS} \rightarrow \text{Entry}$$

Entry Trigger:

- enter on the first pullback after BOS,
- or enter on engulfing candle close if momentum is strong.

Stop Placement

Stops are tight and logical:

- above the sweep high (for shorts),
- below the sweep low (for longs).

If sweep fails, price will continue—and a tight stop protects capital.

Targets

Targets are usually clear:

- opposite range edge,
- nearest liquidity pool,
- VWAP or EMA cluster,
- previous structure point.

Sweeps create sharp moves, so scalpers can scale out aggressively.

$$1R,\ 2R,\ 3R,\ \text{with low drawdown}$$

Confirmation Through Order Flow

Key clues on tape and footprint:

- large volume at the extreme,
- aggressive orders fail to move price further,
- absorption at the swept level.

This means:

> Somebody is selling into aggressive buyers, or buying into aggressive sellers.

This is institutional footprint.

How to Catch Sweeps Without FOMO

Patience is critical.

Do not enter at the sweep itself. Entry comes *after* reversal begins.

Rules:

1. Wait for price to take out the level.
2. Wait for rejection or engulfing candle.
3. Wait for micro BOS.
4. Enter on pullback.

   Sweeps give you time. The trap is for breakout traders, not for you.

Common Traps and Errors

Avoid:

- entering on the breakout,
- entering before confirmation,
- ignoring trend context,
- trading sweeps in dead markets,
- forcing setups where no liquidity exists.

Remember:

$$Asweepwithoutreactionisnotareversal.$$

High-Probability Filters

Sweeps are stronger when:

- session is active (London/New York),
- level is obvious,
- volume spikes at the extreme,
- absorption or divergence appears,
- trend was overextended before sweep.

Why This Setup Works

This setup works because:

- breakout traders enter late and become trapped,
- stop-loss clusters provide liquidity,
- institutions use that liquidity to position,
- price reverses once inventory is filled.

The reversal is mechanical, not magical.

Summary

- Liquidity sweeps happen at obvious levels.
- Price spikes beyond the level to trigger stops.
- Reversal follows when absorption and BOS appear.
- Entry comes on pullback, not at the sweep itself.

Core pattern:

$$\text{Sweep} \rightarrow \text{Rejection} \rightarrow \text{BOS} \rightarrow \text{Entry}$$

The market takes liquidity first. Then it moves.

8.5 Breaker Block Scalping

Breaker Block Scalping is built on a simple observation: before strong moves, price often breaks through a consolidation zone, returns to it, and then continues in the same direction. This zone becomes a *breaker block*—an area where trapped traders sit, providing liquidity for continuation entries.

> A breaker block is the footprint of trapped traders. When price returns, their exit fuels the trend.

This setup is highly effective in trending markets, especially after false breakouts, sweeps, or aggressive impulses.

What Is a Breaker Block?

A breaker block forms when:

1. Price consolidates near a key level.
2. An attempt to break one direction fails.
3. Price reverses strongly in the opposite direction.

That consolidation zone becomes a breaker block.
When price returns to this zone later:

- trapped traders exit,
- new traders enter,
- liquidity fuels continuation.

How Breaker Blocks Trap Traders

During the failed breakout:

- breakout traders enter,
- stop-losses are set on the opposite side,
- institutions fade the move and reverse price.

When price returns:

- breakout traders panic and exit,
- sellers buy back, buyers sell out,
- continuation is fueled.

The breaker block is a liquidity pocket where pain is concentrated.

Recognizing a Breaker Block

Visually, a breaker block appears as:

- a small consolidation,
- usually 3–10 candles,
- located at a key level,
- followed by a strong directional break.

Structure:

$$\text{Range} \rightarrow \text{False Break} \rightarrow \text{Strong Move}$$

The range becomes the breaker block.

Entry Logic

Entry occurs when price retests the breaker block. You are not trading the breakout; you are trading the *return*.

Workflow:

1. Identify the breaker block (post-false-break).
2. Wait for price to return to that zone.
3. Look for rejection and continuation.

Confirmation:

- rejection wicks,
- bearish/bullish engulfing,
- micro BOS,
- absorption on footprint,
- tape showing shift.

Stop Placement

Stops are tight because failure is obvious:

- below the breaker block in an uptrend,
- above the breaker block in a downtrend.

If the block fails, the setup is invalid.

Targets

Targets depend on context:

- session high/low,
- previous swing,
- next liquidity pool,
- measured R multiples.

Scalpers typically scale out:

$$1R,\ 2R,\ \text{then structure.}$$

Ideal Conditions

This setup is strongest when:

- trend is already established,
- the breaker block forms at a key level,
- session is active (London/New York),
- volume expands on initial breakout.

Avoid:

- flat sessions,
- mid-range chop,
- weak impulse after breakout.

Why Breaker Blocks Work

Breaker blocks reflect real market mechanics:

- traders entered during a false breakout,
- their stops sit opposite the move,
- institutions use those stops as liquidity,
- price returns to fill inventory,
- continuation resumes.

It is not magic. It is positioning.

Breaker Block vs Fair Value Gap (FVG)

Breaker blocks often overlap with FVGs:

- breaker block = consolidation zone,
- FVG = imbalance created by displacement.

The highest-probability entries occur when:

- breaker block sits inside an FVG,
- at a session high/low,
- with liquidity swept before return.

Location + imbalance + trap = high-probability continuation.

Common Mistakes

Do not:

- trade every consolidation as a breaker,
- enter before price returns,
- ignore higher timeframe context,
- place stops inside the block,
- trade in low liquidity sessions.

Checklist

Before entry, verify:

1. False breakout occurred earlier.
2. Strong displacement in opposite direction.
3. Clear breaker block zone marked.
4. Price returns to the block.
5. Rejection and micro BOS.

If these align, enter with tight stops.

Summary

Breaker Block Scalping captures continuation after failed breakouts. Key elements:

- consolidation near level,
- false breakout,
- strong displacement,
- return to the block,
- rejection and continuation.

Core pattern:

$$\text{False Break} \rightarrow \text{Displacement} \rightarrow \text{Return} \rightarrow \text{Continuation}$$

The breaker block is where the trapped traders are. Their exit fuels your trade.

8.6 FVG (Imbalance) Scalping

Fair Value Gaps (FVG) are one of the most reliable sources of intraday opportunity. They occur when the market moves so quickly in one direction that there is no opposite-side participation. This creates an *imbalance*—a price region where few trades occurred. Price often returns to this area to rebalance before continuing in the original direction.

> Imbalance is inefficiency. Markets seek efficiency. Rebalancing creates trades.

FVG Scalping exploits these return-to-balance moves.

What Is an FVG?

An FVG occurs when a three-candle sequence forms:

1. Candle A
2. Candle B (strong displacement)
3. Candle C

If Candle C does not overlap Candle A's wick:

$$\text{Candle A Low} > \text{Candle C High} \quad \text{(for bullish)}$$

or

$$\text{Candle A High} < \text{Candle C Low} \quad \text{(for bearish)}$$

This creates a price gap between A and C.
That gap is the FVG.

Why FVGs Matter

FVGs occur because:

- one side of the market dominated,
- liquidity was consumed aggressively,
- no opposite trades filled.

That gap is *unfinished business.*
Price often returns to:

- fill the imbalance,
- collect liquidity,
- then rcsume the trend.

> Imbalance first, then return, then continuation.

Typical FVG Scalping Sequence

The structure is consistent:

$$\text{Displacement} \rightarrow \text{FVG} \rightarrow \text{Return} \rightarrow \text{Continuation}$$

Where:

- displacement = strong impulse,
- return = price pulls back,
- continuation = trend resumes.

Identifying Displacement

Displacement is essential:

- strong momentum candle,
- wide range,
- multiple candles same direction,
- volume spike,
- break of structure.

Weak moves do not create meaningful FVGs.

Ideal Entry Location

The highest-quality entry is:

- at the midpoint of the FVG,
- aligned with the trend,
- after confirmation.

$$\text{Entry Zone} = \frac{\text{Gap High} + \text{Gap Low}}{2}$$

This midpoint is a magnet.

Confirmation Tools

Confirmation improves accuracy:

- EMA cluster support,
- BOS on micro timeframe,
- wick rejection,
- footprint absorption,
- tape slowdown into the gap.

Entry Rules

For a long setup:

1. Trend is up (HH/HL, EMAs stacked).
2. Strong displacement candle creates a bullish FVG.
3. Price returns into the FVG zone.
4. Rejection or engulfing candle forms.
5. Enter long.

For a short setup, invert direction.

Stop Placement

Stops are precise:

- below the FVG low (for longs),
- above the FVG high (for shorts).

If imbalance fails to hold, the setup is invalid.

Targets

Logical targets:

- recent swing high/low,
- next liquidity pool,
- opposing FVG,
- VWAP or ADR levels.

Many scalpers scale out:

$$50\% at 1R,\ 50\% at structure$$

Combining FVG with Other Concepts

FVGs become extremely powerful when combined with:

- breaker blocks,
- liquidity sweeps,
- supply/demand,
- session extremes,
- divergence or exhaustion.

The best FVG trades occur where imbalance meets location.

FVG + Breaker Block

This combination is considered elite:

- displacement creates FVG,
- price returns into breaker block *inside* the FVG,
- reversal or continuation occurs.

The breaker block provides structure. The FVG provides inefficiency. Together they create probability.

Common Mistakes

Avoid:

- trading every gap without displacement,
- ignoring trend context,
- entering before return to the zone,
- trading tiny gaps in chop,
- oversized stops.

Not every gap is imbalance. Only displacement gaps count.

Checklist Before Entry

1. Strong impulse created imbalance.
2. Market structure aligns with direction.
3. Price returns into FVG zone.
4. Rejection or engulfing candle forms.
5. Enter with stop outside gap.

Why This Setup Works

FVG setups work because:

- imbalance signals institutional activity,
- return to FVG provides discounted entry,
- trend continuation provides momentum,
- stops are obvious and tight.

This is not prediction—it is market logic.

Summary

- FVG = inefficiency from displacement.
- Price often returns to fill imbalance.
- Scalpers enter at return and ride continuation.
- Best results come when FVG aligns with structure.

Core pattern:

$$\text{Displacement} \rightarrow \text{Return to FVG} \rightarrow \text{Continuation}$$

> Imbalance shows where the market rushed. The return shows where the opportunity is.

8.7 Range Bound Fade

Markets spend a surprising amount of time in ranges. Inside these ranges, price oscillates between clearly defined highs and lows. When price reaches the extremes of a range and shows rejection, the scalper can fade the move—entering against the immediate direction and targeting the opposite side.

> In a range, price is not trending. It is rotating between liquidity pools.

Range Bound Fade is a precise, logical setup that thrives in balanced, sideways conditions.

Why Ranges Form

Ranges form when:

- buyers and sellers are evenly matched,
- liquidity accumulates at both extremes,
- institutions accumulate or distribute inventory,
- market waits for catalyst or session change.

Inside a range:

- highs act as supply,
- lows act as demand,
- price oscillates between them.

$$\text{High} \to \text{Low} \to \text{High}$$

This repeated behavior provides opportunity.

Ideal Conditions for Range Fades

Range trades work best when:

- EMAs are flat and overlapping,
- VWAP is horizontal,
- price respects the same boundaries multiple times,
- session is balanced (not trending).

Avoid range trades during:

- strong trending sessions,
- high-impact news,
- early breakout conditions.

Identifying the Range

A valid range has:

- at least two touches at top,
- at least two touches at bottom,
- no strong breakouts,
- stable interior structure.

Label:

- range high = resistance,
- range low = support,
- mid-point = equilibrium.

Price tends to revert to equilibrium.

Entry Logic: Fading Extremes

The strategy is straightforward:

1. Price reaches range extreme (top or bottom).
2. Exhaustion or rejection appears.
3. Enter in the opposite direction.

For a fade short:

- price reaches range high,
- rejection wick or bearish engulfing,
- enter short.

For a fade long:

- price reaches range low,
- bullish rejection,
- enter long.

Confirmation Tools

Useful confirmations:

- wicks at extremes,
- bearish/bullish engulfing,
- RSI divergence,
- footprint absorption,
- tape slowdown,
- failed breakout attempt.

One of the strongest clues:

> Breakout attempt fails immediately.

False break → trap → fade.

Stop Placement

Stops are simple and tight:

- above the range high (short),
- below the range low (long).

If price breaks, the setup is invalid.

Targets

Primary target:

Opposite side of the range

Intermediate targets:

- mid-range (equilibrium),
- previous structure,
- partial profit at 1R.

Scalpers often take:

- partial at midpoint,
- remainder at opposite boundary.

Session Timing

Range fades are most effective when:

- after initial impulse,
- during mid-session balance,
- during lunch hours,
- before major sessions overlap.

They should be avoided:

- at market open,
- when momentum is building,
- near high-impact news.

Micro Structure

On small timeframes:

- price pokes beyond range boundary,
- rejection wick forms,
- micro BOS confirms reversal.

Entry is taken on pullback after BOS.

Order Flow Perspective

Inside ranges:

- extremes attract aggressive traders,
- institutional players fade them,
- liquidity accumulates near boundaries.

At the high:

- buyers chase breakout,
- sellers provide inventory,
- price rejects.

At the low:

- sellers chase breakdown,
- buyers accumulate,
- price bounces.

Common Mistakes

Avoid:

- trading inside the middle of the range,
- entering too early without rejection,
- chasing breakouts instead of fading,
- trading in trending conditions,
- tight stops inside noise.

Location is everything. Middle is noise. Edges are opportunity.

High-Probability Filters

Best range fades occur when:

- higher timeframe is balanced,
- liquidity sweeps occur at extremes,
- absorption on footprint,
- slow tape into extremes,
- rejection candle confirms.

Why This Setup Works

The logic is simple:

- traders chase breakout at extremes,
- institutions fade them,
- price returns to balance,
- opposing side is fueled.

Ranged markets reward:

- patience,
- location,
- confirmation.

Summary

Range Bound Fade is ideal when markets are sideways. Key elements:

- identify clear range boundaries,
- wait for price to reach edges,
- look for rejection and failed breakout,
- fade back toward equilibrium or opposite side.

Core pattern:

$$\text{Edge} \rightarrow \text{Rejection} \rightarrow \text{Return to Balance}$$

> In a range, the best trades are at the edges. The middle is noise.

8.8 Trendline Trap Reversal

A trendline trap reversal occurs when traders rely on a trendline for entries, only to be trapped when price breaks it briefly and then reverses in the opposite direction. Many retail traders draw trendlines and wait for breakouts. Markets exploit this predictable behavior by running stops beyond the trendline, filling institutional orders, and then reversing sharply.

> Trendlines attract retail traders. Traps attract liquidity. Reversals attract scalpers.

This setup captures the moment when breakout traders become trapped and their exits fuel the reversal.

Why Trendlines Create Traps

Trendlines are simple and visible:

- connect highs in a downtrend,
- connect lows in an uptrend,
- extend forward to predict continuation.

Because trendlines are obvious, they attract orders:

- breakout traders place entries beyond the line,
- stop losses are placed near the opposite side,
- institutions exploit both.

$$\text{Obvious level} = \text{obvious liquidity}$$

Structure of a Trendline Trap

A typical trap sequence:

1. Price respects a trendline multiple times.
2. Traders expect continuation.
3. Price breaks the trendline.
4. Breakout traders enter.
5. Price immediately reverses.
6. Breakout traders are trapped and exit.

This reversal is often violent:

$$\text{Break} \rightarrow \text{Trap} \rightarrow \text{Reversal}$$

Visual Characteristics

On the chart:

- multiple touches on trendline,
- false break (wick spike or strong candle),
- instant rejection,
- reversal candle or engulfing.

On tape:

- surge of aggression into breakout,
- immediate lack of follow-through,
- opposing aggression steps in,
- trapped orders forced to exit.

Ideal Locations

Trendline traps are powerful at:

- session highs and lows,
- round numbers (00/50),
- supply/demand zones,
- prior swing highs/lows,

- VWAP rejections,
- confluence of levels.

A trendline by itself is weak. A trendline at a meaningful level is strong.

Location gives the trendline its power.

Entry Logic

Entry rules are consistent across sessions:

1. Price breaks the trendline.
2. A rejection candle forms (wick, engulfing).
3. Micro BOS confirms reversal.
4. Enter on pullback into trap zone.

$$\text{Break} \rightarrow \text{Rejection} \rightarrow \text{BOS} \rightarrow \text{Entry}$$

Stop Placement

Stops are simple:

- above the wick that swept the trendline (for shorts),
- below the wick that swept the trendline (for longs).

If price breaks that wick again, the setup is invalid.

Targets

Logical targets:

- opposite structure edge,
- nearest liquidity pool,
- VWAP or EMA cluster,
- 1R, 2R, or more as momentum allows.

Trendline traps often produce fast moves because trapped traders must exit quickly.

Confirmation Tools

Confirmation increases edge:

- wick rejection,
- large stopping volume,
- footprint imbalance,
- absorption at the trap,
- tape slowdown into breakout,
- immediate acceleration opposite direction.

$$\text{Aggressive entry} + \text{Zero follow-through} = \text{Trap}$$

Order Flow Dynamics

At the moment of the trap:

- breakout traders enter late,
- their stops are placed nearby,
- institutions fade their orders,
- price reverses,
- trapped traders exit,
- reversal accelerates.

The reversal is fueled by two flows:

1. new participants entering in direction of reversal,
2. trapped participants being forced to exit.

This dual pressure produces rapid movement.

Advanced Filter: Trend Context

Trendline traps work best when the break occurs:

- against the higher timeframe trend,
- near exhaustion after long move,
- during distribution or accumulation,
- near liquidity pools.

If higher timeframe is strongly trending, avoid fading trendline breaks without additional confluence.

Common Mistakes

Typical errors:

- trading every trendline break as a trap,
- entering before rejection candle forms,
- ignoring context or location,
- using wide stops,
- trading in low-liquidity periods.

A trap is a pattern of behavior, not just a line break.

Checklist

Before entering:

1. Trendline respected multiple times?
2. Obvious breakout level?
3. Clear break and rejection?
4. BOS on micro timeframe?
5. Location at meaningful level?
6. Session active?

If these align, probability increases.

Why This Setup Works

Trendline traps reflect real mechanics:

- retail traders enter breakouts late,
- their stops provide liquidity,
- institutions fill positions,
- reversal is sharp and fast.

It is not random—it is execution.

Summary

Trendline Trap Reversal captures moves where breakout traders become trapped. Key elements:

- multiple touches on trendline,
- false breakout,
- rejection and BOS,
- pullback entry,
- logical targets.

Core pattern:

$$\text{Break} \to \text{Trap} \to \text{Reversal}$$

> The breakout is temptation. The trap is truth. The reversal is your trade.

8.9 Volume Burst Scalping

Volume Burst Scalping is built on a powerful observation: large players reveal their presence through sudden bursts of volume. When volume spikes dramatically, price often follows with sharp, directional movement. A scalper who recognizes this early can enter with precision and capture the momentum while risk remains small.

> Price is the result. Volume is the cause.

This setup seeks to ride the immediate consequence of aggressive participation.

Why Volume Bursts Matter

Volume is not random. Sudden spikes occur when:

- institutions enter positions,
- trapped traders are forced to exit,
- stop clusters are triggered,
- algorithms detect a threshold and activate.

A burst of volume tells us:

- something important just happened,
- attention, aggression, and urgency entered the market,
- continuation is likely in the short term.

Characteristics of a Volume Burst

A valid burst has three elements:

1. **Sharp increase over average volume**
2. **Fast price movement or wide candle body**
3. **Follow-through within the next 1–3 candles**

If volume spikes and price does *not* move, it may indicate:

- absorption,
- exhaustion,
- possible reversal.

Volume bursts without price movement require caution.

Ideal Contexts for Volume Bursts

Volume burst setups thrive during:

- market opens (London, New York),
- news reactions,
- liquidity sweeps,
- breakouts from consolidation,
- strong trending sessions.

Avoid during:

- lunch hour,
- dead Asian session (for indices),
- thin liquidity conditions.

Entry Logic

Entry occurs **after** volume confirms aggression.
Process:

1. Identify a sudden volume spike.
2. Ensure price direction matches aggression.
3. Enter on small pullback or break above/below burst candle.

For a long:

- burst of buying volume,
- strong bullish candle,
- enter on slight retrace or break of high.

For a short, invert direction.

Confirmation Elements

Confirmation strengthens reliability:

- spike is the largest volume of the session,
- price impulse breaks structure,
- follow-through continues in next candle,
- EMAs aligned with direction,
- tape speed increases,
- footprint shows lifting offers (bullish) or hitting bids (bearish).

> Volume without structure is noise. Structure with volume is signal.

Stop Placement

Stops are precise:

- below the low of the volume burst candle (for longs),
- above the high (for shorts).

If price returns inside the burst candle:

- momentum is gone,
- exit immediately.

Targets

Targets reflect immediate momentum:

- next swing,
- liquidity pool,
- VWAP band,
- measured move.

Scalpers often scale out quickly:

$$1R,\ 2R,\ \text{then structure.}$$

Volume bursts create fast trades, not long holds.

Advanced Filter: Accumulation Before Burst

The highest-probability bursts occur after:

- tight consolidation,
- coiling price action,
- multiple failed attempts.

Coiled energy becomes explosive.

$$\text{Compression} \rightarrow \text{Expansion}$$

Volume Burst & News

During news:

- volume is extremely high,
- direction is chaotic,
- spread may widen.

Avoid trading in the first seconds after release. Instead:

1. wait for first burst,
2. wait for retrace,
3. enter on continuation.

Order Flow Perspective

Volume bursts reveal:

- large orders hitting the market,
- stop clusters being triggered,
- liquidity being consumed.

If price moves easily with volume:

- liquidity is thin,
- continuation likely.

If price does *not* move:

- absorption occurs,
- possible trap,
- potential reversal.

Common Mistakes

Avoid:

- entering before volume confirms,
- fading strong volume,
- chasing late without pullback,
- trading during dead sessions,
- ignoring higher timeframe context.

> Volume burst is the beginning, not the whole move. Be early, not late.

Checklist

Before entering:

1. Volume spike is clear and above average?
2. Candle structure confirms direction?
3. Follow-through on next candle?
4. Trend, session, and EMAs align?
5. Logical target with clean R:R?

Why This Setup Works

Volume bursts represent:

- sudden institutional participation,
- liquidation of trapped traders,
- stop cascades,
- algorithmic activation.

The move is not random. It is mechanical and urgent.

Volume is the market speaking loudly. Scalpers listen and act.

Summary

Volume Burst Scalping captures momentum created by sudden, aggressive volume.

Key elements:

- identify volume spike,
- confirm direction and follow-through,
- enter on pullback or break,
- exit before momentum fades.

Core pattern:

$$\text{Volume Spike} \rightarrow \text{Impulse} \rightarrow \text{Continuation}$$

Price follows volume. Volume reveals intention.

8.10 News Spike Reaction Scalping

News events generate sudden bursts of volatility. Markets react violently to economic releases, central bank statements, earnings, or unexpected geopolitical events. This volatility creates fast movement, but also increased risk. Scalpers do not trade the news release itself—they trade the *reaction* after the initial spike.

The spike is chaos. The reaction is opportunity.

News Spike Reaction Scalping focuses on structured setups that appear seconds to minutes after the news, when direction becomes clearer.

Why News Creates Scalping Opportunities

News creates:

- extreme volatility,
- wide candles,
- large volume bursts,
- rapid liquidity rebalancing.

The first move is often emotional and disorganized:

- spreads widen,
- slippage increases,
- aggressive orders hit the book.

Scalpers wait. Once the market absorbs the shock, structure appears, and a high-probability direction forms.

Never Trade the Release

During the release:

- spreads can triple,
- stop-losses may not be honored,
- liquidity disappears,
- execution is unreliable.

Trading during release is gambling.

> Professional scalpers do not trade the news. They trade the reaction.

Post-News Phases

After the initial spike, three phases occur:

1. **Shock:** violent spike, no structure.
2. **Retest:** price returns to the origin or level.
3. **Continuation or reversal:** clean direction emerges.

The safest entries occur in phase 2 or 3.

Ideal Setup Structure

A classic news reaction setup looks like this:

1. Initial spike sweeps liquidity.
2. Price pulls back toward VWAP/FVG/block.
3. Rejection forms (wick/engulfing).
4. Trend resumes or reverses sharply.

Entry is taken on confirmation, not prediction.

Key Confirmation Tools

Use multiple signals:

- footprint showing absorption or exhaustion,
- tape showing aggression shift,
- BOS on micro timeframe,
- clear rejection candle,
- VWAP/EMA confluence,
- FVG return and continuation.

News provides fuel. Structure provides map.

Where to Enter

High-probability zones include:

- the origin of the spike,
- FVG created by displacement,
- breaker block,
- VWAP or session midpoint,
- prior session high/low,
- round numbers (00/50).

Entry comes after price returns to one of these zones and prints rejection.

Stop Placement

Stops must account for wider volatility:

- below rejection wick for longs,
- above rejection wick for shorts,
- or beyond structure if spread is high.

Always adjust for news volatility:

- avoid tiny stops,
- avoid oversized position sizes.

Targets

Targets are logical:

- high/low of spike,
- next liquidity pool,
- VWAP or ADR levels,
- partials at 1R, 2R, 3R.

News moves quickly; scalpers exit quickly.

Session and Instrument Timing

News setups are best on:

- indices: NASDAQ, S&P 500, DAX
- gold (XAUUSD)
- major FX pairs (EURUSD, GBPUSD)
- crypto during major releases

High liquidity makes execution smoother.
Avoid:

- low-volume equities,
- thin overnight sessions.

Types of News

High-impact events include:

- NFP (Non-farm payrolls),
- CPI / inflation data,
- FOMC statements,
- interest rate decisions,
- GDP,
- unemployment reports.

Medium-impact:

- speeches,
- manufacturing indices,
- business sentiment surveys.

Low-impact news usually ignored.

Advanced Considerations

Patterns around news often include:

- liquidity sweeps before release,
- fake breakout in first few seconds,
- strong reversal after retest.

A common sequence:

$$\text{Sweep} \rightarrow \text{Retest} \rightarrow \text{Continuation}$$

Order Flow Interpretation

During the reaction phase:

- if aggressive buyers appear, price rises,
- if aggressive sellers dominate, price drops,
- large orders can be seen in tape and footprint.

The scalper watches:

- does liquidity hold?
- or does price slice through?

Behavior reveals intent.

Common Mistakes

Avoid:

- trading during release,
- chasing the initial spike,
- ignoring spreads,
- oversized positions,
- no confirmation,
- fighting momentum.

Patience after news is profitable. Impulse during news is expensive.

Checklist

Before entering:

1. Has the initial spike happened?
2. Has price returned to structure?
3. Is there rejection or BOS?
4. Is spread stable?
5. Is volatility still high?

Only then enter.

Why This Setup Works

News creates:

- rapid repricing,
- emotional trading,
- liquidity sweeps,
- trapped traders.

Once the noise settles:

- structure returns,
- institutions step in,
- direction becomes clear.

The scalper enters when order returns to chaos.

Summary

News Spike Reaction Scalping is one of the most profitable setups when handled properly.

Key principles:

- do not trade the news release,
- trade the reaction after structure forms,
- wait for retest and rejection,
- use wide stops relative to volatility,
- exit quickly as momentum fades.

Core pattern:

$$\text{Spike} \rightarrow \text{Retest} \rightarrow \text{Continuation}$$

News is energy. Reaction is direction. This is where scalpers profit.

Chapter 9

1-Minute Scalping Mastery

The one-minute chart is where scalping becomes pure speed. Price moves fast, decisions are immediate, and execution must be precise. This chapter explains how to read the 1M chart like a professional scalper, engineer ultra-tight stop-losses, and capture small but consistent movements.

We will focus on high-probability entries, momentum timing, and fast profit-taking, as well as the specific instruments where the 1-minute timeframe offers the highest edge: gold, NASDAQ, US30, EURUSD, and BTC.

9.1 How to Read the 1-Minute Chart Like a Pro

The 1-minute chart is the primary battlefield for scalpers. It is fast, noisy, and unforgiving. To operate skillfully at this level, a trader must learn to extract structure from chaos and identify small but consistent edges in price behavior.

The key is not to *react* to every candle, but to understand the *rhythm* of price: expansion, retracement, continuation, and exhaustion. Professional scalpers read the 1M chart through a structured lens that separates signal from noise.

The Three Layers of the 1M Chart

A professional scalper views the 1-minute chart in three distinct layers:

1. **Trend Layer** — direction using EMA alignment.
2. **Structure Layer** — swings, HH/HL or LH/LL.
3. **Execution Layer** — entry, stop, and partials.

Without all three, trading becomes reactive and random.

Trend Layer: Direction Comes First

Before any entry, the trader must determine the direction of flow.
Use a cluster of EMAs to simplify this:

$$5/8/13/20 \quad \text{aligned upward} \Rightarrow \text{long bias}$$

$$5/8/13/20 \quad \text{aligned downward} \Rightarrow \text{short bias}$$

Flat and overlapping EMAs indicate a range. No trend = no urgency.

> On the 1M chart, direction is everything. Trade with it, never against it.

Structure Layer: Micro Swings

Even on the smallest timeframe, structure matters.
We identify:

- Higher Highs (HH) and Higher Lows (HL) in an uptrend.
- Lower Lows (LL) and Lower Highs (LH) in a downtrend.

These swings reveal the rhythm of the market:

$$\text{Impulse} \rightarrow \text{Pullback} \rightarrow \text{Continuation}$$

When this rhythm breaks, a shift is happening.

Execution Layer: Entry and Stop Engineering

Entries on the 1M chart must be precise. Only three entry conditions matter:

1. **Price pulls back to structure or EMA cluster**
2. **Rejection or engulfing candle forms**
3. **Micro BOS or continuation candle**

Stop-loss placement is mechanical:

- below the rejection wick (long),
- above the rejection wick (short).

This allows extremely small stops, often 0.2%–0.5% on indices and gold. Small risk means large R:R potential.

The Three Candle Model

Professional scalpers often rely on a simple model:

1. **Initiation candle** — impulse in direction of trend.
2. **Retracement candle** — small pullback into structure.
3. **Confirmation candle** — continuation.

Entry occurs at the beginning of the third candle. Stop-loss goes behind the retracement low/high.

$$\text{Initiation} \rightarrow \text{Retrace} \rightarrow \text{Continuation}$$

This pattern repeats hundreds of times per week.

Avoiding Overreaction

The 1-minute chart can mislead inexperienced traders. Every candle looks important in isolation. A professional focuses on:

- context,
- rhythm,
- order flow,
- structure.

Individual candles are just noise unless they occur at *meaningful locations*:

- swing high/low,
- liquidity area,
- EMA cluster,
- VWAP,
- FVG or block.

A candle matters because of location, not shape.

Timing and Momentum

Momentum is critical. On the 1-minute chart:

- price moves in bursts,
- rests,
- then bursts again.

Entries are taken during bursts, not rests.
You want:

- a strong candle,
- clean pullback,
- immediate continuation.

If continuation does not appear within 1–3 candles, exit. Momentum has expired.

Managing Noise and Randomness

The 1-minute chart is full of deception:

- fake wicks,
- tiny breakouts,
- micro-traps,
- false momentum.

To filter noise, scalpers use:

- direction (EMA alignment),
- context (session, location),
- order flow (tape and footprint),
- structure (HH/HL vs LH/LL).

Without context, the 1M chart is chaos. With context, it is a map.

Why Professionals Prefer the 1-Minute Chart

The benefits are enormous:

- faster feedback loop,
- more setups per day,
- tighter stops,
- higher R:R potential,
- less exposure to risk.

One excellent trade can occur within minutes.

> Scalpers do not need many trades. They need one good window.

Summary

Reading the 1M chart like a professional requires:

- identify direction using EMAs,
- track structure with HH/HL or LH/LL,
- enter on pullbacks with rejection and confirmation,
- place tight stops behind structure,
- exit quickly when momentum expires.

Core pattern:

$$\text{Direction} \rightarrow \text{Pullback} \rightarrow \text{Continuation}$$

> The 1-minute chart is not noise when you know its language. It is opportunity, precision, and speed.

9.2 Ultra-Tight Stop-Loss Engineering

Scalping is a game of precision. A small edge repeated many times can produce large results, but only if risk is controlled with discipline. The most powerful advantage of scalping is that stop-loss distances are extremely small. The trader risks very little to capture short bursts of movement.

> A scalper does not need to know the future. They only need a tiny move in their favor.

Ultra-tight stop-loss engineering is the foundation of this edge.

The Philosophy of Tight Stops

A tight stop is not just a smaller number. It is a positional philosophy:

1. Identify location where trade is invalid.
2. Place stop just beyond that location.
3. If price reaches that level, exit instantly.

The goal is not to avoid loss, but to **minimize the cost of being wrong**.

$$\text{Lose small, win often} \Rightarrow \text{edge over time}$$

Where Tight Stops Belong

A tight stop must sit behind structure:

- behind a swing low (for longs),
- behind a swing high (for shorts),
- beyond a rejection wick,
- outside an imbalance or block.

Stops must never sit:

- inside noise,
- directly at the level,
- where market hunts liquidity.

> Stops belong in places the market does not need to visit, unless the idea is wrong.

Microscale Execution

On the 1-minute chart, the scalper can see micro-structure clearly:

- tiny pullbacks,
- wick rejections,
- BOS on micro swings.

Stops often range between:

$$0.10\% \text{ to } 0.50\% \quad \text{on indices and gold}$$

This allows:

- very small risk,
- very high reward-to-risk (R:R),
- more opportunities per session.

Stop Placement Templates

There are three core templates:

1. **Wick-Based Stop**

$$\text{Stop below rejecting wick (long)}$$

2. **Structure-Based Stop**

$$\text{Stop beyond swing low/high}$$

3. **Imbalance/Block Stop**

$$\text{Stop outside FVG or breaker block}$$

If price invalidates that zone, the idea is wrong. Exit.

Never Use Arbitrary Stops

A scalper must never choose a stop based on:

- fixed number of points,
- fixed number of ticks,
- fixed percentage.

The market does not care about round numbers. Stops must follow structure.

> Stops do not protect trades. They protect capital.

ATR Integration

ATR (Average True Range) provides a volatility filter.

If ATR is high:

- use slightly wider stops,
- reduce position size.

If ATR is low:

- tight stops are safe,
- trades may be more frequent.

A practical formula:

$$\text{Stop Distance} = \frac{ATR_{1M}}{2}$$

This adjusts dynamically to volatility.

Scaling In and Out

Many scalpers use two-unit entries:

- Unit 1: take profit early (1R)
- Unit 2: trail behind structure

This maintains:

- positive expectancy,
- lower emotional pressure,
- smoother equity curve.

Even if price returns, risk is already reduced.

How Tight Stops Increase Confidence

A tight stop has psychological benefits:

- fear is reduced,
- losses are small,
- confidence increases,
- discipline improves.

The trader no longer fears being wrong. Being wrong costs little.

$$\text{Less fear} \rightarrow \text{More clarity} \rightarrow \text{Better execution}$$

When Tight Stops Fail

Tight stops are not appropriate when:

- liquidity is thin,
- market is chopping,
- session is quiet,
- spread is wide,
- news is imminent.

In these conditions:

- widen stops,
- reduce size,
- or do not trade.

Checklist Before Entry

1. Is structure clear?
2. Is liquidity nearby?
3. Are EMAs aligned?
4. Is spread stable?
5. Can stop be placed beyond structure?

If any answer is no, skip the trade.

Summary

Ultra-tight stop engineering allows:

- very small risk,
- frequent opportunity,
- large R:R outcomes,
- psychological clarity.

Core principles:

- Stops belong beyond structure, not inside noise.
- Size decreases as stop tightens.

- Exit immediately if invalidated.

$$\text{Tiny risk} \rightarrow \text{Large potential reward}$$

A scalper is not trying to be right. A scalper is trying to be disciplined, consistent, and small in loss.

9.3 High-Probability Entry Techniques

On the 1-minute chart, price moves quickly and unpredictably. To succeed, a scalper must only take trades where probability is clearly tilted in their favor. High-probability entries occur when three elements align:

1. **Directional bias is clear**
2. **Price reaches a meaningful location**
3. **A precise trigger confirms entry**

Without all three, the trade becomes random. This section outlines the most reliable entry techniques used by professional scalpers.

1. Direction First: Flow Detection

Before entering a trade, the scalper determines:

- trend direction,
- session momentum,
- liquidity context.

The simplest and fastest method:

$$\text{EMA Alignment} \Rightarrow \text{Directional Bias}$$

If EMAs (5/8/13/20) are:

- stacked upward: long-only
- stacked downward: short-only
- flat and overlapping: no trade

Never fight the flow. High-probability means high alignment.

2. Location: Price Must Reach a Zone

Entries come from location, not prediction.

High-value zones include:

- previous swing highs/lows,
- VWAP,
- EMA clusters,
- FVG midpoint,
- breaker block,
- liquidity sweep area,
- session high/low.

The scalper waits for price to **reach the zone**, then looks for confirmation. No level = no trade.

3. Trigger: Candlestick Confirmation

Once price is in the zone, a trigger must appear. Typical triggers:

- rejection wick,
- pin bar,
- engulfing candle,
- BOS on micro-structure,
- shift in order flow velocity.

Without a trigger, the risk is too high.

$$\text{Zone} + \text{Trigger} = \text{Entry}$$

4. Entry After Pullback, Not at Extremes

The safest entries occur on pullbacks.

Sequence:

1. Impulse move in trend direction.
2. Price returns to structure (pullback).
3. Confirmation candle forms.
4. Enter on continuation.

This provides:

- tight stops,
- logical invalidation,
- strong R:R.

Do not chase. Wait for price to come to you.

5. BOS (Break of Structure) as Confirmation

A strong entry signal is a micro-BOS:

- for longs: break above previous micro-high,
- for shorts: break below previous micro-low.

$$\text{Pullback} \rightarrow \text{BOS} \rightarrow \text{Continuation}$$

This confirms that:

- trapped traders are exiting,
- momentum is shifting,
- direction is valid.

6. Using Imbalances (FVG) as Entry Zones

Imbalance shows urgency. Price often returns to fill a portion of the gap.
Best entry:

$$\text{At the midpoint of the FVG}$$

Look for:

- rejection wick,
- engulfing,
- volume burst.

FVG entries are particularly effective in trending conditions.

7. Tape & Order Flow Confirmation

For scalpers who use tape or footprint:

- absorption = reversal,
- exhaustion = reversal,
- aggression = continuation.

A strong confirmation:

- buyers lifting offers aggressively (long)
- sellers hitting bids aggressively (short)

If tape slows down into a level, a reversal is likely.

8. Volume Spike + Structure

A sudden burst of volume at structure provides:

- clear intention,
- energy for movement,
- strong continuation.

Volume spike alone is not enough. Volume spike at a meaningful level is ideal.

Volume gives power to price.

9. Entry After Stop Hunt

A powerful entry occurs when price sweeps liquidity:

1. stops are taken beyond swing,
2. rejection wick forms,
3. BOS confirms reversal,
4. enter on pullback.

This traps late traders.

$$\text{Sweep} \rightarrow \text{Rejection} \rightarrow \text{BOS} \rightarrow \text{Entry}$$

10. Multi-Timeframe Alignment

Even on the 1M chart, higher timeframes matter.

Simple rule:

- 1M follows 5M
- 5M follows 15M

If 5M is trending up, 1M longs are safer. If 5M is trending down, 1M shorts are safer.

11. Immediate Invalidation

A high-probability entry must have clear invalidation:

- if price goes beyond rejection wick, exit,
- if momentum dies, exit,
- if BOS fails, exit.

Never widen stops. Invalid is invalid.

> Small losses are strategic. Large losses are emotional.

Checklist for Entry

Before entering:

1. Trend direction confirmed?
2. Price at meaningful level?
3. Trigger candle visible?
4. Tight stop available behind structure?
5. Spread stable?

If any answer is **no** — skip.

Summary

High-probability entries require:

- direction,
- location,
- confirmation.

The core formula:

$$\text{Bias} + \text{Zone} + \text{Trigger} = \text{Entry}$$

This reduces randomness and increases expectancy.

> You are not trading candles. You are trading behavior at location with confirmation.

9.4 Fast Profit-Taking & Momentum Timing

Scalping does not aim for large moves. It aims for fast, controlled profits during brief moments of momentum. The key is to exit while the market is still moving in your direction, before volatility fades and price snaps back.

> Momentum is temporary. Profit must be captured while it exists.

Fast profit-taking is not fear — it is strategy. Momentum timing separates the expert scalper from the emotional trader.

Understanding Momentum Windows

Momentum on the 1-minute chart appears in short bursts. These bursts are generated by:

- aggressive order flow,
- trapped traders exiting,
- stop clusters triggering,
- news or session transitions.

These bursts are brief:

$$\text{20 seconds to 3 minutes}$$

After the burst, price often:

- consolidates,
- retraces,
- reverses.

You do not want to be holding when momentum is gone.

The Momentum Curve

Momentum follows a simple curve:

$$\text{Ignition} \rightarrow \text{Acceleration} \rightarrow \text{Exhaustion}$$

Profits are taken during acceleration. Not before exhaustion.

> When price hesitates, exit. Hesitation is the first sign of exhaustion.

When to Take Profit

There are only three high-probability profit events:

1. **1R to 2R move**
2. **Approaching structure / liquidity**
3. **Momentum slowing**

If price reaches any of these conditions:

Take profit.

Scaling Out Improves Expectancy

Professional scalpers scale out:

- Take partial profit early (1R or structure)
- Move stop to breakeven
- Hold runner for momentum

This provides psychological and statistical benefit:

- reduces risk,
- maintains upside,
- stabilizes equity curve.

$$\text{Small win} + \text{breakeven} + \text{big win} = \text{consistency}$$

Advanced Timing: Candle Rhythm

Momentum timing is visible through candle rhythm:

- strong candle → continuation,
- small candle → hesitation,
- opposing wick → exhaustion,
- engulfing opposite → reversal.

Three small candles signal a stall. Exit is prudent.

Order Flow Clues

Order flow reveals momentum loss:

- tape slows,
- fewer aggressive prints,
- imbalance disappears,
- liquidity absorbs.

If price cannot progress with volume, exit immediately.

> Momentum is effort. No effort, no continuation.

Profit Target Locations

High-probability target zones include:

- previous swing high/low,
- opposing liquidity pools,
- VWAP bands,
- session levels,
- FVG edges,
- round numbers (00, 50).

Price reacts strongly at these levels. Take profit before the reaction happens.

Time Stops

In scalping, time itself is risk.

If a trade does not move quickly:

Exit.

A useful rule:

If trade does not progress within 3–5 candles, close it.

Because:

- momentum is gone,
- opportunity is fading,
- risk is accumulating.

Avoiding Greed

Greed is the enemy of the scalper. Holding for a large move on a small timeframe invites drawdown.

Scalpers are paid for precision, not patience.

The goal is not to capture the entire move. It is to capture the *best part* of the move.

Exit Techniques

Three clean exit techniques:

1. **Structure Exit**

   Exit at obvious level:

   - swing high/low,
   - liquidity,
   - VWAP.

2. **Momentum Exit**

   Exit when momentum slows:

   - smaller candles,
   - wicks,
   - opposite prints.

3. **Time Exit**

   If no movement:

   Close.

Use whichever comes first.

The Emotionless Exit

Professional scalpers exit with zero emotion. They are not attached to outcomes.

Because:

- they risk little,
- they exit quickly,
- they can re-enter.

Summary

Fast profit-taking is essential in scalping:

- momentum bursts are short,
- hesitation signals exhaustion,
- exit at structure or 1–2R,
- scale out to reduce risk,
- use time as a stop.

Core principle:

Enter fast, exit faster.

> A scalper does not need big wins. A scalper needs small, consistent, controlled wins.

9.5 Best Pairs and Indices for 1M Trading (Gold, NASDAQ, US30, EURUSD, BTC)

Not all instruments are suitable for 1-minute scalping. Some move too slowly, others have poor liquidity or wide spreads, and many do not produce enough intraday volatility to justify the risk.

The best instruments for 1M scalping share three characteristics:

1. **High liquidity**
2. **Tight spreads**
3. **Frequent directional bursts**

The following five instruments consistently offer these qualities, making them ideal for fast, precise scalping.

Gold (XAUUSD)

Gold is a favorite of scalpers due to:

- high volume,
- frequent volatility spikes,
- strong reactions to news,
- very clean technical behavior.

Gold provides multiple clean setups per day on 1M, especially around:

- London open,
- New York open,
- macroeconomic news.

Key points:

- momentum moves are fast and large
- spreads are usually acceptable
- tight stop-losses perform well

When gold moves, it moves with purpose.

NASDAQ (NAS100 / NQ)

NASDAQ offers explosive momentum and clean structure. It is highly responsive to:

- technology sector sentiment,
- US economic data,
- market open dynamics.

Advantages:

- strong trends,
- frequent pullbacks,
- excellent rhythm.

Ideal for:

- breakout continuation,
- FVG reactions,
- micro pullbacks.

NASDAQ is a scalper's playground.

US30 (Dow Jones)

US30 moves differently from NASDAQ:

- slower,
- heavier,
- more stable rhythm.

This makes it ideal for traders who prefer:

- cleaner structure,
- slightly slower decision cycles,
- clearer swing points.

It reacts well to:

- session levels,
- liquidity sweeps,
- VWAP interactions.

US30 rewards patience and precision.

EURUSD

EURUSD is the most liquid currency pair in the world. On the 1M chart it provides:

- tight spreads,
- smooth intraday flow,
- excellent pullbacks.

Best during:

- London session,
- London → New York overlap.

Entry techniques align well with:

- EMA pullbacks,
- liquidity sweeps,
- micro break of structure.

EURUSD is the most disciplined instrument for 1-minute structure.

Bitcoin (BTC)

BTC has a unique intraday behavior:

- 24/7 movement,
- frequent micro-trends,
- sudden bursts of volatility.

It is ideal for:

- weekend scalping,
- Asian session activity,
- breakout continuation patterns.

However, BTC requires caution:

- spreads can widen,
- volatility can spike without warning,
- liquidity pockets may be thin.

BTC is a scalper's opportunity, and a scalper's danger.

Session Timing Matters

Each instrument has ideal active windows:

- Gold: London → New York
- NASDAQ: New York open
- US30: New York open + early afternoon
- EURUSD: London + overlap
- BTC: Asia + weekends + breakouts

Trading outside these windows reduces probability.

When Not to Trade

Avoid 1M scalping during:

- very low liquidity (lunch hours),
- major news release seconds,
- widened spreads,
- directionless chop.

If the market is not moving, there is no edge.

Summary

The best instruments for 1M scalping share three properties:

- liquidity,
- volatility,
- structure.

Gold, NASDAQ, US30, EURUSD, and BTC deliver:

- clean rhythm,
- frequent setups,
- fast momentum,
- tight stop-loss opportunities.

Core principle:

> Choose instruments that move fast, clean, and often.

The right instrument makes scalping easier. The wrong instrument makes it impossible.

Chapter 10

5-Minute Scalping Systems

The 5-minute chart offers a powerful balance between speed and accuracy. It provides enough structure to reduce noise while remaining fast enough for active intraday trading. This chapter focuses on slower but highly stable setups, swing-scalp hybrids, momentum confirmation signals, and advanced structure patterns that form on the 5M chart. We will also explore how the 5M timeframe serves as an anchor for precision execution on the 1M chart.

10.1 Slower but More Stable Setups

While the 1-minute chart offers speed and frequency, the 5-minute chart provides a calmer and more structured environment. Price patterns take longer to form, swings are wider, and noise is significantly reduced. This makes the 5M chart ideal for traders who prefer fewer decisions and clearer structure, without sacrificing intraday opportunity.

> The 5-minute chart is slower, but far more stable. It rewards preparation, patience, and timing.

Why the 5-Minute Chart Is Stable

The 5M timeframe filters out much of the randomness that appears on 1M. Each candle represents more data:

- more trades executed,
- clearer directional intent,
- stronger structural levels,
- cleaner trend development.

On the 1M, a single wick may be noise. On the 5M, the same wick is meaningful rejection.

Reduced Emotional Pressure

The slower rhythm of the 5M timeframe reduces psychological stress:

- fewer decisions per minute,
- less impulse trading,
- more time to evaluate context,
- clearer stops and targets.

The trader can think more, react less.

The 5M Candle Is a Micro Trend

Each 5M candle often contains:

- a full micro-impulse,
- retracement,
- continuation.

This means:

- identifying direction becomes easier,
- precision entry points are clearer,
- stop-loss locations are cleaner.

$$\text{One 5M candle} = \text{five micro-cycles of the 1M}$$

Stability from Structure

Stable setups form around clear structure:

- swing highs and swing lows,
- liquidity edges,
- VWAP,
- session levels,
- fair value gaps,
- breaker blocks.

These levels hold more weight on 5M than they do on 1M. When price reacts, continuation is stronger and smoother.

Entry Timing Is Cleaner

A stable 5M setup typically follows this sequence:

1. Trend forms on EMAs.
2. A pullback reaches structure.
3. Rejection candle prints.
4. Volume supports direction.
5. Entry is taken on continuation.

Stops are placed behind the swing, not inside noise.

The 5M chart gives more time for clarity, confirmation, and execution.

Wider Stop, Bigger Target

Because candles are larger, stops must be slightly wider:

- typically 0.30% to 1.00%
- depending on instrument and volatility.

However, reward expands proportionally:

- 2R, 3R, even 5R moves are common,
- especially during trending sessions.

Risk remains controlled because frequency is lower.

Fewer Trades, Higher Quality

The 5M chart favors:

- patience,
- selectivity,
- focus on best structure.

A professional might take:

$$\text{2 to 6 trades per session}$$

But each trade has:

- clear justification,
- strong location,
- high-quality setup,
- better R:R potential.

Less Noise, More Signal

On the 5M:

- fewer false breaks,
- fewer traps,
- fewer random spikes.

This gives greater confidence.
The trader observes:

- impulsive candles,
- wicks at structure,
- true BOS/CHOCH,
- clean continuation.

Psychological Advantages

The emotional benefits are enormous:

- less urgency,
- more control,
- reduced cognitive load,
- easier routine building.

This is especially valuable for:

- new scalpers,
- traders with anxiety,
- those who struggle with impulse.

Ideal Use Case

The 5M chart excels in:

- trending sessions,
- news reaction swings,
- opening range breakouts,
- structure-based pullbacks,
- swing-scalp hybrids.

It is also the best anchor for executing entries on the 1M.

$$\text{5M for structure} \Rightarrow \text{1M for precision}$$

Summary

The 5-minute chart offers:

- slower rhythm,
- clearer structure,
- reduced noise,
- better emotional stability,
- higher quality setups.

Core principle:

> Trade less often, with higher conviction and clearer logic.

The 5M chart rewards patience, discipline, and strategic timing. It serves as the balance point between the speed of scalping and the clarity of structure.

10.2 Swing-Scalp Hybrid Strategies

Swing-scalp hybrid strategies combine the structure of swing trading with the precision and timing of scalping. They use higher timeframe direction (5M, 15M, or even 1H) to establish bias, and then execute entries on the lower timeframe (1M or 5M) with tight stops and fast profit-taking. This approach offers larger R:R potential while keeping risk extremely small.

> Swing logic provides direction. Scalping execution provides precision.

This method is especially effective for traders who want fewer trades with higher conviction, without sacrificing intraday opportunity.

Why Hybrid Strategies Work

Swing-scalp hybrids resolve the main problem of both styles:

- pure scalping = too much noise
- pure swing = too much waiting

The hybrid model uses:

1. Higher timeframe for bias and structure
2. Lower timeframe for entry precision

This creates:

- cleaner setups,
- smaller stops,
- larger targets,
- higher expectancy.

$$\text{HTF direction} + \text{LTF entry} = \text{best of both worlds}$$

Anchor Chart for Direction

The 5M (or 15M) chart acts as the anchor:

- trend detection,
- major swing structure,
- liquidity zones,
- VWAP positioning,
- fair value gaps.

The trader waits for:

- pullback into structure,
- rejection or confirmation,
- entry on lower timeframe.

> Structure comes from the anchor. Execution comes from the trigger.

Execution Chart for Entry

Most entries are executed on 1M or 2M charts.
Look for:

- wick rejection,
- micro BOS,
- engulfing candle,
- inducement sweep.

Stops are extremely tight:

$$\text{3 to 12 ticks on indices}$$

Example Entry Sequence

A classic hybrid sequence:

1. 5M trend is up (HH/HL).
2. Price pulls back into demand block.
3. 1M prints rejection wick.
4. Micro-BOS to upside.
5. Enter long on continuation.

Stops go beneath the wick or structure.

$$\text{Stop} \approx 0.20\% - 0.45\%$$

Targets can be significantly larger:

$$2R,\ 3R,\ 5R,\ \text{or more}$$

Best Market Conditions

Hybrid strategies thrive when:

- higher timeframe is trending,
- pullbacks are orderly,
- volatility is moderate to high,
- session overlap (London $\rightarrow$ New York).

Avoid during:

- flat session,
- choppy structure,
- lunch hours,
- low volatility.

Key Technical Tools

Hybrids benefit from confluence:

- HTF swing structure
- HTF FVG or breaker block
- LTF rejection wick
- LTF BOS or continuation
- ATR and momentum confirmation

Every trade has logic:

$$\text{Reason for direction} + \text{Reason for entry}$$

Benefits of the Hybrid Approach

This method creates a powerful combination:

- fewer trades, higher quality
- tight risk, large targets
- easy psychology
- strong math expectancy

It suits traders who prefer:

- patience over speed,
- clarity over chaos,
- precision over prediction.

Example Target Model

Targets are determined by higher timeframe levels:

- previous swing high/low,
- liquidity pool,
- VWAP band,
- ADR levels,
- session boundaries.

Scaling out increases stability:

$$\text{Partial at 1R, hold for 3R+}$$

Psychological Advantage

Hybrid strategies reduce stress:

- clearer direction,
- fewer decisions,
- more time between setups,
- less impulse trading.

You are not chasing price. You are letting price come to your zone.

Common Mistakes

Avoid:

- entering without direction,
- ignoring structure,
- oversized risk,
- forcing trades,
- trading in chop.

Patience is critical.

Summary

Swing-scalp hybrid strategies combine:

- direction from higher timeframe,
- precision from lower timeframe,
- small stop-losses,
- large targets.

Core formula:

$$\text{HTF Bias} + \text{LTF Trigger} = \text{Optimal Trade}$$

Trade the higher timeframe idea with lower timeframe execution.

10.3 Momentum Confirmation Signals

Momentum is the engine that drives scalping. A setup can be technically perfect, located at structure, with clear rejection — yet without momentum, price will stall, chop, or reverse. Momentum confirmation ensures that when the trader enters, the market is already moving with force in the intended direction.

> Structure tells you where. Momentum tells you when.

This section explains how to confirm momentum before execution.

Understanding Momentum

Momentum is the combination of:

- direction,
- velocity,
- volume,
- participation.

When momentum exists:

- price moves cleanly,
- pullbacks are shallow,
- continuation is swift.

When momentum is absent:

- price hesitates,
- candles become small,
- wicks increase,
- reversals become likely.

Three Pillars of Momentum Confirmation

Professional scalpers rely on three pillars to confirm momentum:

1. **Candle Structure**
2. **Order Flow**
3. **Volume Behavior**

If all three align, confidence is high.

1. Candle Structure Confirmation

Momentum candles have clear characteristics:

- wide body,
- small wicks,
- clean direction,
- close near the extreme.

A strong candle closing at the high (bullish) or low (bearish) signals:

Aggressive participation

Continuation is likely.
Opposite characteristics show weak momentum:

- tiny bodies,
- long wicks,
- indecision,
- hesitation.

2. Order Flow Confirmation

Order flow reveals whether buyers or sellers are pushing market:

- **lifting offers** = buyers aggressive
- **hitting bids** = sellers aggressive

Momentum is confirmed when:

- tape speed increases,
- prints become clustered,
- directional aggression is visible.

If tape slows or becomes uncertain, momentum is fading.

3. Volume Behavior

Volume spikes confirm real participation. Strong moves occur when volume aligns with direction.

Rules:

- **Price up** + **Volume up** = bullish continuation.
- **Price down** + **Volume up** = bearish continuation.
- **Price up** + **Volume down** = exhaustion.
- **Price down** + **Volume down** = indecision.

Volume gives power to price.

Multi-Candle Momentum Signals

Momentum rarely appears in a single candle. Professional scalpers watch for patterns:

- two or three consecutive strong candles,
- shallow pullback,
- immediate continuation.

This rhythm signals flow and direction.

Micro BOS as Momentum Trigger

Break of structure confirms momentum shift.

For longs:

$$\text{Break above micro-high}$$

For shorts:

$$\text{Break below micro-low}$$

Micro BOS shows trapped traders being forced to exit, adding fuel.

Wick Logic and Rejection

Wicks reveal rejection:

- wick against trend = trap/pullback
- wick with trend = continuation

If price rejects strongly from a level and continues:

$$Momentum is active.$$

If price hovers:

$$Momentum is weak.$$

Momentum at Location

Momentum must occur in the right place:

- at structure,
- at EMA cluster,
- at VWAP band,
- at supply/demand block,
- after liquidity sweep.

Momentum without context is dangerous. Context without momentum is ineffective.

Location + Momentum = Entry

Session Momentum

Certain times generate natural momentum:

- London open,
- New York open,
- London → NY overlap,
- after news reaction,
- session extremes.

Outside these windows, momentum may be weak.

Momentum Fade Signals

Watch for momentum dying:

- candle bodies shrink,
- wicks increase,
- tape slows,
- footprint shows absorption,
- volume drops.

When momentum fades:

$$Exit quickly.$$

Time is risk on small timeframes.

Checklist Before Entry

1. Is direction clear?
2. Is structure aligned (HH/HL or LH/LL)?
3. Are EMAs pointing and separated?
4. Is there impulsive candle movement?
5. Did volume increase?
6. Did tape speed up?

If these align, probability is high.

Summary

Momentum confirmation ensures that the market is actually moving when a trade is taken.

Key principles:

- direction must be obvious,
- strong candles confirm aggression,
- volume supports movement,
- order flow shows intention,
- hesitation = exit.

Core formula:

> Structure + Location + Momentum = High-Probability Trade
>
> Trade where price wants to go, when it already began moving there.

10.4 Advanced 5M Structure Patterns

The 5-minute chart provides a unique balance of clarity and speed, allowing patterns to form in a way that is both readable and actionable. Advanced structure patterns on this timeframe offer high-probability setups with clear logic, clean invalidation, and strong momentum follow-through. These patterns form repeatedly every trading session, especially during active hours.

> On the 5M chart, structure is not theory — it is geometry in motion.

This section explains the most reliable and repeatable structure patterns.

1. Opening Range Breakout (ORB)

The first 5–15 minutes of London and New York sessions create a structure known as the *opening range*. Price often:

- consolidates,
- sweeps one side,
- then breaks with momentum.

Reliable sequence:

1. Opening range forms.
2. Sweep of highs or lows.
3. Strong break in opposite direction.
4. Pullback to retest the range.
5. Continuation.

$$\text{Sweep} \rightarrow \text{Break} \rightarrow \text{Retest} \rightarrow \text{Go}$$

Targets:

- liquidity pools,
- session high/low,
- VWAP bands.

2. Mid-Session Trend Channel

Once direction establishes, price often moves within a channel:

- higher highs and higher lows, or
- lower highs and lower lows.

Characteristics:

- momentum candles with shallow pullbacks,
- clear diagonal structure,
- easy continuation entries.

Entry:

$$\text{Buy dips in bullish channel, sell rallies in bearish channel}$$

Stops:

$$\text{Below swing structure}$$

3. Consolidation $\rightarrow$ Breakout $\rightarrow$ Retest

This pattern is the backbone of intraday trading:

- consolidation forms,
- range compresses,
- break occurs,
- retest,
- continuation.

On the 5M chart:

1. Price tightens,
2. wicks reduce,
3. volatility compresses,
4. then a breakout candle erupts.

$$\text{Break without retest is lower probability}$$

4. Micro Double Bottom / Top at Structure

When price retests a level twice:

- buyers/sellers defend zone,
- liquidity is absorbed,
- reversal follows.

Best when aligned with:

- session levels,
- VWAP,
- FVG boundaries,
- swing highs/lows.

Entry confirmation:

1. wick rejection,
2. engulfing candle,
3. micro BOS.

5. Fair Value Gap (FVG) Refill and Continuation

On 5M, FVGs form constantly due to:

- high-speed moves,
- imbalance,
- aggressive participation.

The pattern:

1. impulse creates imbalance,
2. price pulls back into the gap,
3. continues with trend.

Best entry:

$$\text{Midpoint of the gap}$$

Stops behind structure.

6. Breaker Block Reversal

Breaker blocks are powerful reversal zones:

- previous high/low,
- structure sweep,
- flip from support to resistance.

Sequence:

1. strong level breaks,
2. price retests it,
3. momentum confirms.

This traps countertrend traders.

Breaker blocks are footprints of failed positions.

7. Liquidity Sweep + Rejection

Liqudity is often swept before a move.
Setup:

1. price reaches key high/low,
2. wicks sweep stops,
3. rejection candle forms,
4. fast continuation.

Confirmation:

$$\text{BOS on lower timeframe}$$

Sweep → BOS → pullback → entry.

8. VWAP Magnet + Expansion

VWAP acts as a gravity center:

- price compresses around VWAP,
- then expands away,
- especially at session transitions.

Strong setups when:

- compression,
- breakout,
- retest,
- continuation.

9. Exhaustion → Reversal

Exhaustion is visible on 5M:

- candles shrink,
- wicks increase,
- bodies weaken,
- momentum fades.

Then:

$$\text{Sudden reversal with volume}$$

Especially effective after:

- trend climax,
- liquidity sweep,
- news spike.

10. Session High/Low Interaction

Price respects session extremes:

- London High/Low
- New York High/Low

Three behaviors occur:

1. breakout and continuation,
2. sweep and reversal,
3. chop and compression.

The 5M structure makes it obvious which one is happening.

Summary

Advanced 5M structure patterns offer:

- clarity,
- predictability,
- high-probability setups,
- clear invalidation.

They form repeatedly every day across liquid instruments.
Core cycle:

$$\text{Consolidation} \rightarrow \text{Expansion} \rightarrow \text{Retracement} \rightarrow \text{Continuation}$$

The 5M chart reveals the rhythm of the market. Learn the rhythm, and entries become obvious.

10.5 Using 5M as Anchor for 1M Execution

The most powerful way to scalp is to separate *decision-making* from *execution*. The 5-minute chart provides the strategic view (direction, structure, key levels), while the 1-minute chart handles tactical precision (entries, stops, and exits).

Think in 5M. Execute in 1M.

This top-down approach turns random 1M noise into a guided, structured trading plan.

Why the 5M Chart Should Be the Anchor

The 5M timeframe filters out much of the randomness of the 1M:

- trends are clearer,
- structure is more reliable,
- levels hold more weight,
- false signals are reduced.

By using 5M as the anchor, a scalper:

- avoids overtrading in chop,
- focuses only on high-quality locations,
- aligns trades with the dominant intraday flow.

The 1M chart then becomes a tool for *precision timing*, not for guessing direction.

The Anchor–Trigger Framework

A simple and powerful model:

Anchor timeframe: 5M (bias, levels, structure)

Trigger timeframe: 1M (entries, stops, fine timing)

Workflow:

1. Use 5M to define:
    - trend direction (HH/HL or LH/LL),
    - key levels (swing highs/lows, VWAP, FVG, blocks),
    - current phase (impulse, pullback, or consolidation).
2. Mark the zones where you *might* trade.
3. Drop to 1M only when price is at or near those zones.
4. Wait for 1M confirmation (rejection, BOS, momentum).
5. Execute with tight stops and clear targets.

The 5M tells you *where* to look. The 1M tells you *when* to act.

Step 1: Define 5M Bias

On the 5M chart, determine:

- Is the market trending or ranging?
- Are we printing HH/HL (bullish) or LH/LL (bearish)?
- Are EMAs (e.g. 9/20/50) aligned clearly?

Rules:

- If 5M is clearly bullish, focus on long setups on 1M.
- If 5M is clearly bearish, focus on shorts on 1M.
- If 5M is flat and messy, reduce size or stand aside.

Step 2: Mark 5M Levels and Zones

On 5M, highlight:

- recent swing highs and lows,
- demand/supply zones,
- fair value gaps (FVGs),
- breaker blocks,
- VWAP and session highs/lows.

These become your "battle zones" where you will look for trades. Every 1M trade must be anchored to a 5M context.

Step 3: Wait for Price to Reach the Zone

Patience is critical.

- Do *not* watch 1M all the time.
- Only drop down when price is near a 5M level.

This eliminates random, emotional 1M trades and focuses attention on meaningful moments.

Step 4: 1M Confirmation and Trigger

Once price is in the 5M zone, zoom into 1M.

Look for:

- rejection wicks at the level,
- 1M micro BOS in direction of 5M bias,
- engulfing candles,
- small inducement sweeps (stop hunts),
- volume or tape acceleration.

Example (bullish):

1. 5M bullish trend.
2. Price pulls back into 5M demand or FVG.
3. On 1M, price sweeps low, prints strong bullish engulfing.
4. Micro BOS to the upside.
5. Long entry with stop below 1M low / 5M zone.

Stop-Loss and Target Logic Using 5M

Stops:

- placed using 1M structure (tight),
- validated by 5M zone (logical).

For a long:

- stop below 1M swing low,
- which lies inside/just below 5M demand or block.

Targets:

- next 5M swing high/low,
- 5M liquidity pools,
- VWAP or session extremes.

Thus:

Risk is 1M-based, reward is 5M-based.

This asymmetry makes R:R very favorable.

Examples of Anchor–Trigger Combinations

Example 1: 5M FVG + 1M Rejection

- 5M bullish impulse creates FVG.
- Price returns into FVG.
- On 1M, liquidity sweep and bullish engulfing.
- Enter long; stop below 1M low; target next 5M high.

Example 2: 5M Breaker Block + 1M BOS

- 5M level breaks and flips from resistance to support.
- Price retests breaker block.
- 1M prints micro BOS back in trend direction.
- Enter with tight 1M stop and 5M target.

Psychological Benefits of Anchoring to 5M

Using 5M as anchor:

- reduces noise and overtrading,
- creates clear rules and locations,
- lowers emotional swings,
- makes losses easier to accept (idea was valid and structured),
- increases patience and discipline.

  You are no longer reacting to every 1M candle. You are executing a 5M plan with 1M precision.

Common Mistakes

Avoid:

- taking 1M trades without 5M context,
- switching bias every few candles,
- forcing trades in the middle of nowhere,
- ignoring 5M trend just to "catch" reversals on 1M,
- placing stops only by feel, not structure.

Checklist: 5M Anchor, 1M Execution

Before entering:

1. Is 5M bias clear (trend or range)?
2. Is price at/near a 5M level or zone?
3. Has 1M shown rejection or BOS in bias direction?
4. Is there a logical, tight 1M stop beyond structure?
5. Is a 5M-based target available with at least 2R?

If any answer is no, wait.

Summary

Using 5M as anchor and 1M as execution chart combines:

- higher timeframe clarity,
- lower timeframe precision,
- smaller risk,
- larger structured targets.

Core formula:

$$\text{5M Bias \& Levels} + \text{1M Trigger} = \text{High-Quality Scalping Setup}$$

Trade like a swing trader in your analysis. Trade like a scalper in your execution.

Chapter 11

High-Volatility Scalping

Explosive markets offer the fastest opportunities and the fastest risks. High-volatility environments—especially during major news releases—can create rapid directional moves, deep wicks, and dramatic reversals within seconds. This chapter focuses on how to scalp safely when volatility is high, how to handle spreads and slippage, and how to recognize when movement is opportunity versus danger. We will study news event scalping, volatility filters, and the difference between safe and dangerous volatility zones.

11.1 News Event Scalping (NFP, CPI, FOMC)

Macroeconomic news releases create some of the most explosive movements in financial markets. Events such as NFP (Non-Farm Payrolls), CPI (inflation), and FOMC (Federal Reserve interest rate announcements) can produce violent spikes, rapid reversals, and temporary breakdowns of normal market behavior.

For the scalper, these moments can offer tremendous opportunity — but only when handled with discipline and strong risk control. This section explains how to prepare, execute, and protect capital during such events.

Why News Events Are Unique

During major releases:

- spreads widen,
- liquidity withdraws,
- slippage increases,
- moves become erratic.

This happens because:

- market makers reduce exposure,
- large players reposition,
- algorithms dominate order flow,
- retail orders are second in priority.

In the first seconds after release:

The market is wild, not tradable.

However, shortly after the initial chaos, clean opportunity emerges.

The Three Phases of a News Event

Every major news release follows a pattern:

1. **Pre-release positioning**
2. **Initial spike and whipsaw**
3. **Post-release trend**

1. Pre-release Positioning Minutes before release:

- spreads widen,
- volatility drops,
- price compresses.

Professional rule:

Do not open new trades.

2. Initial Spike and Whipsaw When data is released:

- price explodes,
- both sides get hunted,
- spreads are extreme,
- slippage is guaranteed.

This is where most retail traders blow accounts.
Professional rule:

Do not trade the spike.

3. Post-release Trend After the spike:

- direction becomes clear,
- liquidity returns,
- structure forms,
- continuation or reversal appears.

This is where high-probability scalping is possible.

> Wait for the chaos to settle. Trade the structure, not the reaction.

The Best Opportunities Happen *After* the Spike

The safest approach:

1. mark pre-news high and low,
2. wait for spike to take liquidity,
3. wait for structure to form,
4. enter on retracement or continuation.

Entry techniques on 1M/5M:

- pullback to FVG,
- breaker block retest,
- VWAP rejection,
- BOS continuation.

Stops are tight and logical:

Behind spike wick or structure

Liquidity Sweeps Around News

News spikes sweep liquidity:

- stops above prior highs,
- stops below prior lows.

These sweeps are predictable.
A typical pattern:

1. price sweeps one side,
2. reverses sharply,
3. structure forms,
4. continuation in opposite direction.

This traps early traders.

Volatility Windows

Different events have different volatility windows:

- NFP: explosive first 2–5 minutes,
- CPI: steady trend post-release,
- FOMC: range → breakout → trend.

Never assume normal conditions.

Risk Management Rules for News

Non-negotiable safety rules:

- reduce size or avoid initial spike,
- never widen stops,
- avoid market orders at release,
- wait for structure,
- exit fast when momentum fades.

Professional traders often use:

half size or less

until market normalizes.

Execution Strategy After Release

A clean execution model:

1. Wait for the spike.
2. Identify sweep of highs or lows.
3. Observe rejection wick.

4. Confirm with BOS or volume.
5. Enter on retracement to structure.

Targets:

- opposite liquidity pool,
- session level,
- VWAP band.

Tools That Help During News

Useful indicators:

- ATR (volatility filter),
- VWAP (mean reversion anchor),
- footprint or tape (order flow),
- economic calendar (timing).

Session lines matter:

- London,
- New York,
- overlap.

When *Not* to Trade News

Avoid trading when:

- spreads are wide,
- platform is lagging,
- broker execution is uncertain,
- price has no direction or structure.

Three red flags:

1. erratic candles,
2. repeated whipsaws,
3. low liquidity.

Safety first.

Summary

News events offer the biggest momentum, but also the highest danger. The best trades occur *after* the initial spike, when structure returns and liquidity stabilizes.

Key ideas:

- never trade the immediate spike,
- wait for structure to form,
- enter on retracement,
- keep stops tight,
- take profits quickly.

Fundamental principle:

Trade the response, not the release.

> News does not create trends — it accelerates existing imbalance.

11.2 Handling Spreads, Slippage, and Wicks

High-volatility markets create conditions that are very different from normal trading. Price moves faster, order execution becomes less predictable, and the relationship between the chart and the fill price is not always linear. A scalper must understand how spreads, slippage, and wicks affect risk and how to protect capital in these conditions.

> Volatility creates opportunity — and invisible cost.

Spreads: The Hidden Fee of Volatility

The spread is the difference between the bid and ask price. During normal conditions, spreads are tight and predictable. During volatile events, spreads widen dramatically.

Examples during news:

- Gold: from 1.5 pips → 15–30 pips
- NASDAQ: from 2–4 ticks → 20–40 ticks
- EURUSD: from 0.2 pips → 3–8 pips

These widenings are *normal*. The scalper must anticipate them.

Practical Rules for Spreads

- Do not open trades when spread suddenly expands.
- Reduce size during high-spread periods.
- Check spread before placing stop-loss and target.

If spread is bigger than normal, risk is multiplied.

> A wide spread turns a good entry into a losing position before the first tick.

Slippage: When the Market Moves Faster Than You Do

Slippage means your order is filled at a worse price than requested. This happens because:

- price jumped,
- liquidity disappeared,
- broker repriced your request.

Slippage is most common in:

- market orders,
- high-speed moves,
- news releases,
- thin liquidity moments.

How to Minimize Slippage

- Avoid market orders during news.
- Use limit or stop-limit orders for entries.
- Do not chase price *after* the breakout.

Executing at the wrong time creates negative expectancy.

$$\text{Late entries} = \text{guaranteed slippage}$$

Wicks: The Language of Volatility

Wicks show rejection and imbalance. They are especially important on 1M and 5M charts during high volatility.

A large wick means:

- price traded there,
- orders were absorbed,
- direction changed rapidly.

Two Wick Types

There are two critical wick behaviors:

1. Exhaustion Wick Large wick at the end of a move:

- indicates climactic action,
- trapped traders,
- reversal is likely.

$$\text{Exhaustion wick} = \text{stop hunting complete}$$

2. Rejection Wick at Structure Wick into a level followed by strong candle:

- confirms rejection,
- ideal entry trigger,
- tight stop behind wick.

> Rejection wicks are excellent signals — when they occur in the right place.

Wick Safety on Small Timeframes

On 1M charts, wick rules are critical:

- Do not enter during wick formation.
- Wait for candle close.

If the wick is still forming, you have no information. Only the close tells the truth.

$$\text{Wick} = \text{emotion, close} = \text{intention}$$

Spread + Wick Interaction

Widened spreads exaggerate wick size visually. The trader must understand the difference between:

- true rejection,
- spread distortion,
- thin liquidity illusion.

Always check:

$$\text{spread} + \text{volume} + \text{order flow}$$

before trusting a wick.

Execution Rules for Safety

Practical rules:

1. Reduce position size in high volatility.
2. Place stops beyond structure, not inside noise.
3. Never enter inside a wick.
4. Avoid market orders when spread widens.
5. If price hesitates, exit immediately.

Stop-Loss Placement in Volatility

Stops must be outside danger zones:

- beyond wick,
- beyond structure,
- beyond liquidity pool.

Never tighten stops because spreads are wide — that guarantees a loss.

When Not to Trade

Avoid trading when:

- spreads are expanding rapidly,
- chart is printing erratic wicks,
- liquidity is missing,

- slippage is frequent.

The best decision sometimes is to stand aside.

No trade = 100% capital protection.

Summary

Handling spreads, slippage, and wicks is essential for safe scalping. High-volatility markets require discipline, awareness, and respect for execution risk.

Key principles:

- Spreads widen during volatility — reduce size.
- Slippage is common — avoid late entries.
- Wicks provide information — wait for candle close.
- Safety first — protect capital above all.

> Profit is earned by precision. Capital is preserved by caution.

11.3 Identifying Dangerous vs Safe Volatility Zones

Not all volatility is equal. Some volatility provides clean directional movement with order flow support, while other volatility is chaotic, unpredictable, and designed to trap traders. A scalper's edge comes from knowing which volatility to trust and which to avoid.

> Volatility is profitable when it has direction. It is dangerous when it is random.

This section explains how to distinguish between safe and dangerous volatility zones.

What Makes a Volatility Zone Dangerous?

Dangerous volatility has three characteristics:

1. **No clear direction**
2. **Erratic wicks on both sides**
3. **Low liquidity**

In these conditions:

- price whipsaws,
- stops are hunted,
- fills are uncertain,
- patterns fail.

These zones occur frequently:

- immediately after news release,
- during lunch hours,
- inside tight ranges with no breakout,
- near session transitions without volume.

Avoid : no structure, no direction, no liquidity

What Makes a Volatility Zone Safe?

Safe volatility has:

1. clear structure,
2. strong direction,
3. sustained volume.

Clean conditions show:

- momentum candles,
- shallow pullbacks,
- continuation behavior.

This is the environment where scalping thrives.

> Safe volatility has rhythm. Dangerous volatility has randomness.

Examples of Dangerous Zones

Dangerous zones include:

1. News Spike Chaos The first 1–3 minutes after major news:

- spreads explode,
- slippage is guaranteed,
- charts are unreadable.

2. Choppy Mid-Range When price is stuck between two levels:

- random swings,
- no clear continuation,
- false signals.

3. Low Volume Hours Especially:

- Asia session (unless trading crypto),
- lunch time New York,
- pre-market after gap.

No volume = no movement = no edge.

Examples of Safe Zones

Safe volatility zones are predictable:

1. Post-News Trend After the initial spike:

- direction emerges,
- structure forms,
- opportunity appears.

2. Breakout with Retest Clean sequence:

$$\text{Breakout} \rightarrow \text{Retest} \rightarrow \text{Continuation}$$

These are high-probability trades.

3. Strong Trend Session When trend is active:

- pullbacks are shallow,
- continuation is frequent,
- stops can be tight.

How to Detect Chaos vs Structure

Key tools:

ATR (Average True Range)

ATR spike + no direction = chaos. ATR spike + structure = opportunity.

ATR must be high AND directional.

VWAP and Session Levels

Safe zones form around:

- VWAP reaction,
- session high/low,
- FVG midpoints.

If price respects structure — safer.
If price ignores everything — dangerous.

Wick Logic for Safety

- Long wicks on both sides = trap.
- Long wick against trend = exhaustion.
- Long wick with trend = continuation.

Multiple alternating wicks mean:

no commitment, no trade

Volume as the Final Filter

Volume tells the truth.

- High volume + direction = safe volatility
- High volume + no direction = danger
- Low volume + movement = unreliable

A move without volume is a lie.

The Rule of Three

Before trading in volatility, ask:

1. Is direction obvious?
2. Is structure clear?
3. Is volume supporting?

If all three are yes — safe. If any is no — wait.

Summary

Safe volatility is where scalping profit exists. Dangerous volatility is where accounts are destroyed.

Dangerous Zones:

- post-news chaos,
- chop in mid-range,
- low volume hours,
- wide spreads and wicks.

Safe Zones:

- post-reaction structure,
- breakout + retest,
- trending sessions with volume,
- clean pullbacks with continuation.

Core principle:

$$\text{Volatility} + \text{Structure} + \text{Volume} = \text{Opportunity}$$

Trade volatility only when it is controlled, directed, and supported by liquidity.

Part IV

Advanced Scalping

Chapter 12

Options Scalping & Gamma Scalping

Options provide a unique arena for scalping: fast movement, leveraged exposure, and deep liquidity on major indices. This chapter introduces a simplified and practical entry into derivatives scalping, focusing on gamma, market maker hedging behavior, and 0DTE dynamics. We will explore high-speed options setups, execution rules, and the risk management principles required to survive in this highly volatile environment.

12.1 What Gamma Is and Why It Matters

In options trading, three Greeks dominate short-term price behavior: delta, gamma, and theta. For scalping, gamma is the most important because it measures how *fast* delta changes when the underlying price moves. Gamma is the acceleration of option sensitivity, and it becomes extremely powerful near expiration.

> Gamma is the force behind fast option price movement. When gamma is high, small changes in the underlying create large changes in option prices.

Delta vs Gamma: A Short Primer

Delta: how much the option price changes when the underlying moves.

Gamma: how much *delta* changes when the underlying moves.

In mathematical form:

$$\Gamma = \frac{\partial \Delta}{\partial S}$$

Where:

- Γ = gamma
- Δ = delta
- S = price of the underlying

Implication

- High gamma = delta changes rapidly.
- Low gamma = delta changes slowly.

For scalpers, high gamma means:

- fast profit potential,
- tight stop-loss tolerance,
- high responsiveness to price.

> Gamma is volatility *within the volatility.*

Where Gamma Is Highest

Gamma increases as expiration approaches.

$$\Gamma \uparrow \text{ when time-to-expiration } \downarrow$$

That means:

- 0DTE options (expire today)
- weekly expirations
- near-the-money strikes

have the highest gamma.

> This is why scalpers love 0DTE: tiny moves in price create large changes in option value.

Why Market Makers Care About Gamma

Market makers are not directional traders. They hedge risk.

When gamma is high, they must adjust hedges rapidly. This creates feedback loops in price.

$$\text{Underlying moves} \Rightarrow \text{MM hedges} \Rightarrow \text{Underlying moves more}$$

This can create explosive momentum.

Positive Gamma vs Negative Gamma

Positive Gamma When gamma is positive:

- hedging stabilizes price,
- market behaves smoothly,
- reversals are less violent.

This happens mostly when options are:

- long premium,
- before expiration,
- away from spot.

Negative Gamma When gamma is negative:

- hedging amplifies movement,
- breakouts can accelerate,
- volatility becomes self-reinforcing.

This happens mostly near:

- at-the-money strikes,
- towards expiration,
- on 0DTE.

$$\text{Negative gamma} = \text{fast, directional markets}$$

Why Gamma Matters for Scalpers

Gamma amplifies price movements:

- Small underlying movement,
- Big option premium change.

This gives scalpers:

- large percentage returns,
- tight risk control,
- high conviction setups.

But it also increases danger:

- rapid premium decay,
- wide spreads,
- slippage.

Gamma is a double-edged sword. It makes fast profits possible — and fast losses unavoidable if misused.

Expiration Mathematics

As expiration approaches:

$$\Gamma \uparrow, \quad \Theta \uparrow, \quad Vega \downarrow$$

Meaning:

- gamma sensitivity increases,
- time decay accelerates,
- volatility premium collapses.

This is why 0DTE scalping is high skill:

Direction must be correct quickly, or decay will eat value.

Gamma and Liquidity Pools

Gamma increases near key strikes:

- round numbers (4000, 4050, 4100),
- high open interest strikes,
- max pain zones.

These levels attract:

- price magnet behavior,
- abrupt reversals,
- momentum bursts.

Gamma clusters create battlefield zones for intraday scalping.

Gamma and Market Behavior

High gamma environments produce:

- sharp directional moves,
- violent squeezes,
- large intraday ranges,
- heavy stop-hunting.

Common patterns:

- liquidity sweep before trend,
- breakout continuation,
- fast retest and extension.

Summary

Gamma measures how fast delta changes. It is the engine of option acceleration.

Key points:

- Gamma increases near expiration.
- 0DTE = highest gamma.
- High gamma = fast moves, high opportunity.
- Market makers hedge aggressively near high gamma strikes.
- This hedging amplifies direction and momentum.

Core principle:

Options scalping edge = trade where gamma is strongest.

Gamma is not theory. It is the fuel that drives intraday motion.

12.2 Market Maker Hedging Dynamics

Market makers sit at the center of options pricing and execution. They do not speculate on direction – they provide liquidity. Their job is to stand between buyers and sellers, quote prices, and remain as market-neutral as possible. To achieve this neutrality, market makers continuously hedge their exposure. This hedging activity creates force on the underlying price and is one of the most powerful drivers of intraday momentum.

> Market makers do not predict direction. They react to order flow. Their reaction often *creates* direction.

Why Market Makers Hedge

When traders buy calls or puts, market makers usually take the opposite side. This means that any directional exposure is passed to them first:

$$\text{Trader buys call} \Rightarrow \text{Market maker becomes short call}$$

A short call has *negative delta.* To neutralize it, the market maker must buy the underlying.

$$\text{MM hedges: buys the underlying to balance delta}$$

This buying pressure can push price higher.
Similarly:

$$\text{Trader buys puts} \Rightarrow \text{MM becomes short put} \Rightarrow \text{MM sells underlying}$$

Hedging Creates Feedback Loops

Hedging flows can create self-reinforcing moves:

$$\text{Price rises} \Rightarrow \text{MM buys more to hedge} \Rightarrow \text{Price rises more}$$

Or the opposite:

$$\text{Price falls} \Rightarrow \text{MM sells more to hedge} \Rightarrow \text{Price falls more}$$

This is especially strong when gamma is high.

Hedging does not follow price — it accelerates price.

When Hedging Is Most Aggressive

Hedging intensity increases when:

- options are near expiration,
- strikes are near-the-money,
- open interest is large,
- direction changes quickly.

This creates sudden, powerful intraday trends.

$$\Gamma \uparrow \Rightarrow \text{Hedging urgency} \uparrow$$

This is the core of gamma scalping.

Delta Hedging Explained Simply

Market makers hedge by adjusting delta. If delta becomes too positive or negative, they offset.

Example:

- If price rises, delta increases.
- Market maker must buy more underlying to stay neutral.

Neutrality is dynamic.

As a result:

- price movement forces hedging,
- hedging forces more price movement.

This is why breakouts are often explosive near option strikes.

Pinned and Magnetic Levels

High open interest strikes act as magnets:

$$\text{Large OI at 4000} \Rightarrow \text{price gravitates toward 4000}$$

Market makers hedge around these levels.

Effects:

- price slow-grinds toward strike,
- volatility compresses near strike,
- large move after break.

> High OI strikes create gravity. When price escapes, the move is sudden.

Dealers Switching from Long to Short Gamma

When dealers are **long gamma**:

- their hedging stabilizes price,
- they sell when price rises and buy when price falls.

This creates mean reversion.

When dealers are **short gamma**:

- they amplify movement,

- they buy when price rises and sell when price falls.

This creates trends and momentum.

$$\text{Short gamma} = \text{trending days}$$

This is why 0DTE days often have large directional moves.

0DTE and Hedging Feedback

On expiration days:

- gamma is extremely high,
- hedging adjustments are constant,
- price becomes sensitive to option flow.

A small move in the underlying can create:

- large dealer hedging flows,
- which create a larger move,
- which requires more hedging,
- and so on.

This feedback loop is the engine of intraday momentum.

Why This Matters for Scalpers

Scalpers thrive on:

- short bursts of directional movement,
- liquidity-driven continuation,
- strong momentum windows.

Market maker hedging creates exactly this behavior. When hedging is aggressive:

- trends are clean,
- pullbacks are shallow,
- continuation is frequent.

These are ideal conditions for scalping.

Where Hedging Forces Are Visible

Hedging flows show up around:

- round numbers,
- daily strikes,
- high open interest strikes,
- VWAP,
- previous day high/low,
- session boundaries.

Scalpers can use these lines as targets and entries.

Summary

Market makers hedge to stay neutral. Their hedging is reactive and often accelerates price movement.

Key insights:

- Hedging is strongest near expiration and at-the-money.
- Positive gamma stabilizes price.
- Negative gamma amplifies trends.
- 0DTE = highest hedging pressure.
- Hedging creates momentum bursts ideal for scalping.

Core principle:

Scalp in the direction of hedging flow.

> Market makers are not predicting the market — they are stabilizing exposure. In doing so, they create the very moves we trade.

12.3 0DTE (Zero-Day Options) Explained

Zero-day options — commonly called **0DTE** — are options that expire on the same day they are traded. These products have exploded in popularity because they offer:

- high leverage,
- fast movement,

- deep liquidity,
- clear intraday structure.

For scalpers, 0DTE represents a powerful opportunity — but only when handled with discipline and risk management.

What Makes 0DTE Unique

Most options lose value gradually over days or weeks. 0DTE options, however, decay within hours — even minutes. All time value must disappear by the market close.

This produces three important effects:

1. **Gamma is extremely high**
2. **Theta decays extremely fast**
3. **Volatility is concentrated intraday**

$$\text{High gamma} + \text{fast theta} = \text{explosive yet fragile behavior}$$

Why 0DTE Moves So Fast

Because expiration is near, small moves in the underlying cause large changes in option delta. This magnifies price movement:

$$\Delta \uparrow \Rightarrow \text{Premium moves faster}$$

Additionally, market makers must hedge aggressively, which creates feedback loops:

$$\text{Underlying moves} \Rightarrow \text{Hedge} \Rightarrow \text{Underlying moves more}$$

This is why 0DTE often produces:

- sudden breakouts,
- violent squeezes,
- large intraday trends.

Why Scalpers Love 0DTE

0DTE options react quickly:

- price responds immediately to movement,
- premium expansion can be dramatic,
- small underlying moves = large percentage gains.

This allows scalpers to:

- trade small timeframes,
- use tight stops,
- take fast profits.

0DTE compresses premium movement into a single trading session — creating opportunity.

The Risk Side: Theta Decay

The downside is equally powerful. Time value decays rapidly:

$$\Theta \gg \text{normal}$$

If direction is wrong or movement stalls:

- premium collapses,
- position loses value quickly,
- even if underlying barely moves.

A common mistake:

$$\text{Buying options and waiting} \Rightarrow \text{Death by decay}$$

0DTE is not for holding — it is for executing.

Strike Selection for 0DTE

The best strikes are:

- **at-the-money (ATM)**, or
- **slightly in-the-money (ITM)**.

Deep out-of-the-money strikes decay too fast and often expire worthless.

Timing Principles

0DTE trades occur in windows:

- After open: high volatility
- Midday: decay dominates
- Power Hour: final expiration runs

Patterns:

- morning = momentum,
- midday = chop or decay,
- close = gamma squeezes.

The open and the close contain the most opportunity.

Directional vs Non-Directional

There are two primary ways to scalp 0DTE:

1. Directional Scalping

- buy call or put
- ride momentum
- exit quickly

2. Mean Reversion with Credit Spreads

- sell premium
- profit from theta decay

Directional is faster and more aggressive. Credit spreads are slower and safer.

Execution Rules for Safety

Because of high leverage, 0DTE demands strict discipline:

1. Enter only on structure confirmation.
2. Use tight stops.
3. Scale out profits quickly.
4. Never average losers.

A useful rule:

If momentum stops, exit.

Time decay punishes hesitation.

Why 0DTE Works for Scalping

0DTE compresses all option behavior into one session:

- high gamma amplifies movement,
- market maker hedging accelerates direction,
- theta forces exit decisions,
- volatility creates waves.

Scalpers do not need multi-day prediction. They only need:

$$\text{Direction} + \text{Momentum} + \text{Risk Control}$$

Summary

0DTE options are powerful tools for intraday traders.
Core principles:

- Gamma makes them move quickly.
- Theta makes them decay quickly.
- Hedging creates volatility and trends.
- Precision and speed are essential.

0DTE is a tool for scalpers who act decisively, not for traders who hesitate.

> 0DTE is the purest expression of intraday opportunity — fast, leveraged, and unforgiving.

12.4 High-Speed Options Setups

0DTE and near-expiration options create powerful intraday edges when combined with tight execution and structure. This section presents the most reliable high-speed setups used by professional options scalpers. Each is built around a simple principle:

> Trade direction only when price, flow, and gamma align.

Setup 1: Breakout + Retest with Momentum

This is the most consistent setup for directional scalping.

Conditions

- clear level (previous high/low, session level, VWAP)
- strong breakout candle
- follow-through volume
- quick retest to structure

Entry

- buy ATM call above breakout
- buy ATM put below breakdown

Stop

- behind structure (wick or level)

Targets

- opposing liquidity pool
- next strike level

Breakouts without retests are traps. Retests with momentum are gold.

Setup 2: Liquidity Sweep Reversal

This setup exploits typical stop-hunting behavior around key levels.

Conditions

- price sweeps prior high/low
- large rejection wick
- shift in order flow (BOS)

Entry

- enter after BOS confirmation
- buy call after sweep low
- buy put after sweep high

Stop

- behind the sweep wick

Targets

- VWAP
- session midpoint
- major strike

Sweeps trap traders — reversals release energy.

Setup 3: VWAP Bounce with Trend

VWAP is the institutional mean. When price respects it with trend, continuation is likely.

Conditions

- trending day
- price bounces from VWAP
- volume supports direction

Entry

- buy call near VWAP on uptrend
- buy put near VWAP on downtrend

Stop

- slightly beyond VWAP

Targets

- previous swing
- session high/low

VWAP is gravity — price swings around it.

Setup 4: Gamma Squeeze Breakout

When negative gamma dominates and price moves through a high open interest strike, market maker hedging accelerates the move.

Conditions

- price approaches major strike (e.g., 4000)
- high open interest
- rapid acceleration

Entry

- enter after breakout
- strike-to-strike momentum

Stop

- below breakout level

Targets

- next strike level (4000 $\rightarrow$ 4010 $\rightarrow$ 4020)

  Squeezes are fast — scale out quickly.

Setup 5: Power Hour Expiration Run

The final hour of trading often produces large directional moves because:

- gamma is maximum,
- theta is maximum,
- hedging adjustments are constant.

Conditions

- 0DTE near close
- order flow becomes one-sided

Entry

- join momentum in direction of hedging flow

Stop

- tight behind structure

Targets

- next liquidity zone
- session high/low

  Expiration is acceleration — if direction is clear, movement is powerful.

Setup 6: Trendline Trap & Reversal

Trendlines often fail because they are obvious. When they break sharply, option momentum can be explosive.

Conditions

- trendline forms cleanly
- price consolidates beneath/above
- violent breakout opposite direction

Entry

- enter after trap spring

Stop

- behind trap candle

Targets

- prior swing or liquidity pool

  Traps fuel reversals.

Execution Framework

All setups follow the same model:

$$\text{Structure} \rightarrow \text{Trigger} \rightarrow \text{Confirmation} \rightarrow \text{Exit}$$

Structure

- levels
- liquidity
- session lines

Trigger

- breakout
- sweep
- VWAP reaction

Confirmation

- volume
- momentum
- hedging behavior

Exit

- take profit early
- scale out
- never hold into expiration blindly

Summary

High-speed setups work because they combine:

- price structure,
- order flow,
- gamma behavior,
- tight execution.

These setups offer:

- fast reactions,
- controlled risk,
- high reward potential.

Core principle:

> Speed alone is not an edge — precision is the edge.

The most profitable options scalpers do not trade more — they trade better.

12.5 Risk Management for Options Scalpers

Options scalping is a high-leverage, high-speed environment. It offers rapid returns, but equally rapid losses if discipline is weak. Risk management is therefore not an accessory — it is the core operating principle.

> You do not survive options scalping by being right. You survive by controlling loss.

This section explains the rules and frameworks that professional scalpers use to stay safe.

The Prime Directive: Small Size, Fast Exit

Options expand and decay with speed. To withstand variance, size must be controlled.

$$\text{Position size: small \& repeatable}$$

General guideline:

$$1\% \text{ risk per trade or less}$$

Because:

- spreads shift,
- slippage occurs,
- theta burns premium,
- gamma accelerates loss if wrong.

The goal is survival first, profit second.

The Two-Timer Rule

A simple and powerful safety heuristic:

$$\text{If the trade has not worked within 2–3 minutes, exit.}$$

Why?

- theta decay accelerates,
- momentum has faded,
- conditions have changed.

Never Average Down

Averaging down in options is lethal. Premium decay means:

Adding size increases loss faster than price recovery.

Professional rule:

Never add to losers.

Stop-Loss Logic

Stops must be:

- based on structure, not emotion,
- placed behind wicks or levels,
- honored without exception.

In execution:

Hard stop + mental exit

Example:

- if structure breaks,
- leave immediately,
- regardless of hope or opinion.

Profit-Taking Principles

Scalpers do not wait for home runs.

Aim: small win, quickly, repeatedly

Common exit models:

- 20–30% = partial scale-out
- 50–70% = second scale
- remainder = trail with structure

Never allow a winning trade to become a loser.

Daily Stop-Loss Limits

To avoid emotional spiral:

One max loss day per week can erase a full month.

Professional rule:

Stop trading if:

- 2 losses in a row, or
- -2R or -3R for the day.

After that:

Day is over. No exceptions.

Spread Awareness

Options spreads widen during:

- fast moves,
- news,
- lunch hours,
- low liquidity periods.

Always check:

$$\text{Bid/Ask Spread} > \text{Expected Gain?}$$

If yes:

No trade.

Slippage Preparedness

Market orders during volatility cause slippage.
Rules:

- use limit or stop-limit orders,
- avoid chasing price,
- do not enter inside wicks.

If price has already moved:

Missed is better than murdered.

Avoid Holding Through Expiration (Usually)

0DTE decay near the close is violent.

If the option is out-of-the-money:

Premium collapses to zero.

The safest rule:

Exit before expiration unless it is intentional strategy.

Risk Framework

Professional scalpers use a simple model:

$$\textbf{Risk:Reward} = \textbf{1:R}$$

Where R is defined before entry.

Common R values:

- 2R = realistic,
- 3R = excellent,
- 1:1 = acceptable if winrate is high.

Emotional Risk: The Silent Killer

Options scalping is psychologically intense:

- fast decisions,
- fast swings,
- real money moving rapidly.

Rules for emotional safety:

1. Breathe before entry.
2. Trade only planned setups.
3. Avoid revenge trading.
4. Stop after max loss.

Most losses are emotional, not technical.

Session Boundaries

Risk changes by time of day:

- Open = opportunity + chaos
- Midday = decay + chop
- Close = gamma squeeze

Trade the windows where:

$$\text{Flow} + \text{Liquidity} + \text{Volume}$$

align.

Summary

Options scalping offers rapid profit, but risk must be controlled.

Core principles:

- small size, repeatable setups,
- tight stops based on structure,
- exit losers fast,
- scale profits quickly,
- daily limits to avoid damage.

Final rule:

Protect capital at all costs.

You can always enter the next trade — but only if you still have capital.

Chapter 13

Crypto Scalping & Bot Scalping

Cryptocurrency markets offer unmatched volatility, deep intraday movement, and 24/7 accessibility. For scalpers, this presents extraordinary opportunity, but also requires a strong understanding of crypto market microstructure, funding rates, and liquidity behavior. This chapter explores how to scalp crypto effectively, how spot and futures differ, when to use or avoid automated bots, and how AI filters can enhance precision and timing in a fast-moving environment.

13.1 Crypto Microstructure

Cryptocurrency markets behave differently from traditional markets. There is no centralized exchange, no single order book, and no unified liquidity. Instead, crypto is a distributed ecosystem where prices emerge from multiple venues, each with its own depth, fees, and market participants.

To scalp crypto successfully, a trader must understand how this microstructure influences price, volatility, and execution.

> Crypto is not one market — it is a network of markets synchronized by arbitrage, bots, and liquidity flows.

Decentralized Liquidity Across Exchanges

Unlike stocks or futures which trade on a single regulated exchange, crypto trades simultaneously on multiple platforms:

- Binance
- Bybit

- Coinbase
- OKX
- Kraken
- Deribit

Each exchange has:

- different order books,
- different liquidity,
- different fee structures,
- different participants.

Prices remain similar across exchanges because of arbitrage:

$$\text{Buy cheap on Exchange A} \to \text{Sell high on Exchange B}$$

This mechanism keeps the system aligned, but it creates unique scalping behavior:

Price can move on one exchange before the others follow.

High-Frequency Bots Dominate Order Flow

A major difference in crypto microstructure:

Bots make up most of the volume.

HFT systems operate 24/7:

- arbitraging price differences,
- detecting liquidity imbalances,
- front-running order flow,
- managing funding and basis trades.

This means many patterns are algorithmic:

- stop-hunts,
- sweep + reverse,
- breakout traps,
- liquidity raids.

Scalpers must think in terms of machines, not humans.

Perpetual Futures (Perps) Drive the Market

Crypto has a unique instrument:

Perpetual Futures (Perps)

These contracts:

- have no expiration,
- allow high leverage (up to 100x),
- track spot price via funding rates.

For scalpers, perps matter because they control:

- volume,
- direction,
- volatility.

Spot market often follows perp flows.

> In crypto, futures lead — spot follows.

Funding Rates and Position Imbalances

Funding rates keep perp prices close to spot:

$$\text{Longs pay / receive funding} \quad \text{vs} \quad \text{Shorts}$$

When funding is extreme:

- too many traders are on one side,
- market often squeezes them.

Examples:

- If long positions are crowded → downside squeeze.
- If short positions are crowded → upside squeeze.

Funding creates scalping opportunities:

$$\text{Market hunts the side with greatest stress.}$$

Order Book Characteristics in Crypto

Crypto order books are:

- thinner than traditional markets,
- more reactive,
- more easily manipulated.

Large players can:

- spoof bids and asks,
- pull liquidity,
- create false signals.

Wicks are not mistakes — they are strategies.

The Role of Stablecoins

Stablecoins act as the settlement currency:

- USDT
- USDC
- BUSD (historically)

Capital flows between stablecoins and risk assets create price movement. For example:

$$\text{Stablecoin inflow} \Rightarrow \text{Potential rally}$$

$$\text{Stablecoin outflow} \Rightarrow \text{Potential selloff}$$

Large inflows into exchanges often precede volatility.

24/7 Trading and Session Behavior

Crypto trades without closure. However, volume still follows timezone patterns:

- Asian session: accumulation, range
- London session: breakout, trend development
- New York session: volatility and continuation

Weekends are dangerous:

- lower institutional participation,
- thinner books,
- unpredictable moves.

Weekend = traps, not trends

Internal vs External Liquidity

Crypto respects liquidity just like forex:

- swing highs/lows
- stop clusters
- imbalance zones

But it also has **exchange-specific liquidity**:

- Binance order book,
- Deribit delta hedging,
- Bybit liquidation walls.

Sometimes price reacts to hidden liquidity you cannot see on your chart.

The chart is not the only battlefield — order books matter.

Implication for Scalpers

Understanding microstructure reveals a crucial insight:

Crypto is driven by liquidity, not news

Scalpers who succeed:

- follow liquidity flows,
- avoid thin books,
- understand funding cycles,
- trade perp-led direction.

Summary

Crypto microstructure is shaped by:

- multiple exchanges,
- high-frequency bots,
- perpetual futures,
- funding rates,
- thin order books,
- 24/7 sessions.

Key principle:

Trade where liquidity is thick, momentum is clean, and bots are driving direction.

> Crypto rewards precision and punishes hesitation. It is the fastest arena in modern trading.

13.2 Funding Rates, Volatility Cycles, and Liquidity Traps

Crypto markets are heavily influenced by funding rates, cyclical volatility patterns, and deliberate liquidity traps engineered by large players and automated systems. To scalp effectively, a trader must understand how these forces interact to create opportunity, danger, and predictable behavioral patterns.

> Funding drives position pressure, volatility cycles drive timing, liquidity traps drive profit.

Funding Rates: The Hidden Engine of Crypto Movement

Perpetual futures (perps) have no expiration, so a *funding mechanism* keeps their price aligned with the spot market.

Funding is paid periodically:

$$\text{Longs pay Shorts} \quad \text{or} \quad \text{Shorts pay Longs}$$

This transfer creates incentives:

- If funding is positive, longs are paying.
- If funding is negative, shorts are paying.

Key insight:

When one side pays too much, it becomes trapped.

Extreme funding often precedes reversals:

- If funding is high (too many longs), market often drops.
- If funding is negative (too many shorts), market often rallies.

Funding does not predict direction — it reveals pressure.

Volatility Cycles in Crypto

Crypto volatility is cyclical. It oscillates between:

- accumulation,
- expansion,
- distribution,
- liquidation,

These cycles repeat across all timeframes.

1. Accumulation

Price compresses:

- tight ranges,
- low volume,
- low volatility.

Market prepares for expansion.

2. Expansion

Volatility bursts:

- strong candles,
- liquidity breaks,
- trending conditions.

This is where scalpers profit.

3. Distribution

Price pauses and rotates:

- open interest builds,
- liquidity traps form,
- next direction is prepared.

4. Liquidation

Excess leverage is flushed:

- rapid moves,
- stop cascades,
- forced exits.

After liquidation, new accumulation begins.

$$\text{Cycle: Accumulate} \rightarrow \text{Expand} \rightarrow \text{Distribute} \rightarrow \text{Liquidate} \rightarrow \text{Repeat}$$

How Funding and Volatility Interact

When funding is extreme and volatility compresses:

- a violent move is likely,
- trapped traders will be liquidated,
- trend can be sudden and directional.

Combination signal:

$$\text{High funding} + \text{low volatility} = \text{incoming squeeze}$$

The market hunts imbalance.

Liquidity Traps: How the Market Hunts Traders

Crypto markets often engineer traps:

- price sweeps highs/lows,
- triggers stops and liquidations,
- reverses sharply into trend.

These traps exploit predictable behavior:

- breakout traders chase late entries,
- stop clusters sit at obvious levels,
- bots sweep both sides before moving.

$$\text{Trap} \rightarrow \text{Liquidation} \rightarrow \text{Trend}$$

Common Liquidity Trap Patterns

Pattern 1: Stop-Run Sweep

- price spikes above previous high,
- triggers stops and buy orders,
- reverses immediately.

Scalping opportunity:

$$\text{Enter counter trend after sweep + rejection}$$

Pattern 2: Fake Breakout

- breakout candle,
- no follow-through,
- immediate reverse.

The intent is to:

- bait breakout traders,
- trap them,
- run stops.

Pattern 3: Liquidity Vacuum When the order book thins:

- price jumps rapidly,
- both sides hunted,
- liquidity restored afterward.

Where Liquidity Traps Form

Most traps occur at:

- prior highs/lows,
- swing levels,
- round numbers,
- psychological levels,
- funding event times,
- session transitions.

Add futures funding windows:

$$\text{Every 8 hours: funding cycles}$$

Execution windows:

- just before funding,
- just after funding,
- near major liquidation clusters.

Funding windows create price reaction.

Practical Scalping Principle

Do not trade the breakout — trade the reaction.

Typical sequence for opportunity:

1. trap forms,
2. liquidation occurs,
3. trend resumes,
4. scalp continuation.

Risk Management in Traps

To stay safe:

- tight stops beyond structure,
- do not enter during wick formation,
- wait for candle close,
- confirm with volume or delta.

If uncertain, stand aside.

No trade is a winning trade if it avoids loss.

Summary

Funding, volatility cycles, and liquidity traps are the core drivers of crypto behavior.

Key insights:

- funding reveals crowding and pressure,
- volatility cycles reveal timing,
- traps reveal opportunity.

Core formula:

$$\text{Trapped traders} \Rightarrow \text{Forced exits} \Rightarrow \text{Momentum}$$

> Crypto moves not because of prediction, but because of pressure, imbalance, and liquidation.

13.3 Spot vs Futures Scalping

Scalping in crypto can be executed through two primary market types:

1. **Spot markets**
2. **Futures markets**

Both offer advantages, but they behave differently in terms of leverage, fees, risk, and liquidity. Understanding these differences is essential for choosing the right approach.

> Spot is slow but safe. Futures are fast but dangerous. A scalper must know when to use each.

Spot Scalping

Spot trading means buying and selling the asset directly (BTC, ETH, etc.). No leverage is used unless borrowed manually (margin).

Advantages of Spot

- lower risk,
- no liquidations,
- no funding fees,
- smoother price action.

Spot is ideal for:

- beginners,
- trend-following scalps,
- small account protection.

Disadvantages of Spot

- slower movement,
- smaller returns,
- cannot short easily (without margin),
- capital requirements are higher.

$$\text{Spot} = \text{safety and simplicity}$$

Futures Scalping

Futures allow leveraged exposure to crypto price without owning the underlying. Perpetual futures (perps) are dominant.

Advantages of Futures

- leverage (up to 100x),
- ability to go long or short instantly,
- high liquidity,
- no settlement delay.

Futures are ideal for:

- fast scalps,
- breakout continuation,
- mean reversion plays,
- liquidation hunts.

Disadvantages of Futures

- liquidation risk,
- funding payments,
- higher fees,
- spread and slippage during volatility.

$$\text{Futures} = \text{speed and risk}$$

Execution Differences

Spot execution:

- slower,
- larger position sizing,
- less stressful,
- fewer false signals.

Futures execution:

- rapid entries and exits,
- smaller size due to leverage,
- tighter stops,
- more pressure.

Spot lets you breathe. Futures demand precision.

Price Behaviour Difference

Spot price is smoothed by real liquidity.

Futures price is sensitive to:

- funding,
- liquidations,
- order book gaps,
- short-term hedging.

This produces characteristics:

Spot

- cleaner trends,
- steadier movement.

Futures

- faster spikes,
- deeper wicks,
- more stop hunts.

Futures exaggerate real price action.

When to Use Spot vs Futures

Use Spot When:

- market is trending cleanly,
- you want reduced risk,
- scalping small swings,
- avoiding liquidation.

Use Futures When:

- volatility is high,
- directional moves are strong,
- you want speed and leverage,
- short-term opportunity exists.

Hybrid Approach

Many professional scalpers use both:

- spot for swing bias,
- futures for intraday scalps.

For example:

- long ETH spot,
- short ETH futures for hedge during retracement.

This protects capital and captures movement.

$$\text{Spot} = \text{anchor} \quad \text{Futures} = \text{weapon}$$

Risk Differences

Spot Risk:

- no liquidation,
- loss only if price drops,
- easier psychologically.

Futures Risk:

- liquidation can wipe the account,
- over-leverage is common,
- emotional pressure is higher.

Rule:

$$\text{Lower leverage} = \text{longer survival}$$

Summary

Spot and futures serve different purposes.

Spot:

- safer,
- slower,
- ideal for trend scalps.

Futures:

- faster,
- more powerful,
- ideal for momentum scalps.

Key principle:

Choose based on volatility, not preference.

> Trade spot for stability. Trade futures for speed. Master both for maximum edge.

13.4 Using Scalping Bots (Benefits + Dangers)

Scalping bots are automated systems that execute trades at high speed based on predefined rules. They are widely used in crypto, especially on futures exchanges, where fast market movement makes manual execution difficult. Bots can capture opportunities that are impossible for humans — but they can also create sudden and unexpected losses.

> Bots are tools, not magic. They amplify edge — or amplify mistakes.

Why Bots Are Effective in Crypto

Crypto microstructure favors automation:

- markets run 24/7,
- price moves quickly,
- order books change in milliseconds,
- funding and liquidation cycles are constant.

Bots can:

- enter instantly,
- exit with precision,
- maintain discipline,
- avoid emotional impulsiveness.

Bots make fast decisions without fear or greed.

Typical Scalping Bot Strategies

Common bot strategies include:

1. **Market-making bots**
2. **Arbitrage bots**
3. **Grid scalpers**
4. **Trend-following scalpers**
5. **Mean-reversion bots**
6. **Liquidation hunters**

Each uses different logic:

Market-Making Bots

- place bids/asks around mid-price,
- collect spread repeatedly.

Grid Bots

- buy low, sell high within a defined range.

Trend Bots

- follow momentum using moving averages or breakouts.

Benefits of Scalping Bots

1. Speed Bots execute faster than humans:

- no hesitation,
- no reaction delay,
- nanosecond order submission.

This is critical in volatile markets.

2. Consistency Bots never deviate from rules:

- no fear,
- no greed,
- no revenge trading.

3. 24/7 Operation Bots can trade during:

- night hours,
- weekends,
- multiple exchanges simultaneously.

4. Perfect Discipline Bots execute the plan exactly as defined.

They do not break rules. Humans do.

Dangers of Scalping Bots

1. Market Regime Change Bots are rule-based systems. They break when regime changes:

- range → trend,
- low-volatility → high-volatility,
- correlation breakdown.

A profitable bot can become unprofitable instantly.

2. Liquidation Risk in Futures With leverage, bots can:

- enter multiple positions,
- stack margin exposure,
- get liquidated in spikes.

Liquidation happens faster than a bot can react.

3. Overfitting Bots are often optimized on past data:

Perfect on history, terrible in real-time.

4. API or Exchange Failure Risks include:

- API disconnection,
- exchange outage,
- order stuck,
- execution freeze.

The bot cannot adapt to technical failure.

5. Hidden Fees Bots may trade frequently:

- fees accumulate,
- profit shrinks,
- strategy becomes negative.

A profitable bot on paper may lose money after fees.

Bot Safety Principles

To use bots safely:

1. Start with small size.
2. Use low leverage.
3. Avoid illiquid assets.
4. Monitor drawdowns.
5. Stop immediately if behavior deviates.

Always combine bots with:

- manual supervision,
- kill-switches,
- daily limits.

Automation without oversight is gambling.

Hybrid Bot Usage

The best approach is hybrid:

- use bots for execution and speed,
- use humans for strategy and context.

Example:

- human identifies setup,
- bot executes instantly,
- bot exits when rules hit.

This is common in professional trading firms.

AI-Enhanced Filters

AI can help:

- detect volatility changes,
- classify regime,
- identify liquidity traps,
- prevent entries during dangerous conditions.

AI is not for prediction — it is for filtering.

AI filters reduce bad trades. Bots execute the good trades faster.

Summary

Scalping bots are powerful tools when used correctly.

Benefits:

- speed
- consistency
- discipline
- 24/7 execution

Dangers:

- regime shifts,
- liquidation risk,
- exchange failure,
- over-optimization,
- hidden fees.

Core principle:

Bots amplify your edge — or amplify your mistakes.

Bots are servants, not masters. The trader provides intelligence — the bot provides execution.

13.5 AI-Enhanced Scalping Filters

Artificial Intelligence (AI) has become a powerful addition to the scalper's toolkit. AI is not used to predict price direction with certainty — instead, it is used to filter trades, detect changing market conditions, and prevent entries during dangerous regimes. In scalping, the highest value of AI is **risk reduction**, not forecasting.

> AI does not replace strategy. It prevents bad trades from ever happening.

Why AI Helps Scalpers

Scalping requires:

- split–second decisions,
- fast signal processing,
- filtering noise,
- reacting to volatility.

AI can analyze:

- order flow,
- volatility clusters,
- liquidity pockets,
- regime changes,
- patterns in accelerations/pauses.

A human trader simply cannot process all of this in real-time. AI acts as a *guardian layer* that filters the environment.

AI is Used for Filtering, Not Prediction

A central principle:

AI is best at classifying conditions — not predicting prices.

AI excels at answering questions like:

- Is volatility stable or chaotic?
- Is volume rising or falling?

- Is order flow supportive or resistant?
- Is the market trending or ranging?
- Are spreads normal or dangerous?

These answers are often enough to form a decision:

Avoid trading in noise.

Key AI Filters in Scalping

1. Volatility Regime Detection AI models detect volatility clusters:

- low volatility = wait,
- rising volatility = prepare,
- explosive volatility = opportunity or danger.

This avoids entries during:

- chop,
- sideways noise,
- unpredictable wick behavior.

2. Liquidity Depth Monitoring AI monitors order book in real time:

- thickness of bids/asks,
- hidden liquidity,
- sudden withdrawal of orders.

When liquidity thins:

AI blocks trading

because thin books create:

- slippage,
- erratic spikes,
- stop hunting.

3. Spread Detection A simple but powerful filter:

$$\text{Spread} > \text{Threshold} \Rightarrow \text{No trade}$$

AI observes average spread by instrument and time, avoiding:

- low-liquidity hours,
- bad fills,
- untradeable wicks.

4. Order Flow Sentiment AI examines:

- delta,
- market buy/sell pressure,
- speed of aggressive orders.

It detects when:

$$\text{Flow shifts direction}$$

before price visibly moves.

Flow changes come first. Price reacts later.

5. Pattern Recognition AI finds repeating micro-patterns:

- liquidity sweeps,
- trap candles,
- exhaustion wicks,
- VWAP reversion,
- breaker blocks,
- imbalance fills.

These patterns occur thousands of times — AI sees them instantly.

The Role of Machine Learning

Machine Learning models can:

- classify chart states,
- detect reversal signatures,
- score probability of continuation,
- identify regime transitions.

Important note:

> ML improves filtering accuracy, not prediction accuracy.

Large Language Models (LLMs) as Meta-Traders

Modern LLMs can:

- summarize order flow,
- explain context,
- detect anomalies,
- analyze risk scenarios,
- generate checklists before entry.

They complement:

- human intuition,
- bot execution,
- statistical edge.

AI Does Not Replace Human Strategy

Human strengths:

- intuition,
- narrative thinking,
- pattern understanding,
- risk perception.

AI strengths:

- speed,
- consistency,
- calculation,
- noise filtering.

Best results come from **hybrid usage**:

Human identifies setupAI filters environmentBot executes instantly

This forms a triangle:

Human + AI + Bot

Practical Use Cases

AI filters can block trades when:

- volatility is chaotic,
- volume is low,
- order book is thin,
- spread widens suddenly,
- momentum fades,
- news risk is present.

AI can also approve trades when:

- direction is clear,
- flow confirms,
- volatility is stable,
- liquidity is thick.

Summary

AI is a powerful addition to scalping because:

- it filters bad conditions,
- it detects regime change early,
- it prevents emotional errors,

- it enhances safety.

Core principle:

AI increases selectivity — not aggression.

AI protects capital by removing low-probability trades. You trade less, win more, and survive longer.

Chapter 14

Forex, Index & Gold Scalping Playbooks

Different markets behave differently. A scalper must adapt tools, timing, and expectations to each instrument. This chapter provides precision playbooks for the most popular scalping assets, including major currency pairs, gold, and high-volatility indices. We will study micro-structure, volatility rhythms, session behavior, and execution timing for each market.

14.1 EURUSD & GBPUSD Micro Setups

EURUSD and GBPUSD are two of the best instruments for scalping in the Forex market. They offer deep liquidity, tight spreads, and consistent intraday movement during active sessions. A trader who understands their micro-structure can capture precise entries multiple times per day with disciplined execution.

> These pairs reward structure, patience, and timing — not aggression.

Why These Pairs Are Ideal for Scalping

EURUSD and GBPUSD have characteristics that favor scalpers:

- very tight spreads (often < 1 pip),
- high liquidity during London / New York overlap,
- cleaner technical behavior compared to exotic pairs,
- reduced slippage relative to other markets.

Their volume and structure create predictable movements around:

- previous day high/low,
- session open levels,
- VWAP,
- round numbers (00, 50).

$$\text{Structure} + \text{Liquidity} = \text{Opportunity}$$

Session-Based Edge

These pairs move best during:

- London Open (08:00–10:00 GMT),
- New York Open (13:30–15:30 GMT),
- London–New York overlap (13:00–16:00 GMT).

Behavior pattern:

1. Asian session → range and accumulation
2. London open → sweep, reversal, or breakout
3. NY open → continuation or trend shift

Avoid Asian when scalping: too quiet.

Micro Pullback Scalps

A reliable tactic:

1. Identify trend on 5M,
2. Wait for pullback on 1M into EMA cluster (9/20),
3. Enter on rejection wick or breaker candle,
4. Target previous swing or VWAP.

Stop-loss logic:

$$\text{Below pullback low (long)} \quad \text{or} \quad \text{above pullback high (short)}$$

This strategy is high-frequency and repeatable.

Liquidity Sweep Setups

EURUSD and GBPUSD frequently sweep:

- Asian high / low,
- previous day extremes,
- session open price.

Typical pattern:

1. Price sweeps level,
2. Triggers stops,
3. Reverses sharply,
4. Trend continues or forms.

Entry:

- wait for wick,
- enter on rejection,
- stop beyond sweep.

Round Number Reactions

These pairs respect psychological levels:

$$1.0800,\ 1.0850,\ 1.0900 \quad \text{(EURUSD)}$$
$$1.2600,\ 1.2650,\ 1.2700 \quad \text{(GBPUSD)}$$

Behavior:

- liquidity builds,
- market sweeps,
- fast reaction follows.

Scalp reaction, not breakout.

VWAP Interaction

EURUSD/GBPUSD frequently return to VWAP:

- morning sweep away,
- midday mean reversion,
- afternoon expansion.

Scalping logic:

$$\text{Above VWAP} = \text{buy pullbacks}$$
$$\text{Below VWAP} = \text{sell rallies}$$

If price is flat around VWAP:

$$\text{Stand aside: chop zone.}$$

Key Micro Patterns

1. BOS + Pullback Entry

$$\text{Break of structure} \rightarrow \text{Pullback} \rightarrow \text{Continuation}$$

Confirmation:

- 1M candle rejection,
- volume spike,
- EMA alignment.

2. Double Tap Reversal

1. sweep of lows,
2. small bounce,
3. second touch fails to break,
4. reversal begins.

3. London Open Whipsaw Typical sequence:

1. fake breakout,
2. swift reversal,
3. trend emerges.

This pattern repeats daily.

Risk Management

Safe guidelines:

- never chase breakouts,
- wait for wick or retest,
- scale out near previous swing,
- avoid low-volatility periods.

Stop-loss:

$$3\text{–}6 \text{ pips for EURUSD/GBPUSD}$$

Targets:

$$6\text{–}12 \text{ pips} \quad (1R \text{ to } 2R)$$

Summary

EURUSD and GBPUSD are ideal for scalping because they combine:

- deep liquidity,
- tight spreads,
- predictable session structure,
- respect for levels.

Core playbook:

1. Use 5M for structure.
2. Execute on 1M at pullbacks or sweeps.
3. Trade reaction, not breakout.
4. Take profit quickly.

These pairs reward precision and timing. Small moves, repeated often, create consistent profit.

14.2 XAUUSD (Gold) Volatility Blueprint

XAUUSD is one of the most profitable instruments for scalping because it combines:

- deep liquidity,
- explosive volatility,
- clear reactions at levels,
- frequent intraday swings.

However, gold can move violently, with fast spikes and deep wicks. To scalp it safely, a trader needs a structured volatility blueprint.

Gold rewards precision. It punishes hesitation.

Why Gold Is Ideal for Scalping

Gold has a unique market structure:

- traded globally,
- influenced by macro flows (rates, risk sentiment),
- liquid at all sessions,
- extremely active during New York.

It responds cleanly to:

- session opens,
- economic news,
- liquidity sweeps,
- institutional levels.

Gold is momentum + liquidity.

Session Behavior

Gold has distinct rhythms:

Asian Session:

- slow,
- range-bound,
- accumulation.

London Open:

- first volatility expansion,
- sweeps of Asian high/low.

New York Session:

- strongest movement of the day,
- high volume,
- explosive trends.

Prime time: 13:30–16:00 GMT (NY Open)

Key Levels for Gold

Gold reacts strongly to:

- round numbers (e.g. $2300, $2320, $2350),
- previous day high/low,
- session open price,
- weekly/monthly levels,
- VWAP and deviations,
- imbalance zones (FVG).

$$\text{Level} + \text{Reaction} = \text{Trade}$$

Gold Loves Liquidity Sweeps

The most reliable gold pattern:

1. Sweep of stop clusters,
2. Strong wick,
3. Immediate reversal.

Common traps:

- false breakouts,
- wick hunting,
- news spikes with sharp reversals.

Do not trade the breakout. Trade the reaction after the sweep.

Volatility Compression and Expansion

Gold cycles between:

- tight range (compression),
- violent breakout (expansion).

Pattern:

$$\text{Triangle} \rightarrow \text{Breakout} \rightarrow \text{Trend}$$

Inside compression:

- do less,
- avoid chop.

On expansion:

- scalp momentum,
- follow structure,
- exit on exhaustion wick.

VWAP Playbook

VWAP acts as an institutional magnet.

Rules:

- Price above VWAP = long pullbacks.
- Price below VWAP = short rallies.
- Price stuck at VWAP = no trade.

Gold typically returns to VWAP at least once per session.

$$\text{VWAP} = \text{mean reversion anchor}$$

XAUUSD Stop-Loss Engineering

Gold requires slightly larger stops than Forex:

$$\text{Typical stop: 10–25 pips (1.0–2.5 USD)}$$

Because:

- wicks are deep,

- volatility is high,
- stop-hunts are frequent.

But targets are larger:

$$20\check{}60 \text{ pips}$$

$$\text{Risk:Reward} = 1{:}2 \text{ or better}$$

Best Entry Models for Gold

1. Pullback to Structure

1. identify trend on 5M,
2. wait for pullback into EMA/VWAP zone,
3. rejection wick,
4. enter in direction of trend.

2. Breaker Block Trade After sweep:

- strong reversal candle,
- pullback into block,
- continuation.

3. Session Open Sweep Typical daily behavior:

1. London sweeps range,
2. New York drives trend.

Trade direction after sweep, not during.

Filtering Bad Conditions

Avoid gold during:

- narrow range chop,
- no volatility,
- midday lull,
- pre-major news suspense.

Better to wait than to bleed.

Scalping Gold During News

Gold reacts explosively to:

- NFP,
- CPI,
- FOMC,
- rate decisions.

Rules:

- do not enter during spike,
- wait for wick,
- trade the second move.

The first move is trap. The second move is trend.

Summary

Gold offers scalpers:

- high volatility,
- clean execution windows,
- strong reactions at levels,
- clear intraday rhythm.

Core blueprint:

1. Use 5M for structure.
2. Enter on 1M pullbacks or sweeps.
3. Respect volatility cycles.
4. Use VWAP as bias anchor.
5. Take profit quickly.

XAUUSD is a battlefield of volatility. With discipline, it becomes a consistent edge.

14.3 NASDAQ/US30 Impulse Scalping

NASDAQ (NQ) and US30 (Dow Jones) are among the fastest-moving index futures and CFDs. They deliver powerful intraday impulses, sharp bursts of momentum, and frequent directional runs. For scalpers, these markets are a goldmine — but they can also be unforgiving if risk is not controlled.

> Index scalping is the art of catching bursts, not trends.

Why NASDAQ and US30 Are Ideal for Scalping

Both instruments offer:

- deep liquidity,
- strong reaction to session opens,
- clean momentum bursts,
- sensitivity to economic news.

However:

$$\text{US30} = \text{fast, wicky, emotional}$$
$$\text{NASDAQ} = \text{smoother, more technical}$$

> US30 hunts stops; NASDAQ respects structure.

Session Timing: Prime Execution Windows

Index scalping is best during:

- US Pre-Market (13:30–14:30 GMT),
- New York Open (14:30–15:30 GMT),
- Power Hour (19:00–20:00 GMT).

Patterns:

1. Pre-market sets bias,
2. NY open triggers momentum,
3. afternoon shows trend continuation or reversal.

Avoid:

- midday chop (16:00–18:00 GMT).

Impulse Behavior

NASDAQ and US30 move in impulses:

$$\text{Expansion} \rightarrow \text{Retracement} \rightarrow \text{Continuation}$$

Impulse scalping is capturing these:

- strong directional bursts,
- defined legs,
- rapid volume acceleration.

Each impulse often begins with:

- liquidity sweep,
- rejection wick,
- breaker block.

$$\text{Sweep} \rightarrow \text{Rejection} \rightarrow \text{Burst}$$

Structure Recognition

5M provides structure:

- trend direction,
- key swing highs and lows,
- BOS/CHOCH transitions.

1M provides entries:

- micro pullbacks,
- imbalance fills,
- candle rejections.

Structure on 5M, execution on 1M.

Preferred Entry Models

1. Pullback to EMA Cluster Use:

- EMA 9/20/50 cluster,
- wick rejection,
- continuation candle.

Entry:

Break of micro-structure in direction of trend

2. Breaker Block Setup After sweep:

- strong reversal,
- pullback into breaker zone,
- impulse continuation.

Target:

- previous high/low,
- next liquidity pool.

3. VWAP Bounce/Reject VWAP acts as institutional bias:

- above = buy pullbacks,
- below = sell rallies.

Avoid when price is stuck at VWAP (chop zone).

Risk Engineering on Indices

Because indices move fast:

Stops must be tight, logical, and pre-planned.

Typical stops:

- NASDAQ: 8–15 points
- US30: 20–40 points

Targets:

$2R$ or more during impulse

Key rule:

Never widen stop on indices.

News Sensitivity

Indices react violently to:

- NFP,
- CPI,
- rate decisions,
- FOMC.

Execution rule:

- do not enter during spike,
- wait for second move,
- confirm direction with order flow.

$$\text{First move} = \text{trap, second move} = \text{trend}$$

Trap Zones

Common traps on indices:

- pre-market highs/lows,
- round numbers (100s on US30, 50s on NASDAQ),
- opening drive fake breakouts.

Execution logic:

- let trap form,
- enter after rejection,
- scalp impulse.

Scalping Psychology

Index scalping demands:

- calm mind,
- fast execution,
- emotional detachment.

Never chase candles.

If you missed it, wait for the next one.

Summary

NASDAQ and US30 offer:

- frequent impulses,
- deep liquidity,
- fast profits,
- clear session patterns.

Core blueprint:

1. Define trend on 5M.
2. Enter on 1M pullbacks or sweeps.
3. Trade impulse bursts.
4. Manage risk tightly.

Indices reward speed and structure. Trade bursts, not noise.

14.4 NIFTY/BANKNIFTY Precision Setups

NIFTY and BANKNIFTY are highly attractive for scalpers because they combine:

- strong intraday movement,
- clear institutional levels,
- predictable opening behaviors,
- deep liquidity during market hours.

They offer multiple clean setups each day, especially around the open and during trend continuation phases.

BANKNIFTY is volatility. NIFTY is structure.

Session Behavior in Indian Markets

The key trading window is:

$$09{:}15 \rightarrow 10{:}15 \text{ (first hour)}$$

This period provides:

- opening volatility,

- liquidity sweep,
- early trend formation.

Midday behavior:

- slower,
- narrower range,
- mean reversion.

Afternoon session:

$$14{:}00 \rightarrow 15{:}15$$

- trend continuation,
- breakout opportunities,
- closing volatility.

NIFTY vs BANKNIFTY Characteristics

NIFTY:

- smoother movement,
- more controlled retracements,
- excellent for trend pullbacks.

BANKNIFTY:

- explosive,
- aggressive spikes,
- deeper wicks,
- more emotional.

$$\text{NIFTY} = \text{technique}. \quad \text{BANKNIFTY} = \text{aggression}.$$

Opening Range Playbook

Typical pattern:

1. Opening candle forms large range,
2. Price sweeps top or bottom,
3. Reversal or continuation follows,
4. Trend emerges.

Execution:

- wait for sweep of high/low,
- enter on rejection candle,
- stop beyond sweep.

Do not chase the first candle. Trade the reaction to liquidity.

VWAP Anchored Trend Scalping

VWAP is extremely effective in Indian indices.
Logic:

- Above VWAP = Long bias,
- Below VWAP = Short bias.

Best entries:

- pullback to VWAP,
- rejection wick,
- continuation.

Targets:

- session high/low,
- previous swing,
- round numbers.

Round Number Reactions

Both NIFTY and BANKNIFTY respect psychological levels:

$$\text{BANKNIFTY: 500, 1000 levels}$$

$$\text{NIFTY: 50, 100 levels}$$

Behavior:

- liquidity builds,
- price spikes,
- reversal or breakout forms.

$$\text{Scalp reaction, not breakout.}$$

Pullback Setup (High Probability)

Steps:

1. Identify trend on 5M.
2. Wait for pullback to EMA cluster (9/20).
3. Look for rejection wick or reversal candle.
4. Enter with structure.
5. Target previous swing.

Stop placement:

$$\text{Below pullback low (long)} \quad \text{or} \quad \text{above pullback high (short)}$$

BANKNIFTY requires wider stops:

$$\text{15–30 points}$$

NIFTY can use tighter:

$$\text{8–15 points}$$

Breakout Continuation on BANKNIFTY

BANKNIFTY offers breakout continuation during:

- strong trending days,
- after news events,
- when institutions are active.

Execution:

- breakout
- small pullback
- continuation burst

One candle pullback is enough.

Avoiding Traps

Both indices frequently produce:

- fake breakouts,
- mid-range chop,
- lunch session drift.

No-trade zones:

- price around VWAP with no direction,
- overlapping candles,
- wicks on both sides,
- inside previous range.

Boredom is not a signal.

Risk Control

Indices move quickly — risk must be controlled.

Principles:

- define stop before entry,
- never widen stop,
- avoid averaging down,
- stop after 2 losses.

Profit-taking:

Scale out in momentum.

Targets:

- 1R = safe,
- 2R = strong,
- 3R = excellent.

Summary

NIFTY and BANKNIFTY provide consistent opportunities for scalpers because they combine:

- opening volatility,
- clean session structure,
- respect for levels,
- strong intraday trends.

Core blueprint:

1. Trade opening sweeps.
2. Use VWAP for bias.
3. Pullback entries are high probability.
4. Respect round numbers.

Precision matters: NIFTY requires patience; BANKNIFTY demands bravery — with risk under control.

14.5 Session-Based Scalping Frameworks

Market sessions create the rhythm of intraday trading. Each session has unique characteristics in terms of:

- volatility,
- liquidity,
- institutional participation,
- trap behavior,
- trend development.

A scalper who understands session dynamics can anticipate when movement will be clean and when it will be dangerous.

Right timing is more important than the right signal.

Three Major Global Sessions

The primary trading sessions are:

1. Asian Session
2. London Session
3. New York Session

Each session contributes differently to price action.

Asian Session: Accumulation and Range

Time window:

$$23:00 - 07:00 \text{ GMT (approx.)}$$

Characteristics:

- low volatility,
- tight ranges,
- accumulation behavior.

Patterns:

- price builds liquidity,
- slow drift,

- false breakouts.

Scalping advice:

Wait, observe, do not force trades.

Best use case:

- mark highs/lows for London sweeps.

London Session: Expansion and Trend Formation

Time window:

07:00 – 11:00 GMT

Behavior:

- volatility increases,
- liquidity enters,
- trend begins.

Typical pattern:

1. sweep of Asian high/low,
2. reversal or continuation,
3. clean trend emerges.

Ideal scalping setups:

- break of structure (BOS),
- pullback to EMA/VWAP,
- continuation burst.

London = first clean move of the day.

New York Session: Momentum and Continuation

Time window:

12:30 – 16:00 GMT

New York adds:

- volume,
- speed,
- emotional movement.

Typical structure:

1. consolidation before open,
2. opening impulse,
3. continuation or reversals,
4. afternoon trend follow-through.

This is where scalping is most profitable:

London sets direction. New York expands it.

London–New York Overlap: Prime Scalping Window

Overlap window:

12:00 – 14:00 GMT

Characteristics:

- deepest liquidity,
- strongest volatility,
- clearest structure.

Ideal trades:

- trend continuation,
- pullback to VWAP,
- liquidity sweeps.

This is the best 2-hour scalping window in the world.

Session Transitions Create Traps

Transitions between sessions often create:

- false breakouts,
- stop runs,
- reversal signals.

Examples:

- Asian → London: sweep of liquidity
- London → NY: expansion burst

Rules:

Never enter during transition candle.

Instead:

- wait for direction,
- enter on pullback.

No-Trade Zones by Session

Avoid trading:

- low-liquidity Asian chop,
- midday NY lull,
- pre-news suspense,
- price stuck at VWAP.

No trade is profitable if it avoids loss.

Session Anchors: High/Low and VWAP

Every session creates:

- session high,
- session low,
- session VWAP.

These become:

- magnets,
- reversal zones,
- breakout targets.

Playbook:

1. Mark Asian high/low
2. Watch London for sweep and direction
3. Trade continuation in NY

Session levels = scaffolding of the day.

Summary

Session frameworks provide clarity:

- Asian = buildup,
- London = breakout,
- New York = continuation.

A scalper who respects session behavior avoids noise and focuses on the best windows.

Core principles:

- do not trade when market is asleep,
- trade when liquidity arrives,
- avoid transitions,
- scalp impulses, not chop.

Scalping is timing. Sessions provide the clock.

Part V

Building a Scalping Business

Chapter 15

Risk Management for Scalpers

In scalping, the goal is not to be right — the goal is to protect capital long enough to allow your edge to compound. Fast markets produce fast profits, but they can also produce fast losses if risk is unmanaged. This chapter presents a practical framework for position sizing, stop placement, scaling, and daily limits, designed to help scalpers survive volatility and grow consistently over time.

15.1 R-Multiple Thinking

Traditional traders think in terms of dollars, points, or pips. Professional scalpers think in terms of R. The concept of R-multiples transforms trading from emotional uncertainty into mathematical consistency.

> R is the distance between your entry and your stop-loss. Every profit or loss is measured relative to R.

What is R?

R is defined as:

$$R = \text{Risk per trade}$$

For example:

$$\text{Entry: } 100 \quad \text{Stop: } 99.5$$

Risk = 0.5
So:

$$1R = 0.5$$

If you risk \$100 per trade, then:

$$1R = \$100$$

A profit of \$200 is:

$$+2R$$

A loss of \$50 is:

$$-0.5R$$

Why R-Multiples Matter

R thinking creates:

- clarity,
- consistency,
- scalability,
- unemotional execution.

Using R removes attachment to money:

> You are not trading money. You are trading risk units.

This allows a trader to repeat a winning process regardless of account size.

Profit Becomes Multiplicative

When traders think in money, they say:

- "I made \$200."
- "I lost \$150."

This is subjective.
When traders think in R, they say:

- "I made +2R."
- "I lost -1R."

This is objective.

A system with 2R average reward and 1R average loss is profitable.

Winrate + R = Edge Formula

A profitable trading system must satisfy:

$$(\text{Winrate} \times \text{Average Win}) > (\text{Lossrate} \times \text{Average Loss})$$

Using R-multiples:

$$(0.40 \times 2R) > (0.60 \times 1R)$$

$$0.8R > 0.6R$$

$$\text{Edge} = \text{Profit}$$

This system is profitable despite:

- 40% win rate,
- 60% loss rate.

You can lose more trades than you win and still make money.

Stop-Loss Determines R

R is fixed the moment you choose a stop-loss.
Steps:

1. Identify structure for stop.
2. Measure distance from entry.
3. Define risk = that distance.

Then you know:

$$1R = \text{your defined risk}$$

If you change stop after entering:

You change R. You destroy the math.

Targets Are Multiples of R

Profit targets are not random:

$$1R,\ 2R,\ 3R,\ 4R,\ \ldots$$

Example:

- Stop = 5 points
- Target = 10 points

$$\text{Target} = 2\text{R}$$

This simplifies decision-making:

$$\text{Hit 2R} \rightarrow \text{take partials}$$
$$\text{Trail stop on remaining}$$

Position Sizing with R

Position size = risk / stop distance.
Formula:

$$\text{Position Size} = \frac{\$\ \text{Risk}}{\text{Stop Distance}}$$

Example:

- Willing to risk = \$200
- Stop = 0.5 points

$$\text{Position Size} = \frac{200}{0.5} = 400 \text{ units}$$

Scaling R-Multiples Over Time

The beauty of the R approach:

$$\text{Account grows} \Rightarrow \text{R grows}$$

If you risk 1% per trade:

- \$10,000 account → \$100 per R
- \$50,000 account → \$500 per R
- \$200,000 account → \$2,000 per R

Same strategy. Same R. Only position size changes.

Emotional Benefit

R thinking removes emotional noise:

- no fear of money,
- no attachment to profit,
- no revenge trading.

You no longer think:

- "I need to make $1,000 today."

You think:

I need 2R today.

This is stable, repeatable, and scalable.

Summary

R-multiple thinking creates:

- mathematical consistency,
- clarity of risk,
- scalable results,
- emotional stability.

The framework:

1. Define stop = define risk.
2. Every trade = risk 1R.
3. Measure profit as multiples of R.
4. Scale position size as account grows.

Do not think in money. Think in R. This is how scalpers survive and thrive.

15.2 Stop-Loss Precision & Volatility-Adjusted Stops

For a scalper, the stop-loss is not just a protection tool — it is the *definition of risk.* Every R, every position size, every expectation is built on where the stop is placed. A sloppy stop turns a good strategy into a losing one. A precise, volatility-aware stop transforms the same strategy into a robust, scalable system.

> Your edge lives between your entry and your stop. If the stop is wrong, the edge is gone.

The Purpose of a Stop-Loss

A professional stop-loss must satisfy three conditions:

1. It must be placed **beyond noise** (so normal fluctuations do not hit it).
2. It must be placed **at structural invalidation** (where your idea is proven wrong).
3. It must be **known in advance** (no moving after entry).

In other words:

$$\text{Stop-loss} = \text{Price level where your trade idea is invalid}$$

If price reaches the stop, you are not "unlucky" — you are wrong. And that is acceptable, as long as risk is controlled.

Structure-Based Stop Placement

The most important principle:

Stops belong behind structure, not behind hope.

For longs:

- below a swing low,
- below a demand zone,
- below a breaker or FVG boundary,
- below VWAP or key support line (when used as anchor).

For shorts:

- above a swing high,

- above a supply zone,
- above a breaker or FVG boundary,
- above VWAP or key resistance line.

If your stop is inside the structure you are trading from, you are placing it **inside noise**, and normal fluctuations will hit it repeatedly.

The Role of Wicks in Stop Placement

Wicks are the footprints of liquidity grabs. In high-volatility scalping, wicks often:

- reach into stop clusters,
- sweep liquidity,
- reverse instantly.

Stop rules:

- Never place the stop *inside* a wick.
- Place the stop slightly beyond the wick (for safety).

For a long trade after a downside sweep:

- wick low = liquidity hunt,
- stop = just below that wick (not at the exact low).

This helps avoid being part of the hunted liquidity.

Volatility-Adjusted Stops

Volatility is not constant. A stop size that works in calm conditions becomes too tight in high-volatility markets. To adapt, scalpers use volatility metrics like ATR (Average True Range).

ATR-Based Adjustment

ATR measures the average range of price movement over a chosen period. For scalping, common choices:

- ATR(14) on the 1M or 5M chart,
- ATR(10) for more sensitivity.

Basic rule of thumb:

$$\text{Stop distance} \approx k \times \text{ATR}$$

Where k is usually between 0.5 and 1.5, depending on:

- instrument,
- session,
- volatility regime.

Examples:

- For gold in normal volatility: stop $\approx 1.0 \times \text{ATR}_{1M}$.
- For EURUSD: stop $\approx 0.5\text{–}0.8 \times \text{ATR}_{1M}$.

Combining Structure + ATR

The most robust method:

1. Place stop beyond structural invalidation (swing, zone, wick).
2. Confirm that distance is reasonable relative to current ATR.
3. If the distance is less than a minimum ATR multiple, widen slightly.

This ensures:

- you are not too tight for current volatility,
- you are not so wide that R becomes huge and meaningless.

$$\text{Stop} = \max(\text{Structure},\ k \times \text{ATR})$$

Instrument-Specific Stop Logic

Different instruments require different stop scales.

Forex Majors (EURUSD, GBPUSD):

- typically low to moderate volatility,
- 3–6 pips per stop for 1M scalps,
- 6–12 pips per stop for 5M setups.

Gold (XAUUSD):

- high volatility with deep wicks,
- 10–25 pips (1.0–2.5 USD) per stop,
- always outside obvious stop-hunt wicks.

Indices (NASDAQ, US30):

- fast spikes, strong impulses,
- NASDAQ: 8–15 points,
- US30: 20–40 points,
- must be placed beyond micro structure.

Crypto:

- very regime-dependent,
- use ATR + structure,
- when volatility is extreme, widen stops or reduce size.

Common Stop-Loss Mistakes

1. **Stops based on account balance, not structure** e.g. "I will place a 5-pip stop because I only want to lose $50." This ignores volatility and structure.

2. **Moving stops further away to avoid being hit** This converts defined risk into unlimited risk. One trade can undo an entire month.

3. **Placing stops at obvious round numbers** Institutions and algos hunt stops at those levels. Slightly beyond structure is safer than exactly at the level.

4. **Using fixed pip/point stops in all conditions** The same 5 pips behave differently in low vs high volatility. Static stops in dynamic markets are dangerous.

5. **No stop at all (mental stops only)** Fast markets can move more than expected before you react. Mental stops often fail under stress.

Tight vs Too Tight

As scalpers, we want tight stops. But there is a difference between:

- *tight and logical*, and
- *tight and suicidal.*

A tight, logical stop:

- sits just beyond a well-defined structure,
- respects current volatility,
- is consistent across trades.

A too-tight stop:

- sits inside noise,
- ignores ATR and session behavior,
- gets hit repeatedly before real move.

If your stop is hit often and price then goes your way, your stops are too tight.

Volatility Filters Before Entering

Good risk management starts *before* you place a stop:

- If ATR is extremely high, reduce size or skip trades.
- If spread widens, increase caution.
- If candles show chaotic wicks on both sides, stand aside.

Sometimes the best stop-loss is:

No trade at all.

Stop-Loss and R Integration

Once stop distance is chosen, R is defined:

$$1R = \text{Stop Distance} \times \text{Position Size}$$

Then:

- Targets are expressed as 1R, 2R, 3R, etc.
- Daily losses are capped in R (e.g. -2R or -3R).
- Weekly, monthly performance is tracked in R-multiples.

Summary

Stop-loss precision and volatility adjustment are central to professional scalping.

Key principles:

- place stops beyond structure, not randomly;
- respect volatility using ATR or similar measures;
- adapt stop size by instrument and session;
- never move stops wider after entry;
- integrate stops into your R-multiple framework.

> You cannot control the market. You can only control where you exit when you are wrong. Master that, and your edge can finally breathe.

15.3 Scaling In/Out Without Increasing Risk

Scaling is a powerful technique for improving trade performance — *if done correctly.* Most traders scale emotionally, adding to winning trades too late or adding to losing trades to "average down." A professional scalper scales mathematically, ensuring that total risk never exceeds the predefined $1R$.

> Scaling is not about taking more risk — it is about allocating risk more efficiently.

Core Principles of Safe Scaling

There are three rules that govern professional scaling:

1. Total risk across all entries must never exceed $1R$.
2. Scaling must follow structure, not emotion.
3. Scaling occurs only when the original trade thesis is still valid.

This allows the trader to increase position size while maintaining controlled risk.

Scaling In: The Right Way

Scaling in means building a position *as the market confirms your direction.*

Do not add size while price moves against you. This is averaging down. It increases risk. It destroys accounts.

Averaging down = emotionally comfortable, mathematically disastrous.

Correct scaling follows:

Add size only after confirmation.

Structure-Based Scaling

A high-quality scaling model:

1. Enter initial position at high-probability setup.
2. Let price move in your favor.
3. On pullback to structure (EMA, FVG, VWAP), add size.

Rules:

- Stop-loss for entire position stays at original invalidation point.
- New size is calculated so that total risk $\leq 1R$.

Risk remains constant. Size increases.

Position Sizing Mathematics

If original stop distance is d and the trader risks \$R:

- First entry: size $= \frac{R}{d}$
- After movement and pullback, second entry stop is closer to break-even.

The new size is:

$$\text{Size}_2 = \frac{R - \text{risk consumed}}{\text{new stop distance}}$$

This ensures:

$$\text{Total Risk} \leq R$$

Scaling is not free — it is funded by unrealized profit.

Scaling Out: Profits Lock-In Momentum

Scaling out means taking partial profits to:

- secure gains,
- reduce emotional stress,
- let the remainder run.

Common method:

1. Take partial at $1R$.
2. Move stop-loss to break-even.
3. Let remaining position target $2R, 3R$.

This achieves:

Small winners guaranteed, large winners allowed.

Advantages of Scaling Out

Scaling out provides:

- psychological relief — some profit secured,
- emotional detachment — easier to hold winners,
- compounding — large R multiples possible.

When some profit is locked:

Greed decreases, clarity increases.

When NOT to Scale

Bad times to scale:

- during chop,
- at major news release,
- inside imbalance,
- into obvious supply/demand levels,
- when spread widens,
- when internal pressure forces you emotionally.

If you feel the urge to scale $\rightarrow$ Do not scale.

Scaling Up After Stop Movement

A key method used by professionals:

- once partial profits are taken,
- stop-loss is moved to break-even,
- new risk budget opens up.

You can now add size again:

$$\text{New scale} = \text{new risk budget generated by profits}$$

This allows position growth without additional account risk.

The Scaling Flywheel

The goal of scaling is to build a *compounding flywheel*:

1. Enter small size with tight stop.
2. Market confirms.
3. Add size on structure.
4. Move stop to break-even.
5. Let winners expand.

This allows the trader to:

- control risk tightly,
- increase payout,
- reduce emotional stress.

$$\text{Small risk} \rightarrow \text{large return potential.}$$

What Scaling Is Not

- It is not averaging down.
- It is not gambling.
- It is not emotionally adding size because price "looks good."

Scaling is:

- strategic,
- mathematical,
- structure-based.

Summary

Scaling in/out is a professional tool, not a hack.

Key principles:

- Risk must never exceed $1R$.
- Add only after confirmation.
- Scale out to secure profit and reduce stress.
- Use partial exits + break-even stop to allow runners.

> Scaling is the art of increasing size without increasing risk. Done correctly, it transforms a good system into a compounding engine.

15.4 Avoiding Overtrading

Overtrading is one of the greatest threats to scalpers. The fast pace of short-term charts creates the illusion of opportunity everywhere, but in reality:

> Only a few moments each day are truly high probability. Everything else is noise.

Professional scalpers learn that discipline is not found in doing more, but in doing less with precision.

What Is Overtrading?

Overtrading occurs when a trader:

- takes too many trades,
- trades outside the plan,
- enters without valid setup,
- chases movement,
- forces trades due to boredom or emotion.

It is not defined by the number of trades, but by the *quality of decisions.*

Why Scalpers Are Vulnerable

Scalpers experience:

- fast charts,
- constant price movement,
- frequent candles,
- micro-changes.

This creates a psychological trap:

$$\text{Movement} \neq \text{Opportunity}$$

The market is always moving, but not always in a tradeable way.

The Cost of Overtrading

Overtrading creates damage in multiple dimensions:

Financial cost:

- commissions,
- spread costs,
- slippage increases,
- death by small losses.

Mental cost:

- emotional fatigue,
- stress,
- frustration,
- impulsive revenge trading.

Opportunity cost:

> When you are trading low-probability setups, you are not available for high-probability ones.

The Overtrading Cycle

Many traders fall into this destructive loop:

1. Take impulsive trades.
2. Lose small amounts repeatedly.
3. Get frustrated.
4. Increase size or chase trades.
5. Create larger losses.

Then the trader thinks:

I must trade more to recover.

And the cycle repeats.

How Professionals Avoid Overtrading

Professionals use structure, not emotion.

Rule 1: Predefined Playbook A scalper must know:

- what setups they trade,
- when they trade them,
- what invalidates them.

If a setup is not in the playbook:

It is not a setup.

Rule 2: Session Windows Only trade when:

- liquidity is high,
- volume increases,
- volatility is clean.

Examples:

- NY Open,
- London Expansion,
- 1-hour windows of clean movement.

Rule 3: Daily Trade Limit A simple rule:

3–5 trades per session, maximum.

Not because fewer trades is always better, but because beyond a certain point:

Decision quality degrades.

Rule 4: Time-Out After Losses If two consecutive losses occur:

Stop. Step away. Reset.

This prevents emotional escalation.

The "Boredom Trade" Problem

The most dangerous trades are the ones taken due to boredom:

I haven't traded for 30 minutes... this looks okay...

But:

Okay is not enough. Only excellent is profitable.

Professional scalpers learn to sit through boredom with calm.

The Discipline of Waiting

Waiting is a skill.
A scalper often spends:

- 80% of time waiting,
- 20% of time executing.

This is normal.

The market pays the patient, not the active.

Metrics to Detect Overtrading

Red flags:

- number of trades increasing daily,
- decreasing average R,
- trading outside peak sessions,

- trading during chop,
- urge to "make it back."

Two key questions:

1. Did I follow my plan?
2. Was this a setup from my playbook?

If the answer is "no" to either:

It was overtrading.

Build Boundaries: A Scalper's Shield

Boundaries reduce emotional exposure:

- Daily loss limit ($-2R$ or $-3R$)
- Daily win goal ($+2R$ or $+3R$)
- Maximum trades per session (3–5)
- Break after loss streak

Boundaries transform chaos into structure.

Summary

Avoiding overtrading is a core skill of a professional scalper.

- Movement does not equal opportunity.
- Trade only when conditions align.
- Use a predefined playbook.
- Limit trades per session.
- Stop after consecutive losses.
- Protect emotional capital as much as financial capital.

  Scalping is not about catching every move. It is about catching the right moves.

15.5 Daily Win/Loss Limits and Personal Circuit Breakers

A professional scalper treats risk like an engineer treats physics: the environment must be controlled before performance is possible. Daily limits and circuit breakers are not signs of weakness — they are the foundation of longevity.

> Your goal is not to win every day. Your goal is to be able to trade tomorrow.

Daily Loss Limits: The Safety Net

Every scalper must have a predefined maximum loss for the day:

$$\text{Daily Loss Limit} = -2R \text{ or } -3R$$

This means:

- After losing $2R$ or $3R$,
- You stop trading,
- No exceptions.

Why?

1. Emotional control collapses after a loss streak.
2. Revenge trading becomes extremely likely.
3. Decision quality deteriorates.

Stopping is not defeat — it is risk mastery.

One bad day should not ruin a month.

Daily Win Limits: Protecting Profits

This concept is less understood, but equally important:

$$\text{Daily Win Limit} = +2R \text{ or } +3R$$

After reaching the target:

- Lock in profits,
- Stop trading,
- Preserve emotional capital.

Because after a big win:

- euphoria increases,
- discipline drops,
- traders overtrade and give money back.

Protecting a win is as important as preventing a loss.

The "Circuit Breaker" Concept

Circuit breakers are predefined stop conditions:

Conditions where trading must stop, immediately.

Examples:

- 2 consecutive losing trades,
- 3 trades in a row with no edge,
- emotional stress or anger,
- boredom trades,
- spread or volatility spikes.

A circuit breaker is not emotional — it is mechanical.

Psychological Rationale

Humans are biologically wired to lose rationality after:

- stress,
- fear,
- frustration,
- greed.

Cognitive overload causes mistakes.
Circuit breakers preserve the trader from:

- revenge trading,
- chasing losses,
- gambling behavior.

Stopping is a professional move, not a weakness.

Example Rule Set

A high-level rule set could be:

1. Maximum losses: $-2R$ per day.
2. Maximum wins: $+3R$ per day.
3. Maximum trades: 5 per session.
4. Stop for the day after:
    - 2 consecutive losses, or
    - emotional deviation detected.

This protects both financial and emotional capital.

Time-Based Circuit Breakers

Time of day matters.
Professional scalpers avoid:

- trading out of session,
- trading in low volume,
- trading while tired.

Time-based circuit breaker:

If market is not moving, stop.

If personal focus drops, stop.

Performance Preservation

The goal is not maximal trading — it is maximal return on discipline.

> One high-quality trade can make the day. Ten low-quality trades can destroy it.

Circuit breakers preserve:

- capital,
- mental energy,
- confidence,
- long-term edge.

Monthly Compounding Effect

A trader who avoids catastrophic days can compound steadily:

$$(+2R, +3R, +1R, -1R, +2R, -2R) \rightarrow \text{consistent growth}$$

A trader who ignores limits will eventually experience:

$$(-8R, -10R) \rightarrow \text{destroyed account}$$

$$\text{Prevention} > \text{Recovery}$$

Summary

Daily limits and circuit breakers create *structural discipline*.

Key principles:

- Daily loss limit: $-2R$ or $-3R$
- Daily win limit: $+2R$ or $+3R$
- Stop after consecutive losses
- Stop when emotional imbalance appears

You do not need to trade all day. You need to trade until you hit your limit — then preserve the edge.

Chapter 16

Performance Optimization

Scalping is not random action — it is a measurable business. The edge is not found only in charts, but in the data you collect about your own behavior. This chapter focuses on how to transform trading into a statistically driven process: what to record, how to tag trades, how to discover performance patterns, and how to refine your strategy through monthly and quarterly review cycles.

16.1 What to Track: Setups, Emotions, Mistakes, Metrics

A scalper's journal is not a diary — it is a data-collection system. The journal exists to reveal what the trader cannot see in real-time:

- strengths,
- weaknesses,
- patterns of success,
- patterns of failure.

Most traders record only entries and exits. Professionals record the *entire decision process.*

> The market leaves footprints. So do you. Your journal is where they become visible.

Track Setups with Precision

Every trade must be classified by setup type.
Examples:

- EMA pullback
- liquidity sweep reversal
- VWAP bounce/reject
- breaker block continuation
- FVG fill

Each setup is tagged with:

- entry conditions,
- timeframe used,
- confluences,
- outcome (in R).

Over time, you learn:

- which setups work best,
- in which sessions,
- under which volatility conditions.

Your best setups become your business model.

Track Emotions

Scalping is a psychological sport. The journal must capture emotional state:

- calm
- confident
- tired
- anxious
- euphoria
- fear of missing out (FOMO)

A simple scale works well:

$$-2, -1, 0, +1, +2$$

Where:

- -2 = emotional stress, no clarity
- 0 = neutral state
- $+2$ = calm, confident, in flow

Patterns often emerge:

+2 = high performance   -2 = mistakes

Trading edge = technical ability + emotional stability.

Track Mistakes (The Most Valuable Data)

Mistakes are more valuable than trades.
Examples:

- entering without setup,
- chasing price,
- widening stops,
- overtrading,
- trading during chop,
- ignoring session behavior.

A simple table can track error types:

Mistake Category	Example
Process	Ignored checklist
Emotional	Revenge trade after loss
Execution	Late entry/exit
Risk	Increased size impulsively
Session	Trading at low liquidity

After weeks of data, patterns are obvious:

80% of losses come from 2 types of mistakes.

Track Metrics (The Math of Improvement)

Key performance metrics:

- Win rate
- Average R per trade
- Max drawdown

- Profit factor
- Expectancy

Expectancy is the most important:

$$E = (W \times AW) - (L \times AL)$$

Where:

- W = win rate
- AW = average win (in R)
- L = loss rate
- AL = average loss (in R)

A system is profitable when:

$$E > 0$$

This approach transforms trading into engineering:

> You do not guess. You measure.

Ideal Tracking Framework

Every trade entry should have:

1. Setup type
2. Time of day/session
3. Emotional state
4. Entry/Stop/Target (in R)
5. Outcome (win/loss + R)
6. Mistake tags (if any)

Example journal entry:

```
Setup: VWAP rejection
Session: London open
Emotion: +1
Stop: 0.5R
Target: 2R
Outcome: +2R
Notes: clean move, followed plan
```

A losing trade entry:

```
Setup: none
Emotion: -1
Mistake: boredom trade
Outcome: -1R
Notes: forced trade, no signal
```

Outcome of Systematic Recording

After a month of data, you will know:

- your best setups,
- your worst behaviors,
- your ideal sessions,
- your emotional triggers,
- your optimal frequency.

You will discover:

> You do not need more signals.You need fewer mistakes.

Summary

Tracking is the foundation of performance improvement.

- record setups,
- tag emotions,
- categorize mistakes,
- measure metrics,
- review patterns monthly.

What gets measured improves. What gets ignored repeats.

16.2 Trade Tagging for Performance Patterns

Tagging trades is a method of transforming raw activity into structured information. When trades are properly labeled, patterns emerge that are otherwise invisible. Trading performance is not random — it has structure. Trade tagging reveals that structure.

> A journal without tags is a diary. A journal with tags is a database.

Why Tag Trades?

Every day, the market produces hundreds of price swings. Only a few of them are worth trading.

To discover which ones are truly high-probability, each trade must be tagged according to:

- setup type,
- entry trigger,
- session,
- direction,
- volatility,
- emotional state,
- outcome (in R),
- mistake category (if any).

With time, this reveals:

- which setups make money,
- which setups lose money,
- when to trade,
- when not to trade.

Patterns emerge only from data.

Core Tag Categories

Every trade should use a consistent category set. A typical list includes:

Setup Tags:

- EMA pullback
- VWAP bounce/reject
- liquidity sweep reversal
- breaker block continuation
- FVG scalping
- range fade
- news spike reaction

Timing Tags:

- Asian session
- London expansion
- NY open
- overlap period

Structure Tags:

- BOS (break of structure)
- CHOCH (change of character)
- HH/LL sweep

Outcome Tags:

- +2R winner
- +1R winner
- break-even
- -1R loss

Emotional Tags:

- calm
- anxious
- confident
- impatient

Tagging emotions is as important as tagging setups.

The biggest failures are emotional, not technical.

Pattern Discovery Through Tagging

After a few weeks, sorting by tags produces insights:

- You may see that VWAP rejections during London are highly profitable.
- You may see that liquidity sweeps during Asian are unprofitable.
- You may see that anxious trades lose money.

A simple example report:

$$\text{EMA Pullback + London} = +5R \text{ per week}$$

$$\text{Range Fade + NY midday} = -4R \text{ per week}$$

This forms the basis of strategic filtering:

Trade more of what works. Trade less of what doesn't.

Mistake Tagging Reveals Leaks

When a losing trade is tagged:

Mistake: No setup

or

Mistake: Traded chop

The trader learns:

Loss was avoidable.

Over time, mistakes form clusters:

Mistake Category	Frequency
Boredom trade	12
Chasing candle	8
Ignored stop discipline	5
Overtrading	4

Now, improvement is obvious:

> Eliminating one mistake category can improve performance dramatically.

Tagging Generates Edge

Edge comes from repetition of high-probability setups.

Tagging allows performance questions:

- Which setup has highest R?
- Which session is most profitable?
- Which emotional states lead to losses?

Examples:

EMA Pullback + NY Open = +3R avg

Liqudity Sweep + Asian Session = -2R avg

Now the system is built on data, not belief.

How to Implement Tagging Efficiently

A simple spreadsheet works:
Columns may include:
Date Setup Session Emotion Outcome (R)
Optionally:
Volatility Mistake Reason Notes
Tags should be:

- fast to apply,
- consistent,
- standardized.

Consistency beats complexity.

Weekly Tag Review

Once per week:

1. Sort by setup.
2. Sort by session.
3. Sort by emotional tag.
4. Sort by mistake type.

Questions:

- What works?
- What does not?
- What patterns repeat?

This transforms trading:

From intuition → to statistics → to edge.

Summary

Trade tagging creates clarity.

It shows:

- which trades produce results,
- which behaviors cause loss,
- how emotion influences decision-making,
- where your edge lives.

> A trader with tags learns from every trade. A trader without tags repeats mistakes forever.

16.3 How to Identify Your Best/Worst Setups

Your trading performance is not evenly distributed across all setups. In fact, most scalpers discover the 80/20 rule:

80% of your profits come from 20% of your setups.

The goal of performance analysis is simple:

> Find the setups that consistently pay you — and eliminate the setups that consistently drain you.

Identifying your best and worst setups transforms your trading from random activity into a focused, high-precision system.

Step 1: Categorize Every Setup

Each trade must be associated with a specific setup label.

Common categories:

- EMA pullback
- VWAP bounce or rejection
- liquidity sweep reversal
- breaker block continuation
- FVG fill
- range-bound fade
- news spike reaction

The accuracy of your analysis depends on the accuracy of your labels.

> If you don't track setups, you can't measure them. If you can't measure them, you can't refine them.

Step 2: Track Performance of Each Setup in R-Multiples

For each setup category, calculate:

$$\text{Total R}, \quad \text{Average R}, \quad \text{Win Rate}, \quad \text{Max Drawdown}$$

A simple example table:

Setup	Avg R	Win Rate	Trades	Verdict
EMA Pullback	+1.6R	55%	32	Excellent
VWAP Reject	+0.9R	48%	20	Good
Liquidity Sweep	-0.3R	38%	18	Avoid
Range Fade	-1.1R	33%	15	Eliminated

From this, your edge becomes obvious.

Step 3: Add Session Filters

Performance varies dramatically by session.
Example:

$$\text{EMA Pullback + London} = +2.1R$$

$$\text{EMA Pullback + Asian} = -0.4R$$

Or:

$$\text{Liquidity Sweep + NY Open} = +1.7R$$

$$\text{Liquidity Sweep + Midday} = -1.2R$$

Session filters reveal:

- which setups work when liquidity is high,
- which setups fail in quiet conditions.

Step 4: Add Volatility Filters

Not all setups work in all volatility environments.
For example:

- EMA pullback works best when volatility is moderate.
- FVG fill works best when volatility is strong.
- VWAP setups fail during extreme spikes.
- Range fades fail when volatility expand.

Track volatility using:

- ATR,
- candle range,
- spread width.

This helps answer:

Which setup works in this regime?

Step 5: Identify Behavioral Triggers

Sometimes the weakness is not the setup — it is the trader's behavior around that setup.

Examples:

- You chase liquidity sweeps instead of waiting for confirmation.
- You exit EMA pullbacks too early due to impatience.
- You misread VWAP bounces because of fear.

Behavior tags help distinguish:

Bad setup vs. bad execution.

Step 6: Rank Setups by Profitability

Rank setups in descending order of profitability:

$$\text{Setup Performance Score} = \text{Avg R} \times \text{Win Rate}$$

Example:

$$\text{EMA Pullback Score} = 1.6 \times 0.55 = 0.88$$

$$\text{Range Fade Score} = -1.1 \times 0.33 = -0.36$$

Now you can clearly see:

- top-performing setups (high score),
- mediocre setups (near zero),
- losing setups (negative score).

Step 7: Create Your Personal "A-List" Setups

Your A-list determines what you trade:

- A-list (top 1–2 setups): trade them aggressively.
- B-list (average setups): trade selectively.
- C-list (losing setups): eliminate completely.

Example A-list:

- EMA pullback in trend
- liquidity sweep + reversal confirmation

Step 8: Build a "Do-Not-Trade" List

A DNT list saves enormous emotional and financial capital.
Example:

- range fades in low volume,
- counter-trend trades during news,
- trades taken during boredom or impatience,
- liquidity sweeps without confirmation.

This prevents repeated mistakes.

> The easiest way to improve performance is to stop doing what consistently loses.

Step 9: Review Monthly and Quarterly

A single week is noise. A single month starts to reveal trends. A quarter provides deep insight.
Questions to ask:

- Which setups produced the most profit?
- Which setups produced the most loss?
- Which setups felt easiest to execute?
- Which setups caused the most stress?

This converts raw data into strategic clarity.

Summary

Identifying best/worst setups allows the scalper to:

- focus on high-probability opportunities,
- eliminate destructive behaviors,
- reduce stress,
- increase consistency,
- scale intelligently.

> Your edge is already in your data. Your job is to uncover it.

16.4 Monthly and Quarterly Performance Reviews

A scalper who does not review performance is not improving — they are repeating. Markets change, volatility shifts, and your emotional state evolves. Monthly and quarterly reviews ensure that your trading process adapts to reality instead of operating from assumptions.

> Weekly data shows noise. Monthly data shows behavior. Quarterly data shows truth.

Purpose of Review Cycles

Performance reviews exist to answer three questions:

1. What worked?
2. What did not?
3. How do we improve next month?

This turns trading from an emotional activity into a scientific one.

> Reviewing is the bridge between experience and improvement.

Monthly Review: Detecting Patterns

At the end of each month, generate a report:

1. Setup Performance Sort trades by setup:

- EMA pullback: +8R
- VWAP bounce: +3R
- Range fade: -4R
- Liquidity sweep without confirmation: -6R

Insights:

- Range fades and premature sweep entries must be eliminated.
- EMA pullbacks should be prioritized.

2. Session Performance Sort trades by session:

- London Open: +7R
- NY Open: +5R
- Midday: -3R
- Asian: -2R

Conclusion:

Avoid midday and Asian sessions.

3. Emotional State Sort by emotional tags:

- Calm: +10R
- Impatient: -6R
- Bored: -3R

Conclusion is obvious:

Do not trade when bored or impatient.

Quarterly Review: Adjusting Strategy and Scaling

Quarterly data provides enough sample size to detect structural performance patterns. This is the cycle where system-level decisions are made:

1. Promote winning setups If EMA pullbacks produce consistent gains:

Increase size or frequency (within risk limits).

2. Retire losing behaviors If liquidity sweeps without confirmation lose, then:

$$\text{Eliminate them from playbook.}$$

3. Session optimization If mid-session trades lose consistently:

$$\text{Trade only during peak windows.}$$

4. Psychological improvements If emotional tags reveal:

$$\text{anger or frustration correlate with losses}$$

Then:

$$\text{Create circuit breaker rules to stop trading when triggered.}$$

Monthly and Quarterly Metrics

Key metrics to report:

- total R
- win rate
- average win / average loss
- profit factor
- max drawdown
- number of trades
- best setup
- worst setup

These metrics reflect whether the trading system is improving.

Profit Factor Formula:

$$\text{Profit Factor} = \frac{\text{Gross Profits}}{\text{Gross Losses}}$$

A stable system has:

$$\text{Profit Factor} > 1.5$$

A strong system has:

$$\text{Profit Factor} > 2.0$$

Strategy Refinement Loop

Performance reviews feed a continuous improvement loop:

1. Measure performance (data).
2. Identify patterns (insight).
3. Make adjustments (action).
4. Trade next month (execution).

This loop builds:

- confidence,
- mastery,
- resilience,
- scalability.

> You do not become a better trader by trading more. You become a better trader by reviewing more.

Annual Reflection

Quarterly reviews form the foundation of the yearly reflection. At the end of the year, assess:

- total growth,
- evolved discipline,
- playbook improvements,
- emotional maturity.

The trader should ask:

> What did I do this year that made the biggest difference? What will I remove next year to grow even faster?

Summary

Monthly and quarterly performance reviews are the backbone of professional improvement.

Key outcomes:

- winning setups are amplified,
- losing behaviors are eliminated,

- emotional leaks are removed,
- trading windows are optimized,
- the system evolves continuously.

Journaling creates memory. Reviewing creates mastery.

16.5 System Refinement Based on Data

A trading system is not something you invent once and follow forever. It is a living process that evolves with the trader's skill, emotional maturity, and market conditions. System refinement is driven not by intuition, but by data collected through journaling and performance reviews.

If you cannot measure it, you cannot improve it.

The Refinement Cycle

The refinement process follows a repeating cycle:

$$\text{Record} \rightarrow \text{Analyze} \rightarrow \text{Improve} \rightarrow \text{Execute}$$

This creates a feedback loop:

1. You record detailed trade data.
2. You analyze which variables correlate with success or failure.
3. You eliminate weak patterns.
4. You reinforce strong patterns.
5. You execute a cleaner system next month.

Every month, your system becomes more efficient.

Refinement Based on Setup Data

If monthly reports show:

$$\text{EMA Pullbacks} = +10\text{R}$$

and:

$$\text{Range Fades} = \text{-6R}$$

Then the system change is obvious:

- Trade more EMA pullbacks.

- Stop trading range fades.

Refinement is not emotional. It is mathematical.

Keep what works. Remove what doesn't.

Refinement Based on Session Data

If data shows:

- London Open = highly profitable,
- Midday = negative.

Then the refinement is:

- Trade during London Open.
- Avoid midday entirely.

A scalper's time becomes optimized.

Refinement Based on Emotional Data

If emotional tagging shows:

Impatient trades = losing trades

Then a personal rule is created:

If emotional state = negative, no trades.

This prevents overtrading and impulsive behavior.

Emotional intelligence is performance intelligence.

Refinement Based on Risk Data

If size increases correlate with inconsistency:

Size too large = fear + hesitation

Then apply a rule:

Reduce size until stability returns.

System improvement comes before size increase.

Refinement Based on Volatility Data

Different setups work in different volatility regimes.
If reports show:

FVG setups work only when ATR is high

then your system adds a volatility filter:

Trade FVG only when ATR $>$ threshold.

This reduces random trades.

Refinement Based on Execution Data

If the trader is consistently late on entries:

Chasing candles $=$ bad fills $=$ losses

Solution:

- Use limit orders at zones.
- Wait for candle close confirmation.

Execution rules are refined.

Building the "Next Version" of Your System

Each month or quarter, create a formal update:

- promote winning setups,
- eliminate failing setups,
- refine entry rules,
- adjust stop placement,
- update trading windows,
- add/remove filters.

Your system evolves through versions:

$$v1.0 \rightarrow v2.0 \rightarrow v3.0$$

Amateurs seek a perfect system. Professionals evolve their system.

Data-Driven Scaling

When consistency is proven:

$$\text{Profit Factor} > 2.0 \quad \Rightarrow \quad \text{Increase size.}$$

Scaling is based on evidence, not emotion.

Growth comes from stability, not aggression.

Summary

System refinement is the engine of long-term success. It requires:

- continuous recording,
- objective review,
- iterative changes,
- emotional discipline,
- patient execution.

The scalper becomes more skilled not through time alone, but through systematic evolution.

Data is the teacher. Refinement is the mastery.

Chapter 17

The Scalper's Operating System

Consistency is not created by indicators or luck. It is created by routine. A scalper must operate like a disciplined professional, following a daily structure, a pre-trade checklist, and a post-trade analysis routine. This chapter presents the operating system used by elite scalpers to maintain focus, reduce mistakes, and achieve long-term profitability.

17.1 Professional-Grade Daily Routine

Successful scalpers treat trading as a performance discipline. They do not wake up randomly and "see what happens." They follow a structured daily routine, similar to professional athletes, pilots, and surgeons. The goal is consistent performance built from consistent process.

> You cannot control the market. You can control your preparation.

Morning Preparation

A professional scalper begins before the market opens.

Key elements:

1. Physical state

- hydration,
- light movement or stretching,
- deep breathing.

The brain needs oxygen and energy. Scalping with a tired or stressed mind is a high-risk activity.

2. Emotional check-in Simple questions:

- Am I calm?
- Am I impatient?
- Am I carrying stress from outside life?

If emotional state is negative:

Do not trade.

3. Market reconnaissance Before trading, the scalper quickly reviews:

- overnight price action,
- key levels,
- volatility conditions,
- economic calendar,
- session opens.

This forms a macro-awareness of where flow may appear.

Session Entry Protocol

At the open of London or New York, focus intensifies.

Checklist:

1. Have I marked my zones?
2. Is volatility expanding or contracting?
3. Are spreads normal?
4. Is news scheduled?
5. Do I have a valid setup?

If any answer is unclear:

Wait.

Patience is a position.

During Trading Hours

The routine during the trading window is minimal by design.

- Trade only primary setups.
- Track emotional state.
- Record trades immediately.

A professional does not multitask:

No social media. No distractions.

The only screens open should contain:

- charts,
- journal,
- news feed (if macro relevant).

Post-Trade Sequence

After a trade closes:

1. Log the trade (setup, entry, stop, outcome).
2. Tag emotional state.
3. Add notes (why this trade).

Losses are recorded neutrally:

$$\text{Loss} = \text{information.}$$

Wins are recorded neutrally:

$$\text{Win} = \text{information.}$$

No celebration, no frustration.

Lunch Break / Reset

Midday is often a low-quality trading window. Professionals stop trading, reset, and prepare for next session.

Activities:

- walk,
- hydration,
- stretch,
- mental reset.

Energy management is as important as risk management.

Session Close Routine

At the end of day:

1. Review chart screenshots.
2. Tag mistakes.
3. Write 3 improvement points.
4. Set intention for next day.

No trading after fatigue sets in.

$$\text{Fatigue} = \text{Danger.}$$

Evening Routine

Evening routine is about restoration:

- light movement,
- stretch,
- read or learn,
- sleep early.

A tired brain cannot scalp well. Sleep is part of trading.

Summary

A professional-grade daily routine consists of:

- preparation,
- execution,
- recovery,
- review.

This structure produces consistent results over time.

$$\text{Routine} \rightarrow \text{Stability} \rightarrow \text{Consistency} \rightarrow \text{Profitability}$$

The market rewards discipline, not intensity.

17.2 Pre-Trade Preparation Checklist

Professionals do not enter the market unprepared. They operate from a structured process that ensures clarity, discipline, and readiness. A pre-trade checklist prevents impulsive decisions, emotional trading, and random entries. Before placing a single trade, the following checklist must be completed.

Preparation reduces uncertainty. Uncertainty increases risk.

1. Personal State Check

Trading requires cognitive precision. Before trading, confirm:

- Physical alertness: rested, hydrated, fed.
- Emotional stability: no stress, anger, fear, or excitement.
- Mental clarity: no external distractions.

If the trader is tired or emotional:

Do not trade.

Your mental state is part of the system.

2. Market Conditions Assessment

The market itself must be ready for scalping. Check:

- Is volatility expanding or contracting?
- Are spreads normal?
- Is the market trending, ranging, or consolidating?
- Are key sessions active (London/NY)?

Scalping during low-liquidity or dead markets is a recipe for frustration.

No volatility = no scalping.

3. Key Levels Marked

Before trading, mark:

- previous day high/low,
- session high/low,

- major support and resistance,
- liquidity pools,
- fair value gaps,
- VWAP.

These levels form the battlefield.

Scalping without levels is gambling.

4. News and Economic Calendar

Verify:

- upcoming events (NFP, CPI, FOMC),
- speeches,
- high-impact releases,
- unexpected news risk.

Rule:

Do not enter large positions immediately before major news.

Post-news scalping may be excellent, but it requires protocol.

5. Setup Identification

Trades must be planned before they happen. Ask:

- Which setup am I waiting for?
- What is my entry trigger?
- What would invalidate the setup?

If no setup exists:

Do not force trades.

6. Risk and Position Size Defined

Before entering:

- stop-loss level is defined,
- take-profit target is clear,
- position size is calculated from risk,
- maximum daily loss is respected.

Rule:

Risk is defined before entry, not after loss.

7. Execution Conditions Clear

A valid trade requires alignment:

1. trend direction,
2. momentum confirmation,
3. clean structure,
4. no obstacles (major levels) ahead.

If conditions are unclear:

Wait for clarity.

Patience is a position. Waiting is profitable.

8. Screens and Workspace Clean

Only essential items should be visible:

- charts,
- DOM or tape,
- journal,
- economic calendar.

Distractions are removed:

- no social media,
- no chat rooms,
- no random videos.

9. Fire Drill Protocol

Before trading, assume:

Something will go wrong.

Plan:

- what if price spikes?
- what if platform freezes?
- what if spread widens?

Have a backup:

- hotkey exits,
- stop orders,
- mobile app,
- broker phone line.

10. Final Check: Am I Ready?

One simple question:

If I lose the next 3 trades, will I be emotionally stable?

If the answer is **yes**, you are ready.
If the answer is **no**, pause.

Summary

A pre-trade checklist ensures:

- discipline,
- clarity,
- structure,
- safety.

It prevents emotional trading and reduces mistakes.

Professionals prepare. Amateurs react.

17.3 Post-Trade Analysis Sequence

Placing a trade is only half of the work. The other half — the part that leads to mastery — happens after the trade is closed. Post-trade analysis reveals whether the trader followed their system, whether the setup was valid, and how execution can be improved.

Each trade is either profit or tuition.

Why Post-Trade Analysis Matters

Without reflection, mistakes repeat. With reflection, improvement compounds.

Scalpers operate in a fast environment; details are easily forgotten. Recording the trade immediately preserves clarity.

Memory fades. Data stays.

Step 1: Capture the Trade Immediately

As soon as the trade closes:

- note the setup,
- mark the entry/exit,
- screenshot the chart,
- record emotional state.

No delay.

Emotion fades quickly. Record now.

Step 2: Tag the Trade

Every trade needs tags for:

- setup type,
- direction (long/short),
- session,
- volatility,
- emotion,
- mistake type (if any).

Tagging enables pattern recognition:

Tags $\rightarrow$ Patterns $\rightarrow$ Insight $\rightarrow$ Improvement

Step 3: Evaluate Validity of Setup

Ask:

- Was the setup real or imagined?
- Did I follow rules?
- Did I skip confirmation?

Sometimes trades are losses but valid:

$$\text{Good setup} + \text{Stop hit} = \text{Good trade}$$

Sometimes trades are wins but invalid:

$$\text{Bad setup} + \text{Lucky win} = \text{Dangerous behavior}$$

Winning is not the goal. Following the system is the goal.

Step 4: Evaluate Execution Quality

Execution is separate from strategy.
Questions:

- Was entry early, late, or perfect?
- Did I chase price?
- Did I widen stop?
- Did I exit emotionally?

Execution quality can be rated:

$$-2, -1, 0, +1, +2$$

Step 5: Evaluate Emotional State

Emotion affects decision quality.
Record:

- confidence,
- fear,
- excitement,
- boredom,
- frustration.

Correlations emerge:

$$\text{Boredom trades lose.Calm trades win.}$$

Step 6: Identify Lessons

Every trade must produce learning.

Simple prompts:

- What went well?
- What went wrong?
- What will I do differently?

Short notes are enough:

```
Lesson: Wait for candle close before entry.
Lesson: Avoid trading into major level.
Lesson: Stop was too wide.
```

Step 7: Archive and Organize

Screenshots are saved to folders:

- by setup,
- by session,
- by month.

This builds a personal library of edge. Over time, patterns become obvious:

This setup works.This setup fails.

Step 8: Weekly Review

At end of week:

1. group screenshots by setup,
2. review emotional tags,
3. analyze mistakes,
4. update rules.

Step 9: Reduce or Remove Problems

Identify recurring issues:

- late entry,
- trading chop,
- trading tired,
- revenge trading.

A rule is created:

If I feel X, I do not trade.

This prevents future losses.

Step 10: Reinforce Strengths

Do not only fix mistakes. Also reinforce strengths:

EMA pullbacks during London work consistently.

Write rules to trade them more:

Trade every valid EMA pullback during London.

Summary

Post-trade analysis converts randomness into mastery.

- capture the trade immediately,
- tag setups and emotions,
- evaluate setup validity,
- analyze execution,
- extract lessons,
- archive evidence,
- refine system weekly.

One trade teaches nothing. One hundred analyzed trades teach everything.

17.4 Weekly Optimization Cycles

Weekly optimization is the engine of consistent progress. It is not enough to journal trades daily — the insights must be reviewed, organized, and translated into new rules. Every week is a feedback loop that strengthens what works and eliminates what harms performance.

Small improvements, repeated weekly, create exponential growth.

Purpose of Weekly Optimization

The goal is simple:

Trade better next week than last week.

Weekly optimization allows the scalper to:

- identify patterns,
- remove repeating mistakes,
- double down on winning setups,
- adjust execution rules,
- maintain emotional balance.

Weekly cycles are small, consistent steps that compound over time:

$$1\% \text{ improvement per week} \Rightarrow 67\% \text{ improvement per year.}$$

Step 1: Aggregate All Trades of the Week

At the end of the week, collect:

- trade list,
- screenshots,
- journal notes,
- emotional tags,
- performance metrics.

This creates a complete picture of performance.

Data is the mirror that shows the truth.

Step 2: Group by Setup

Sort trades by setup type:

- EMA pullbacks,
- VWAP rejections,
- liquidity sweeps,
- range fades,
- news spikes.

For each setup, record:

- win rate,
- total R,
- average R,
- number of trades,
- emotional difficulty.

Patterns emerge quickly:

EMA Pullback = +6RRange Fade = -3R

Conclusion:

Trade more pullbacks, stop fading.

Step 3: Group by Session

Sort by:

- London Open,
- NY Open,
- NY Close,
- Asian Session.

Example:

London Open = +5RMidday = -2R

Rule is updated:

No trades during midday.

Step 4: Group by Emotional Tag

Sort trades by emotional state:

$$\text{Calm} = +8\text{RImpatient} = \text{-3RFrustrated} = \text{-4R}$$

Clear conclusion:

Do not trade when emotional.

Emotional leaks destroy accounts faster than bad setups.

Step 5: Identify 3 Successes and 3 Mistakes

Each week, record:

Top Successes:

- Example: perfect EMA pullback at London open.
- Example: waited patiently for confirmation.
- Example: respected stop without hesitation.

Top Mistakes:

- Example: traded during chop.
- Example: entered early without signal.
- Example: overtraded after loss.

Mistake patterns are targeted for removal.

Step 6: Convert Issues into Rules

Every recurring mistake becomes a rule.
Examples:

```
Rule: No trades during low volatility.
Rule: Wait for candle close before entry.
Rule: Never widen stop-loss.
Rule: Maximum 3 trades per session.
```

Rules reduce uncertainty.

Step 7: Create Next-Week Optimization Plan

Based on insights, define:

- what to do more of,
- what to stop doing,
- what to test or refine.

Example plan:

```
Next Week Focus:
- Trade only EMA pullbacks and VWAP rejections
- Avoid Asian session
- Stop after 2 consecutive losses
```

Clarity increases execution quality.

Step 8: Reset Emotional State

Before the new week begins:

- release losses,
- release wins,
- return to neutral.

A neutral mind is a profitable mind.

Summary

Weekly optimization cycles create:

- continuous improvement,
- reduced mistakes,
- stronger edge,
- increased confidence,
- long-term consistency.

Consistency is not magic — it is maintenance.

Success is the result of weekly habits, not occasional brilliance.

17.5 How Elite Scalpers Sustain Consistency

Elite scalpers are not defined by their best trades — they are defined by their stability. They do not rely on emotional intensity, luck, or random bursts of performance. Consistency is built from systems, discipline, and controlled behavior.

> The average trader seeks excitement. The elite trader seeks stability.

Consistency Comes from Systems, Not Predictions

Elite scalpers do not wake up trying to predict the market. Instead, they follow a structured operating system:

1. pre-trade checklist,
2. execution rules,
3. risk protocols,
4. journaling,
5. weekly optimization.

The market decides direction. The trader decides discipline.

$$\text{Consistency} = \text{Rules} + \text{Execution}$$

They Do Less, Not More

The elite do not trade all setups. They specialize.

Example:

- One trader may master EMA pullbacks only.
- Another may master VWAP rejections only.

Elite scalpers build a narrow edge and repeat it.

Focus beats variety.

They Respect Risk Relentlessly

Elite scalpers do not feel strong emotions after a loss. They feel discomfort only if they violate process.

A losing trade that follows rules is a success.

Their risk rules include:

- fixed R-multiple risk per trade,
- daily loss limit,
- no revenge trading,
- stop-loss never widened,
- sessions avoided when emotional.

Control risk and profit takes care of itself.

They Stop When Conditions Are Bad

Elite scalpers do not try to force wins in bad markets.

They stop trading when:

- volatility is dead,
- structure is unclear,
- spreads widen,
- emotions are unstable,
- mistakes accumulate.

This preserves capital and emotional energy.

Not trading is a position.

They Track Emotional State

Performance is not just technical — it is emotional.

Elite scalpers monitor:

- excitement,
- frustration,
- boredom,
- confidence,
- fatigue.

If emotional conditions deteriorate:

Step back. Reset. Return later.

They Optimize Weekly

After every week, elite scalpers perform:

- data review,
- setup ranking,
- mistake elimination,
- rule updates.

Their systems evolve through cycles:

$$v1.0 \rightarrow v2.0 \rightarrow v3.0$$

They Are Bored

Elite scalpers do not find trading exciting. They find it routine.

> Boredom is a sign of discipline. Excitement is a sign of danger.

Consistency is built from executing boring, high-probability decisions every day.

They Maintain Personal Energy

Scalping is mentally intense. Elite traders protect energy:

- quality sleep,
- hydration,
- movement,
- sunlight,
- mental rest.

They avoid overtrading, avoid screens after fatigue, and finish the session early if clarity fades.

They Scale Slowly and Safely

Elite scalpers never increase size during emotional periods. They increase size only when:

- consistency is proven,
- expectancy is positive,

- drawdown is shallow,
- confidence is stable.

Scaling is patient, structured, and data-driven.

Growth comes from stability, not aggression.

Summary

Elite scalpers sustain consistency through:

- systems,
- specialization,
- risk discipline,
- emotional regulation,
- selective trading,
- weekly optimization,
- energy management,
- slow scaling.

Consistency is not a secret. It is a habit.

Part VI

Master Level

Chapter 18

Flow State, Precision & Discipline

Scalping performance reaches its highest level when execution becomes effortless, emotionless, and precise. This chapter explores the psychology of flow state, how traders act without hesitation or fear, and how confidence emerges through repetition, ritual, and experience. We will unlock the processes that lead to peak performance and long-term mastery.

18.1 Building "Zero Emotion Execution"

Elite scalpers do not trade emotionally. Their decisions are not driven by fear, hope, or excitement. They act with a calm and neutral mind, following a process they trust. This state is called *zero emotion execution* — a condition in which judgment is clear and action is precise.

Emotion is expensive. Neutrality is profitable.

Zero Emotion Does Not Mean Zero Feeling

Zero emotion execution does not mean the trader becomes a robot. It means:

- emotions are acknowledged,
- but they do not influence decisions.

Fear may appear — but it does not decide. Excitement may arise — but it does not dictate action.

Feelings are information. Execution is logic.

Three Pillars of Zero Emotion Execution

1. System Trust A trader must trust their system completely. Trust comes from:

- backtesting,
- journaling,
- statistics,
- repeated execution.

When confidence exists in the plan:

There is no need for emotion.

2. Pre-Defined Decisions All major decisions are made *before* entering the trade:

- setup,
- entry,
- stop loss,
- target,
- risk per trade,
- exit conditions.

Nothing is improvised afterward.

Unplanned decisions invite emotion.

3. Acceptance of Loss Emotion is strongest when loss is feared. Elite scalpers begin each trade with acceptance:

I may lose. That is fine.

Loss becomes a cost of doing business, not a personal failure.

Losses are tuition. Knowledge is the return on investment.

Execution Ritual

85% of execution quality comes from a ritual:

1. Breathe deeply and slowly.
2. Confirm checklist items.
3. Visualize the trade playing out.
4. Place order.
5. Accept outcome.

This ritual anchors the mind.

Reducing Emotional Noise

Several practical techniques reduce emotional interference:

- position size small enough to feel nothing,
- predefined stop-loss,
- no moving stops after entry,
- no "hope" or "fear" decisions,
- maximum number of trades per session.

Neutrality is achieved through boundaries.

When Emotion Arises

Emotion is not the enemy — emotional reaction is.
If anxiety or excitement spikes:

Step away from the screen.

A short break — breathing, stretching, hydration — resets the nervous system.

The brain trades better when the body is calm.

The Role of Discipline

Zero emotion execution is indistinguishable from discipline.

Discipline means:

- follow plan,
- avoid randomness,
- respect stops,
- trade only valid setups,
- stop when tired.

Discipline creates neutrality.

Discipline removes emotion.

The Paradox of Peak Performance

The more emotionally neutral a trader becomes, the better their performance — and the less trading feels like trading.

Elite scalpers often report:

- It feels boring.
- There is no drama.
- It is just repetition.

This is the essence of mastery.

> When trading feels exciting, something is wrong. When trading feels boring, something is right.

Summary

Zero emotion execution is built from:

- trust in the system,
- predefined decisions,
- acceptance of loss,
- rituals that anchor focus,
- small position sizing,
- consistent discipline.

Emotion may exist. Reaction does not.

Mastery is calm. Precision is calm. Profit is calm.

18.2 Speed Without Fear or Anxiety

Scalping demands rapid execution. Decisions are made in seconds — sometimes less. But speed must not be emotional. Speed must be mechanical, confident, and calm.

> Speed is dangerous only when it is emotional. Speed is profitable when it is controlled.

Speed Comes from Preparation, Not Impulse

Fast execution is not "thinking quickly." It is having decisions already made before price reaches the trigger.

Speed is the product of:

- clear rules,
- predefined setups,
- specific entry conditions,
- tight execution rituals.

A prepared trader reacts fast.An unprepared trader reacts emotionally.

Fear and Anxiety Come from Uncertainty

Most fear comes from one root cause:

Not knowing what to do.

When the trader does not know:

- where to enter,
- where to exit,
- how much to risk,
- what invalidates the setup,

Their brain fills the gap with fear.
Speed becomes panic.

Speed Becomes Calm When Rules Exist

When the rules are clear:

If A happens, do B.

There is no fear, because there is no uncertainty.
Speed becomes:

- automatic,
- predictable,
- repeatable.

Speed comes from clarity.

Micro-Decisions, Macro-Mastery

A scalper makes hundreds of micro-decisions:

- enter,
- exit,
- move stop,
- take profit,
- avoid chop.

These decisions cannot be made consciously one by one.
They must be trained into habit.

Fast decisions are not fast thinking.Fast decisions are trained responses.

Drills: Training the Brain for Speed

Like athletes, scalpers train off-market.
Practical drills:

1. replay charts at 2x speed,
2. practice one setup only,
3. one-click execution hotkeys,
4. 20-30 simulated trades per night.

Repetition removes hesitation.

Hesitation is fear. Repetition creates confidence.

Position Size Reduces Fear

Fear is proportional to risk.
If a trader risks too much:

Every tick feels emotional.

The solution is counterintuitive:

Trade smaller.

Smaller positions:

- reduce emotional pressure,
- increase clarity,
- improve execution speed,
- create calm.

Small size = fast mind.

Breathing and Body State

The nervous system influences execution. Two breaths before execution can change everything:

1. inhale slowly,
2. exhale twice as long.

This shifts the body into parasympathetic mode:

Calm body = clear decisions.

The Paradox of Speed

Speed is not a goal. Speed is a result.
It emerges naturally when:

- the system is clear,
- the mind is calm,
- the risk is controlled,
- the setup is familiar.

Speed follows preparation.Speed does not replace it.

Summary

Speed without fear or anxiety is built from:

- predefined rules,
- clarity of setup,
- small position size,
- breathing ritual,
- practice and replay,
- habit formation.

> Speed is a symptom of mastery. Fear is a symptom of uncertainty.

18.3 Confidence Rituals

Confidence in trading is not a feeling — it is a consequence of preparation, routine, and past evidence. Elite scalpers do not rely on motivation or hype. They develop rituals that anchor their mind, stabilize their emotions, and prepare them for execution.

> Confidence is not luck. Confidence is a process.

The Purpose of Rituals

Rituals serve two essential functions:

1. They remove uncertainty.
2. They create psychological safety.

When a trader has a routine, the mind relaxes:

I know what to do next.

This reduces fear, hesitation, and impulsive behavior.

Pre-Trade Ritual Example

Before the first trade, a simple ritual may include:

1. Stretch and breathe.
2. Review levels and setups.

3. Recite risk rules.
4. Visualize one high-quality trade.

This creates clarity and intention.

A mind with intention makes cleaner decisions.

Physical Anchors

The body influences the mind.
Elite scalpers often:

- sit upright,
- keep feet grounded,
- breathe slowly,
- relax shoulders.

These physical anchors signal:

I am calm. I am ready.

Verbal Anchors

Short statements reinforce neutral focus.
Examples:

- "Trade the plan, not the emotion."
- "One setup at a time."
- "Losses are tuition."

These phrases are repeated internally before execution.

Words direct attention. Attention directs action.

Process Anchors

Some traders anchor confidence to specific actions:

- checking checklist,
- marking levels,
- rehearing setups verbally.

When these steps are completed, readiness increases.
The brain knows:

I have done this. I can do this.

Visualization

A powerful ritual is mental rehearsal.

The scalper imagines:

- seeing the setup,
- taking the entry,
- staying calm during pullback,
- closing trade with discipline.

Visualization primes the nervous system.
Athletes use it. Pilots use it. Elite traders use it.

The brain cannot distinguish rehearsal from reality.

Win Ritual vs. Loss Ritual

Confidence rituals must handle both outcomes.

Win Ritual:

1. Breathe.
2. Record trade.
3. Do not celebrate.

Loss Ritual:

1. Breathe.
2. Record trade.
3. Do not punish.

The emotional message:

Wins and losses are equal. Both are information.

End-of-Day Ritual

At session close:

- review screenshots,
- review emotions,
- write one improvement,
- mentally release the day.

This prevents emotional carryover.

Weekly Ritual

At end of week:

- summarize setups,
- update rules,
- plan next week.

Confidence builds as patterns repeat.

Why Rituals Work

Rituals reduce cognitive load.
The brain does not need to decide:

What should I do?

It already knows.
This creates:

- faster execution,
- less hesitation,
- emotional neutrality,
- increased confidence.

Summary

Confidence rituals are not magic. They are systems that create stability.
They include:

- physical anchors,
- verbal anchors,
- process anchors,
- visualization,
- clear win/loss protocol,
- daily and weekly review cycles.

> Confidence is not the absence of fear. Confidence is acting correctly despite fear.

18.4 Developing Instinct Through Experience

Scalping is a fast environment. There is no time for deep analysis during execution. Top traders often appear to act instinctively, as if they simply "feel" the right moment to enter or exit. But instinct is not mystical — it is learned.

Instinct is experience compressed into intuition.

Instinct Is a Result of Pattern Recognition

The human brain is excellent at recognizing patterns after enough exposure. When a trader has seen thousands of price movements, the brain begins to anticipate outcomes automatically.

You do not think. You recognize.

Instinct emerges when:

- setups are repeated hundreds of times,
- patterns are reinforced through journaling,
- mistakes are corrected through review,
- emotional interference is reduced.

Repetition Builds Neural Pathways

Neuroplasticity is real.

Each repeated setup strengthens neural circuits:

See pattern → Execute → Learn

Repetition transforms effort into ease.

The goal is:

Execution without internal debate.

Experience Creates Speed

New traders think too much:

- Is this a pullback?
- Should I enter?
- Will it fail?

Experienced traders simply act.
Speed comes from:

- pre-defined rules,
- pattern familiarity,
- emotional neutrality.

Speed is a symptom of mastery.

Quality of Screen Time Matters

Not all practice is equal.

- Mindless chart watching is not learning.
- High-focus replay produces much more growth.

The most effective practice routines:

- replay charts at high speed,
- take simulated trades,
- annotate levels and reactions,
- save examples.

This accelerates recognition.

Instinct Is Evidence-Based

Intuition is not guessing.
It is:

- subconscious pattern matching,
- based on evidence,
- refined through journaling,
- validated through statistics.

If a trader has seen 200 similar setups, instinct tells them:

This is a good one.

Mistakes Are Training Signals

Mistakes are not failures — they are feedback.

Each mistake teaches:

- where patterns break,
- where traps appear,
- what emotional impulses arise,
- how to avoid them next time.

$$\text{Experience} = \text{mistakes} + \text{analysis}.$$

Screen Time with Intent

Elite traders improve because they observe price with purpose:

- What is structure?
- Where is liquidity?
- What are the traps?
- Where is momentum?

Intentional observation accelerates instinct.

Journaling Converts Experience Into Intelligence

Without journaling, experience is forgotten. With journaling, experience becomes wisdom.

The journal captures:

- setups,
- conditions,
- outcomes,
- emotions,
- mistakes,
- improvements.

This process creates:

Experience with memory.

Flow Emerges from Familiarity

When intuition is developed:

- actions become smooth,
- decisions become fast,
- hesitation disappears.

This is flow state:

The trader is fully present, without thought.

Summary

Instinct is not magic. It is the result of:

- repetition,
- recognition,
- review,
- refinement,
- emotional neutrality.

$$\text{Experience} \rightarrow \text{Instinct} \rightarrow \text{Precision}$$

> You do not develop instinct by thinking. You develop instinct by experiencing.

18.5 Mastery Through Repetition

Scalping is a performance skill. Like martial arts, music, or professional sports, mastery comes only from repetition. The more a trader practices a setup, the more automatic it becomes. At elite levels, execution appears effortless — because it has been repeated hundreds of times.

> Repetition creates familiarity. Familiarity creates confidence. Confidence creates mastery.

The Brain Learns Through Pattern Exposure

Every trade teaches the brain what price does:

- at pullbacks,
- at breakouts,
- in ranges,
- during news,
- at liquidity levels.

These repeated exposures form internal models.

The more you see it, the better you recognize it.

Over time, the brain moves from:

Conscious effort $\rightarrow$ Automatic instinct

This transition is the foundation of mastery.

Narrow Focus Beats Broad Effort

Many beginners try to learn everything:

- every indicator,
- every strategy,
- every setup.

Elite traders do the opposite:

They specialize.

A professional boxer practices one punch thousands of times. A professional scalper practices one setup thousands of times.

Depth beats variety.

Repetition Builds Flow State

Flow state — fast, effortless execution — is a byproduct of repetition.

Repetition creates:

- reduced cognitive load,
- automatic responses,
- instant pattern recognition.

When the brain does not need to think, the trader moves with the market naturally.

Correct Repetition Matters

Not all repetition is useful.

Correct repetition means:

- trade the same setup,
- under the same conditions,
- with the same rules,
- analyze the same metrics.

This creates a refined skill, not a random habit.

Practice must be consistent to produce consistency.

Drills to Build Mastery

Effective drills for scalpers include:

1. replay charts at maximum speed,
2. execute simulated entries and exits,
3. screenshot winning and losing setups,
4. categorize patterns,
5. re-read journal notes weekly.

With time, execution becomes automatic.

The Emotional Impact of Repetition

Repetition does not only train the eyes — it trains the nervous system.

As setups repeat:

- fear decreases,
- confidence rises,
- anxiety disappears,
- neutrality increases.

Emotions calm because the outcome is familiar.

You have seen this before.

Repetition Compounds Over Time

Mastery is not created in a week. It accumulates over months of repetition.

$$1\% improvement per day \rightarrow exponential growth$$

Progress is invisible at first, then undeniable later.

> At first you cannot see the improvement. Then you cannot miss it.

Mastery is Boring

Repetition is not exciting. It is repetitive, predictable, and sometimes dull.

This is a feature, not a flaw.

Elite traders embrace boredom:

$$\text{Boring trading} = \text{profitable trading}$$

Excitement leads to mistakes. Boredom leads to discipline.

Summary

Mastery is a result of:

- repetition,
- specialization,
- pattern recognition,
- emotional neutrality,
- flow state,
- long-term consistency.

Do one thing 1,000 times. Not 1,000 things once.

> Repetition is the mother of mastery.

Chapter 19

The Future of Scalping

Markets evolve. Scalping evolves with them. The next decade will be shaped by artificial intelligence, algorithmic execution, on-chain liquidity, and automation. This chapter explores how the edge of the future will be won: what machines are mastering, what humans still do best, and where the greatest opportunities will emerge.

19.1 AI and Algorithmic Scalping

Artificial intelligence is changing the microstructure of markets. Where scalpers once relied on intuition, today machines operate at microsecond speeds, interpreting order flow, liquidity, and volatility with mathematical precision. AI scalping is not simply faster — it is different. It analyzes more data, reacts instantly, and adapts continuously.

The edge of tomorrow is algorithmic.

What AI Does Better Than Humans

AI excels at tasks that require:

- pattern recognition across large datasets,
- ultra-fast reaction to market conditions,
- continuous optimization,
- emotion-free execution.

These strengths create advantages:

1. microsecond order placement,
2. instant cancellation of wrong trades,

3. statistical arbitrage on tiny spreads,
4. 24/7 monitoring of multiple instruments.

AI removes hesitation, fatigue, and fear.

How AI Scalping Works

An AI scalping engine typically contains:

1. a pattern detection model,
2. a prediction module,
3. an execution engine,
4. a risk manager,
5. continuous learning loops.

The system watches markets tick-by-tick.
When a condition matches its model:

$$\text{Signal detected} \rightarrow \text{Order sent} \rightarrow \text{Risk enforced}$$

All in milliseconds.

Deep Learning on Price Streams

Modern AI does not analyze candlestick images. It analyzes *streams of microstructure data*:

- order book snapshots,
- trade prints,
- spread changes,
- volume bursts,
- liquidity shifts.

These signals are too fast for human reaction. AI thrives on them.

AI scalps the invisible layers of price.

Adaptive Decision Making

Unlike static strategies, AI algorithms adapt.
They continuously:

- measure performance,
- remove losing patterns,
- reinforce profitable patterns,
- adjust to volatility.

This makes them robust in shifting conditions.

AI improves with time. Humans tire.

Execution Advantages

Execution matters as much as logic.
AI offers:

- sub-millisecond order routing,
- hidden liquidity access,
- smart spread crossing,
- iceberg order detection,
- slippage control.

These micro-edges compound.

$$0.1\% edge \times thousandsoftrades = majorprofit$$

Where AI Is Already Dominant

AI dominates in areas where speed and repetition are key:

- index scalping,
- futures scalping,
- crypto arbitrage,
- market making,
- high-frequency trading (HFT).

In many markets, the counterparty is already a machine.

When you scalp, you often trade against algorithms.

What Humans Still Do Better

Humans outperform machines in:

- intuition during regime change,
- interpreting macro news,
- avoiding chaos after data releases,
- adapting to new conditions instantly.

AI is powerful, but narrow.
Humans still excel at:

Non-linear judgment.

AI Plus Human = Superior Edge

The future is not AI vs human.
The future is:

$$\text{AI} + \text{Human}$$

Humans provide:

- context,
- discretion,
- emotional control,
- risk supervision,
- system design.

AI provides:

- speed,
- precision,
- repetition,
- endurance,
- pattern detection.

Together:

$$\text{Judgment} + \text{Automation} = \text{Dominant Competitor}$$

The Rise of Retail AI Scalping

Retail traders now have access to:

- low-latency APIs,
- cloud execution engines,
- Python libraries,
- machine learning frameworks,
- on-chain liquidity data.

This closes the gap with institutional players.

$$The future belongs to the trader who learns technology.$$

Summary

AI and algorithmic scalping bring:

- adaptive execution,
- microsecond speed,
- emotion-free decisions,
- continuous optimization.

Humans bring:

- intuition,
- discretion,
- risk intelligence,
- creativity.

Humans decide the edge. AI executes the edge.

19.2 On-chain Liquidity (Crypto Order Flow)

Cryptocurrency markets are radically different from traditional markets because they are *transparent.* Every transaction, every limit order, every liquidation, and every liquidity pool movement is recorded publicly on-chain. This transparency creates a new form of scalping edge: on-chain order flow.

> On-chain data allows traders to see what exchanges, whales, and algorithms are doing — in real time.

What Is On-Chain Liquidity?

On-chain liquidity refers to the actual capital sitting inside:

- decentralized exchanges (DEX),
- automated market makers (AMM),
- liquidity pools,
- smart contracts.

Instead of hidden books, liquidity is openly visible.
This means:

Scalpers can see where the money is.

Decentralized Order Flow

In centralized markets, order flow is private. In crypto, order flow is public — anyone can observe:

- whale wallets,
- position sizes,
- margin changes,
- liquidations,
- funding rate spikes.

Tools such as:

- Glassnode,
- Nansen,
- Arkham,
- Whale Alerts,
- DexTools

give scalpers direct visibility.

Information asymmetry decreases.

Liquidity Pools Drive Price

On-chain liquidity behaves differently from traditional order books.

In AMM systems:

Price changes as liquidity moves.

When liquidity is added to a pool, price may stabilize. When liquidity is removed, volatility can spike.

This is a scalping signal.

Liquidations Create Scalping Opportunities

Crypto derivatives markets use leverage. When price moves against leveraged traders, liquidations happen:

Forced selling or forced buying.

This creates:

- violent spikes,
- rapid reversals,
- high-momentum setups.

Scalpers use liquidation maps to anticipate volatility bursts.

Whale Activity Matters

On-chain data reveals:

- when whales enter,
- when whales exit,
- which tokens they accumulate,
- which pools they drain.

Large wallets often move price.

A simple rule emerges:

Follow the whales.

DEX Order Flow vs CEX Order Flow

Both environments matter:

- Centralized exchanges (CEX) show order book and depth.
- Decentralized exchanges (DEX) show on-chain liquidity movement.

Scalpers use both:

CEX for microstructure, DEX for liquidity.

Blockchain as a Market Tape

In traditional markets, scalpers watch Level 2 data. In crypto, the blockchain itself becomes the tape:

- transactions,
- swaps,
- LP movements,
- protocol activity,
- MEV bots.

This provides direct insight into intention.

The market is not guessing — it is watching behavior.

Liquidity Traps

On-chain analysis reveals traps:

- fake liquidity added,
- price manipulated upward,
- retail enters,
- liquidity removed,
- price collapses.

These traps are engineered to hunt stop-losses.
Recognizing them creates scalping opportunity.

Cross-Exchange Arbitrage

Because liquidity is fragmented, price differences appear between:

- Binance,
- OKX,
- Bybit,
- DEX pools.

Bots exploit these differences in milliseconds. Scalpers can ride their wake.

Arbitrage is a byproduct of liquidity fragmentation.

Future is On-Chain

As regulation increases and transparency becomes normal:

More liquidity will move on-chain.

Scalpers who understand blockchain fundamentals will have an edge over those who do not.

Summary

On-chain liquidity provides:

- full transparency,
- liquidation signals,
- whale tracking,
- liquidity pool analysis,
- arbitrage opportunities.

This is a new frontier in scalping.

> In crypto, the truth is on-chain. And the traders who read it gain the advantage.

19.3 MEV Bots and Automation Risks

The rise of decentralized finance (DeFi) has created a new class of automated scalpers: *MEV bots.* MEV stands for "Miner / Maximal Extractable Value" — the profit extracted by reordering, inserting, or censoring transactions inside a block.

> MEV bots do not trade price — they trade the ordering of transactions.

They operate invisibly between the trader and the blockchain, extracting value without the trader realizing it.

How MEV Bots Work

When a trader submits a transaction:

1. The transaction enters the mempool.
2. MEV bots scan the mempool instantly.
3. Bots find profitable opportunities:
   - frontrunning,
   - sandwich attacks,
   - backrunning,
   - liquidation sniping.
4. Bots submit custom transactions to capture profit.

They exploit transaction timing, not market direction.

MEV Strategies That Impact Scalpers

The three most common MEV strategies:

1. Frontrunning The bot sees your trade and enters first at a better price.

2. Sandwich Attack

1. Bot buys before you.
2. Your order pushes price up.
3. Bot sells after you at a higher price.

You pay the cost — the bot takes the profit.

3. Backrunning Bots attach their trade immediately after a profitable transaction.

They harvest residual value.

Liquidation Sniping

In leveraged markets, when a liquidation is about to occur:

- bots detect the margin breach,
- trigger liquidation,
- capture the collateral,
- resell for instant profit.

This can cause:

sudden wicks, volatility spikes, forced exits.

Why MEV Bots Matter for Scalpers

Scalpers often operate in:

- low timeframe,
- high volatility,
- tight spreads,
- precise entries.

MEV bots disrupt these conditions.
They can:

- worsen entry,
- increase slippage,
- cause stop hunts,
- create fake volume,
- trigger psychological damage.

A scalper's enemy is not always another human — it may be a bot.

Automation Risks Beyond MEV

Other automation dangers include:

- trading bots misfiring during news,
- API delays,
- execution errors,
- account liquidation,
- infinite order loops.

A system that works in calm markets may fail in chaos.

Automation without supervision is dangerous.

Latency and Network Risks

Scalping bots depend on:

- network speed,
- mempool visibility,
- gas fee optimization.

High gas spikes can:

- delay execution,
- cause missed trades,
- trigger unintended fills.

Speed is critical. Latency is fatal.

MEV-Protected Solutions

To reduce MEV exposure, traders can use:

- private relays (Flashbots),
- gas auctions,
- anti-MEV DEX routers,
- order batching,
- dark pools.

These tools minimize bot interference.

Not all transactions must go through the public mempool.

Human vs Machine

MEV bots are powerful, but limited.

Humans still excel at:

- macro interpretation,
- context awareness,
- adapting to regime change,
- stepping away when conditions are bad.

The strongest combination is:

$$\text{Human discretion} + \text{automated execution}$$

Summary

MEV bots introduce:

- frontrunning,
- sandwich attacks,
- liquidation sniping,
- slippage,
- psychological damage.

The risks can be mitigated through:

- private relays,
- anti-MEV routing,
- careful automation,
- active supervision.

> Automation creates speed. Supervision creates safety.

19.4 Human vs Machine Evolution

The future of scalping is not a conflict between humans and machines. It is a process of co-evolution. Machines are rapidly improving at tasks involving speed, pattern recognition, and execution. Humans remain superior at judgment, adaptability, and understanding market context.

> The winner is not the human or the machine — but the trader who combines both.

Machines Will Dominate Repetition

Anything that is:

- repetitive,
- rules-based,
- extremely fast,
- data-heavy,
- unemotional,

will increasingly be handled by algorithms.
Machines will continue to dominate:

- high-frequency scalping,
- spread capture,
- arbitrage,
- market making,
- execution routing.

If a task is mechanical, a machine will outperform.

Humans Will Dominate Adaptation

Machines struggle when conditions change suddenly.
Humans excel at:

- context,
- intuition,
- ambiguity,
- new information,
- unusual volatility,
- rare events.

Examples:

- unexpected news,
- macro announcements,

- geopolitical shocks,
- regulatory changes.

In these scenarios, machines may fail, while humans adjust instantly.

If conditions are new, humans outperform.

Division of Responsibility

The future trader will divide roles:

Machines:

- scan markets,
- detect patterns,
- place orders,
- enforce risk,
- operate 24/7.

Humans:

- define strategy,
- choose parameters,
- supervise bots,
- cancel trades when necessary,
- manage capital.

This partnership creates an edge greater than either alone.

Decision Hierarchy

A practical framework:

$$\text{Human decides} \rightarrow \text{Machine executes}$$

1. Human chooses:
    - assets,
    - conditions,
    - strategies,
    - risk limits.

2. Machine performs:
    - entry,
    - exit,
    - sizing,
    - monitoring.

Humans think. Machines act.

Emotional Intelligence vs Computational Intelligence

Humans bring emotional intelligence:

- restraint,
- awareness,
- judgment,
- experience.

Machines bring computational intelligence:

- speed,
- precision,
- endurance,
- repetition.

Together they create:

$$\text{Stability} + \text{Efficiency}$$

When Machines Fail

Machines struggle when:

- market regimes shift,
- liquidity disappears,
- spreads explode,
- new patterns emerge,
- external shocks occur.

The trader must override automation.

Human control is a safety valve.

When Humans Fail

Humans struggle when:

- emotions take control,
- impulsive trades appear,
- boredom creates overtrading,
- fatigue reduces judgment.

The machine must enforce:

- risk limits,
- daily stops,
- trade filters,
- timeouts.

Machines protect humans from themselves.

The Evolutionary Path

Today:

- most retail traders are manual,
- some use indicators,
- few use automation,
- very few use AI.

The future:

- most traders will use semi-automation,
- many will supervise bots,
- only experts will remain fully manual.

The edge will belong to the hybrid trader.

Summary

Humans and machines evolve together.

Humans excel at:

- judgment,
- intuition,
- adaptation.

Machines excel at:

- speed,
- repetition,
- execution.

A trader who combines both becomes unstoppable.

Humans decide the strategy. Machines execute the strategy. The future belongs to the hybrid.

19.5 Major Future Opportunities

The landscape of scalping is expanding. New markets, new technologies, and new forms of liquidity are emerging. The trader who understands these shifts will find opportunities that did not exist a few years ago. This section highlights the most promising domains for the next decade.

The future edge belongs to those who see change early.

On-Chain Order Flow and Smart Contracts

As more trading migrates to decentralized finance, liquidity becomes visible on-chain. This transparency allows scalpers to read:

- liquidity pool behavior,
- whale wallet movements,
- liquidation clusters,
- funding rate shifts,
- arbitrage opportunities.

Unlike traditional markets, where order flow is hidden:

Crypto reveals everything.

This creates opportunity for:

- mempool sniping,
- liquidity chasing,
- volatility harvesting.

AI-Driven Execution Engines

Artificial intelligence systems will increasingly:

- detect patterns,
- place orders,
- manage risk,
- adapt automatically.

Already, AI frameworks are used to:

- classify price patterns,
- predict short-term momentum,
- generate execution signals,
- optimize entries and exits.

Future opportunity:

AI operating the strategy, human supervising the risk.

Microstructure Arbitrage

Microstructure edges include:

- spread capture,
- rebate arbitrage,
- latency arbitrage,
- cross-exchange pricing differences.

As exchanges increase in number, fragmentation grows:

More fragmentation = more arbitrage.

Market-Making as a Strategy

Market-making used to be institutional only. Today, crypto and futures allow smaller players to:

- place bids and offers,
- collect spread,
- earn funding,
- avoid directional risk.

This creates income without predicting direction.

$$\text{Income from liquidity, not direction.}$$

Scalping Across Asset Classes

The future is multi-market.

New instruments suitable for scalping:

- volatility indices (VIX, VIX derivatives),
- crypto perpetual futures,
- tokenized forex markets,
- synthetic stock contracts,
- data-based prediction markets.

Volatility will not disappear — it will migrate.

Regime-Based Automation

Markets move through regimes:

- trending,
- ranging,
- volatile,
- illiquid.

Future systems will adapt:

$$\text{Strategy} = \text{automatic based on regime.}$$

Instead of a single strategy:

- the machine detects regime,
- activates correct strategy,
- deactivates when edge disappears.

Retail Access to Institutional Tools

Access to tools once reserved for banks is expanding:

- real-time order flow,
- footprint charts,
- on-chain dashboards,
- execution APIs,
- cloud-based backtesting.

Retail traders will operate with near-institutional technology:

The barrier is now education, not access.

The Rise of Hybrid Traders

The future elite is not purely manual or purely algorithmic.

Hybrid traders outperform both.

They combine:

- human discretion,
- automated execution,
- machine pattern detection,
- risk intelligence.

This hybrid approach reduces weaknesses on both sides.

Global, 24/7 Markets

Traditional markets have limited sessions. Crypto, synthetic indices, and global futures trade 24/7.

This enables:

- multiple time zone opportunities,
- continuous volatility harvesting,
- automated systems running nonstop.

Markets never sleep — systems must evolve.

Summary

Major future opportunities emerge from:

- on-chain liquidity and transparency,
- AI-driven scalping engines,
- microstructure arbitrage,
- market-making and liquidity income,
- regime-based strategy switching,
- hybrid human-machine traders,
- global, 24/7 markets.

The future belongs to prepared traders — those who combine technology with human skill.

Chapter 20

Lifelong Scalping Evolution

Scalping is not a short-term activity. It is a lifelong craft that evolves through stages of skill, maturity, and financial growth. This chapter shows how a trader progresses from beginner to professional, how to grow a small account safely, and how to transform short-term scalping profits into long-term investment wealth. The goal is not only fast trading — but a hybrid identity: scalper, investor, and disciplined operator with a multi-year roadmap to mastery.

20.1 Skill Progression: Beginner → Intermediate → Advanced → Pro

The Scalpers Playbook is not achieved in a single leap. It evolves through clearly defined stages, each with its own challenges, mindset, and milestones. Understanding this progression prevents frustration and sets realistic expectations.

> Growth in trading is not linear. It is layered. Each layer becomes the foundation for the next.

Stage 1: Beginner — Learning the Basics

At the beginner stage, everything is new:

- charts,
- indicators,
- platforms,
- entries and exits,
- emotions.

Core goals at this stage:

1. Learn how price moves.
2. Understand basic setups.
3. Build a routine.
4. Stop blowing accounts.

Typical mistakes:

- overtrading,
- revenge trading,
- moving stops,
- no journaling.

Success is defined simply:

Beginner goal: survive.

Stage 2: Intermediate — Building Systems

The intermediate trader begins to create structure:

- one or two setups,
- fixed stop-loss,
- fixed position size,
- daily routine,
- journal entries.

Key focus:

$$\text{System} > \text{Emotional decisions}$$

This stage often produces:

- small profits,
- small losses,
- some consistency.

The trader begins to understand:

Trading is a business, not entertainment.

Stage 3: Advanced — Refining Edge Through Data

The advanced trader no longer experiments randomly.

They:

- track statistics,
- optimize entries,
- remove bad setups,
- increase size slowly.

The edge becomes measurable:

$$\text{Expectancy} = (\text{Win Rate} \times \text{Average Win}) - (\text{Loss Rate} \times \text{Average Loss})$$

They master:

- risk,
- discipline,
- setup accuracy,
- emotional control.

Trading becomes calm.

Advanced traders look boring. Their results do not.

Stage 4: Pro — Consistency and Income

A professional scalper does not try to be perfect. They try to be consistent.

A pro:

- trades only the best setups,
- has monthly and yearly performance,
- treats trading as a business,
- scales slowly and safely,
- protects capital aggressively.

At this stage:

Your job is not to trade every day — your job is to trade well.

Pros often have multiple income layers:

- scalping income,
- swing/investment account,
- automated systems,
- consulting or prop roles.

The Psychological Shift

Each stage has a psychological transformation:

Beginner: excitement, confusion

Intermediate: structure, discipline

Advanced: calm confidence

Pro: strategic focus, business thinking

As skill increases, emotion decreases.

Timeframe of Evolution

The timeline depends on effort, feedback, and emotional maturity.
Typical ranges:

- Beginner: 0–6 months
- Intermediate: 6–18 months
- Advanced: 18–36 months
- Pro: 3–7 years

Mastery is slow. But it is worth it.

Common Failure Points

Many traders quit during transitions:

- Beginner → Intermediate: frustration from losses
- Intermediate → Advanced: boredom, lack of novelty
- Advanced → Pro: fear of scaling

Knowing these transitions helps you persist.

The path is hard. The reward is freedom.

Summary

Skill progression requires:

- education,
- repetition,
- emotional regulation,
- journaling,
- system refinement,
- time.

Beginner: survive.
Intermediate: structure.
Advanced: optimize.
Pro: scale and sustain.

The Scalpers Playbook is a journey — not a destination.

20.2 Growing a Small Account Safely and Systematically

Many traders begin with a small account and dream of turning it into something meaningful. This is possible — but only with strict risk discipline and a systematic growth plan. The goal is not to "flip" the account with reckless leverage, but to *compound* it intelligently over months and years.

> Small accounts are not a problem. Reckless behavior with small accounts is.

The Reality of Small Accounts

A small account has constraints:

- limited margin,
- higher psychological pressure per loss,
- temptation to use excessive leverage,
- desire for fast growth.

The wrong mindset is:

"I will double this in a week."

The right mindset is:

"I will grow this steadily without blowing it up."

Core Principles for Growing a Small Account

1. Capital Preservation First Rule:

Do not lose the account.

Before thinking about profit, the trader must avoid:

- large drawdowns,
- margin calls,
- account resets,
- emotional tilt.

2. Fixed Fractional Risk Risk per trade must be:

$$0.25\% \text{ to } 1\% \text{ of account balance}$$

For very small accounts, 1–2% is acceptable if discipline is strong. More than this increases the risk of ruin.

3. No "All-In" Behavior Never risk a large portion of capital on a single idea.

One trade should never decide your future.

The Mathematics of Compounding

If a trader can average:

$$2R \text{ to } 4R \text{ per week at } 1\% \text{ risk,}$$

then:

- weekly growth: 2–4%,
- monthly growth (approx): 8–16%,
- yearly compounded growth: very large.

Example:
Even 5% monthly growth compounded:

$$(1.05)^{12} \approx 1.80$$

That is:

80% growth in one year — without crazy risk.

Micro-Risk Scaling Model

A safe progression model:

1. Start with 0.5–1.0% risk per trade.
2. Maintain risk until:
   - at least 3 profitable months in a row, and
   - maximum drawdown stays within predefined limits.
3. Then, optionally increase risk slightly (e.g. from 0.5% to 0.75%, or 1% to 1.25%).

Risk increases only after proven consistency.

Account Milestone Scaling

Instead of randomly increasing lot size, use account milestones.
Example:

- From \$500 to \$750: risk 1% per trade.
- From \$750 to \$1,000: risk 0.75–1.0% per trade (same percent, more dollars).
- From \$1,000 to \$2,000: consider reducing risk to protect gains if psychology is not stable.

The key:

Growth must not break your psychology.

Instrument Selection for Small Accounts

Not all instruments are suitable for small accounts.
Prefer:

- markets with:
  - tight spreads,
  - low commissions,
  - micro-contracts or small position sizing,
  - low margin requirements.

Examples:

- micro futures (e.g. MES, MNQ),
- forex pairs with micro lots,
- crypto with fractional position sizing,
- CFDs with adjustable lot size (if accessible and regulated).

Avoid:

- instruments with huge tick value,
- instruments needing massive stops,
- exotic pairs with wide spreads.

Leverage: Tool or Time Bomb

Leverage is not evil — misuse is.
For small accounts:

- use leverage to gain *flexible sizing*,
- not to overexpose.

Rule:

Leverage is for precision sizing, not gambling size.

Reducing Psychological Pressure

Small accounts feel fragile.

To reduce pressure:

- treat money as risk units (R), not dollars,
- use very small size at first,
- frame early phase as "training capital",
- avoid checking P&L during trades.

Your job is to execute. The math takes care of itself.

Reinvesting Profits vs Withdrawing

In early stages:

- focus on compounding,
- withdraw only if necessary,
- re-invest profits to slowly increase R (in dollar terms).

Later:

- set a rule to withdraw a portion periodically (e.g. 25–50% of monthly profit),
- move withdrawals into long-term investments.

Scalping funds the future. Investing secures it.

Behavior That Destroys Small Accounts

Avoid:

- revenge trading after losses,
- doubling risk to "make it back,"
- martingale strategies,
- trading during emotional stress,
- violating daily loss limits.

One rule:

If you hit -2R or -3R in a day — stop.

Example Growth Path (Conceptual)

Suppose:

- Start: \$500 account.
- Risk: 1% per trade = \$5 per R.
- Average: $+3R$ per week = +\$15/week ($\approx$ 3%).

In 12 weeks:

$$\text{Account} \approx \$500 \times (1.03)^{12} \approx \$711$$

In 52 weeks at 3% per week (theoretically):

$$\$500 \times (1.03)^{52} \approx \$2{,}300+$$

Real results vary, but the principle is:

Small, consistent growth beats explosive risk.

Summary

Growing a small account safely and systematically requires:

- capital preservation first,
- fixed fractional risk per trade,
- realistic compounding expectations,
- milestone-based scaling,
- instrument selection that fits account size,
- controlled use of leverage,
- strict emotional discipline.

You do not need a big account to trade professionally. You need a professional process to grow any account.

20.3 Using Scalping Profits to Build Long-Term Investment Wealth

Scalping generates short-term cash flow. But the real objective is not fast income — it is long-term wealth. The most successful traders do not rely on scalping forever. They use scalping profits as fuel for building durable financial assets.

Scalping is a cash machine. Investing is a wealth machine.

Why Scalping Alone Is Not Enough

Scalping offers:

- high liquidity,
- rapid returns,
- low overnight risk.

However, scalping is:

- mentally intense,
- time-dependent,
- limited by personal energy.

If a trader relies only on scalping, they remain trapped in an endless cycle:

$$\text{Trade} \rightarrow \text{Earn} \rightarrow \text{Trade} \rightarrow \text{Earn}$$

Wealth comes from breaking that cycle.

Convert Income Into Assets

The key principle:

Do not consume trading profits. Convert them into investments.

Use scalping income to buy:

- equities,
- index ETFs,
- gold,
- real estate,
- digital assets,
- bonds,
- business stakes,
- automation systems.

These assets work for you while you sleep.

Short-term trading funds long-term ownership.

The Wealth Flywheel

A simple wealth loop:

1. Scalping generates cash.
2. Cash is transferred into investments.
3. Investments compound over time.
4. Compounding increases net worth.
5. Larger capital enables larger, safer trading.

This creates a positive feedback system:

Trading grows investing. Investing grows trading.

Segregation of Capital

Never mix trading capital with investment capital.
Maintain separate accounts:

- Trading account,
- Investment account,
- Emergency savings.

Rules:

- Do not pull investment money back into trading.
- Trading stays for trading.
- Investing stays for wealth.

Protect your future from your present.

Automated Wealth Transfer

Create a rule-based system for transferring funds.
Example:

Every month: withdraw 25–50% of trading profits and invest.

This builds wealth without emotional decision-making.

Profit → Transfer → Invest → Forget

Investment Instruments for Scalpers

A smart investment portfolio may include:

- index ETFs (broad market exposure),
- dividend stocks (cash flow),
- gold (hedge),
- bonds or T-bills (stability),
- long-term crypto (optional, small allocation),
- rental property,
- business equity or angel investments.

The exact mix depends on comfort and goals.

Time Horizon: Think in Decades

Scalping is days and weeks.
Investing is:

years and decades.

Compounding needs time.

$$(1.15)^{10} \approx 4.05$$

15% annual growth quadruples capital in 10 years. With monthly contributions (from trading), results accelerate dramatically.

Behavioral Shift: From Income to Ownership

When traders begin to invest:

- they stop chasing daily profit,
- they think in bigger timeframes,
- trading pressure decreases,
- mistakes reduce.

This improves trading performance.

Investing calms the trader. Calm traders win.

Using Passive Income to Support Trading

Eventually, investments produce cash flow:

- dividends,
- interest,
- rent,
- yield farming,
- royalties,
- business income.

This income reduces reliance on trading, enabling:

- selectivity,
- patience,
- emotional neutrality.

When you do not need to trade, you trade better.

The Ultimate Goal: Financial Independence

The path:

1. Learn to scalp.
2. Become consistent.
3. Withdraw profits.
4. Invest profits.
5. Build wealth.

Financial independence is reached when:

$$\text{Investment income} \geq \text{lifestyle cost}$$

At this moment:

Trading becomes optional.

Summary

Using scalping to build long-term wealth requires:

- segregation of accounts,
- rule-based withdrawals,
- consistent investing,
- ownership of assets,
- long time horizons.

Scalping funds wealth. Investing compounds it.

Trade for income. Invest for freedom.

20.4 Becoming a Hybrid Scalper + Investor

A trader reaches peak financial power when they combine two roles:

1. **Scalper** — generates short-term income.
2. **Investor** — builds long-term wealth.

This hybrid identity creates a system where short-term execution and long-term compounding work together.

Scalping pays the bills. Investing buys freedom.

Why Hybrid Is Superior

Pure scalpers face limitations:

- income is tied to screen time,
- performance pressure is high,
- no compounding of wealth,
- burnout risk.

Pure investors face:

- slow cashflow,
- limited liquidity,
- drawdowns without income.

The hybrid trader solves both problems.

Scalping produces cash. Investing multiplies it.

Identity Evolution

Early traders identify as:

"I am a trader."

Hybrid traders shift to:

"I am a capital allocator."

This shift is critical.

The job is no longer to simply trade. The job is to deploy capital intelligently.

Flow of Capital Between Roles

The hybrid model works like a machine:

- Scalping generates daily/weekly cash.
- A portion is withdrawn systematically.
- Withdrawn cash is invested.
- Investments grow through compounding.
- Investment income reduces trading pressure.
- Lower pressure improves trading performance.

This becomes a feedback loop.

$$\text{Income} \rightarrow \text{Investment} \rightarrow \text{Freedom} \rightarrow \text{Better Trading}$$

Portfolio Construction Strategy

A hybrid trader maintains:

- **One trading account**
- **One investment account**

The accounts never mix.

Trading account:

- used for executions,
- risk-managed,
- high-liquidity instruments.

Investment account:

- used for compounding,
- long time horizon,
- low stress.

Examples of investment assets:

- index funds,
- dividend stocks,
- gold,
- bonds,
- real estate,
- business ownership.

Cash Extraction Strategy

To be consistent, withdrawals must be rules-based.

Recommended:

Withdraw 25–50% of monthly trading profits.

This creates:

- reward for trading,
- discipline,
- long-term wealth.

But the trading account is not starved:

50–75% remains to grow the account.

Psychological Advantage of Hybrid Traders

Hybrid traders are calmer.

Why?

- They are not desperate for profit.
- They do not force trades.
- They can take days off.
- They do not fear losing streaks.

When trading is optional:

Performance improves dramatically.

Decision-Making Evolution

Hybrid traders behave differently:

- They wait for A+ setups.
- They skip choppy markets.
- They respect loss limits.
- They trade fewer hours.

Their motto is:

"No trade is a position."

Lifestyle Benefit

A hybrid trader:

- builds wealth automatically,
- reduces working hours,
- avoids burnout,
- has multiple income streams.

Freedom increases every year.

Wealth is time, not money.

The End State: Capital Sovereignty

The highest level of mastery:

You own your time.

Trading is no longer a job. It is a skill that funds the life you want.

> The hybrid trader does not chase the market. They build a life that the market funds.

Summary

Becoming a hybrid scalper and investor requires:

- identity shift from trader to allocator,
- separation of trading and investing accounts,
- systematic profit withdrawal,
- disciplined capital deployment,
- long-term compounding,
- psychological maturity.

> Scalping for income. Investing for wealth.Hybrid for freedom.

20.5 Your Multi-Year Roadmap to Mastery

The Scalpers Playbook is not a sprint — it is a strategic, multi-year journey. Progression is measured not by how fast you grow, but by how consistently you refine your edge. This section offers a realistic, step-by-step roadmap from beginner to professional, integrating trading, psychology, and wealth-building.

> You do not rise to the level of your goals. You fall to the level of your systems.

Year 1: Foundation and Survival

The first year is about understanding the game:

- Learn market structure, price action, and indicators.
- Develop a daily trading routine.
- Journal every trade.
- Build emotional control.

Primary objective:

Stop losing through mistakes.

Success is simple:

- Small profits,
- Small losses,
- Zero blow-ups.

Skills Built:

- execution discipline,
- risk management basics,
- chart reading,
- patience.

Trade size remains small.

Year 2: Consistency and Structure

The second year is more systematic:

- Focus on one or two proven setups.
- Use fixed risk per trade.
- Improve stop placement.
- Begin performance tagging.

This is where consistency begins.

Consistency first. Money later.

Evolution:

- The trader stops improvising.
- Rules define entries and exits.
- Losses are accepted, not feared.

Year 3: Optimization and Scaling

Now the trader is profitable with small size.

The goal of this year:

Optimize your edge and slowly scale size.

Steps:

- Increase size only after stability.
- Measure win rate and expectancy.
- Identify best sessions and market conditions.
- Remove low-quality setups.

This stage demands:

- emotional maturity,
- patience with slow growth,
- confidence under pressure.

You scale precision, not emotion.

Year 4: Income and Systemization

By year four, many traders can generate side income or even full income.

Key focus:

- creating routine income,
- systemizing processes,
- removing randomness.

Typical components:

- pre-trade checklist,
- post-trade review,
- weekly optimization.

Begin transferring profits:

$$25\text{–}50\% \text{ withdrawn monthly} \rightarrow \text{investment portfolio.}$$

Wealth-building begins.

Year 5+: Hybrid Mastery and Wealth

After 4–5 years of steady development, the trader becomes a hybrid:

$$\text{Scalper} + \text{Investor}$$

New focus:

- wealth compounding,
- asset ownership,
- time freedom.

Trading pressure disappears:

You do not need to trade.

This creates the highest performance.

Multi-Year Milestones

Every year adds new layers:

- More skill,
- More capital,
- More discipline,
- Less emotion.

Milestone summary:

- Year 1: Learn and survive
- Year 2: Consistency
- Year 3: Optimization and scaling
- Year 4: Income and routine
- Year 5+: Wealth and freedom

Time Horizons: Think Long

A scalper who commits for 5–10 years can achieve:

- elite skill,
- excellent income,
- compounded wealth,
- lifestyle independence.

> Most people underestimate 5 years and overestimate 5 weeks.

Behavioral Expectations

Mastery demands:

- consistency,
- humility,
- discipline,
- patience,
- learning from losses.

The market rewards emotional adults, not impulsive gamblers.

The Reality of Mastery

Mastery is not dramatic. It is repetitive.

> You become a master by repeating basics with excellence.

Pros are predictable:

- same routine,
- same setups,
- same risk,
- same discipline.

The Endgame: Freedom

Mastery delivers freedom:

Time freedomLocation freedomFinancial freedom

Trading becomes a choice, not a necessity.

> The goal is not to trade forever. The goal is to be free forever.

Glossary

This glossary provides concise definitions of key terms used throughout the book. It is designed for quick reference, rapid learning, and deeper technical clarity.

A

Absorption: Large resting orders that absorb aggressive buying or selling, often signaling exhaustion and potential reversal.

Algorithmic Trading: Automated execution using predefined rules to enter and exit trades.

ATR (Average True Range): Volatility indicator used to calibrate stop-loss and position sizing.

B

Bid: The highest price a buyer is willing to pay.

Block Orders: Large institutional orders, often hidden or executed in segments to avoid market impact.

Breaker Block: A price zone where the market reverses after breaking a previous high/low, used for entries.

C

Candle Wick: The thin line showing price movement beyond open/close; indicates rejection or aggression.

CHOCH (Change of Character): Shift in market behavior from trending to reversing or vice-versa.

Compounding: Growth through reinvestment of profits, increasing capital exponentially over time.

D

Dead Market: Low volatility, low volume market conditions where scalping becomes risky and unprofitable.

Discipline: Ability to follow rules and trade plans regardless of emotions.

Drawdown: Reduction in account equity from peak to trough during a series of losses.

E

EMA (Exponential Moving Average): Weighted moving average that reacts faster to price; widely used in scalping.

Execution: The precise entry and exit timing during a trade.

Exhaustion: Point where aggressive buying or selling loses momentum, often leading to reversal.

F

FVG (Fair Value Gap): Imbalance between buyers and sellers, creating a price "gap" that often gets filled.

FOMO (Fear of Missing Out): Emotional impulse to chase trades without edge or signal.

Footprint Chart: Visualization of volume at bid/ask for each price level, used for order flow analysis.

G

Gamma Scalping: Options strategy where traders adjust delta exposure to profit from volatility.

Gap Fill: Price returning to close an imbalance created by fast movement.

Greed: Emotional desire to overtrade or hold too long, leading to losses.

H

HH (Higher High): New swing high above a previous high, signaling bullish structure.

Hidden Liquidity: Orders not visible on the order book, often from institutions or iceberg orders.

HFT (High Frequency Trading): Algorithmic execution at extreme speed, often scalping micro-movements.

I

Imbalance: Unequal buying/selling pressure that creates directional movement.

Institutional Activity: Large-scale trading from banks, funds, or market makers.

Intuition: Pattern recognition built through experience and repetition.

L

Liquidity: Availability of buyers and sellers; high liquidity enables tight spreads and fast execution.

Liquidity Sweep: Price moving beyond a high/low to trigger stops before reversing.

Lot Size: Number of units traded; determines risk and reward.

M

MACD: Momentum indicator used for confirmation of trend strength.

Market Maker: Entity providing liquidity by quoting bid/ask prices.

Micro Pullback: Tiny retracement within a trend, often used for precision entry.

N

Non-Farm Payroll High-impact economic event creating volatility.

News Spike: Rapid price movement after a news release; can be traded but requires strict risk control.

Neutral Bias: State where a trader has no predisposition to direction — essential for clarity.

O

Order Flow: Real-time interaction between bid/ask, showing aggression and intent.

Overtrading: Excess trades without edge, often emotional rather than strategic.

OCO (One Cancels Other): Linked orders where execution of one cancels the other.

P

Price Action: Study of price movement without indicators.

Pullback: Temporary move against trend before continuation.

Psychology: Mental and emotional discipline required for consistent trading.

R

Range: Market oscillating between defined support and resistance with no clear trend.

R-Multiple: Risk-based performance measure: profit/loss in units of risk.

Reversal: Change in direction from up to down or vice versa.

S

Scalping: A trading approach targeting small price movements with high precision and frequency.

Stop-Loss: Predefined exit price that limits risk.

Structure: Sequence of highs and lows defining market direction.

T

Tape Reading: Interpreting incoming orders, speed, and flow for early signals.

Trendline Trap: False breakout designed to trigger stops before reversing.

Tick Chart: Chart that prints a bar after a fixed number of trades, not time.

V

Volume Burst: Sudden influx of volume, often signaling breakouts or reversals.

VWAP (Volume Weighted Average Price): Institutional benchmark average price; acts as dynamic support and resistance.

Volatility: Speed and magnitude of price movement, essential for scalping.

W

Win Rate: Percentage of winning trades.

Wick Rejection: Candle wick showing rejection at a price level, often used for entries.

Weekly Optimization: Scheduled review of performance to refine systems.

Z

Zero-Sum Game: In many markets, one participant's gain equals another's loss; edge is required to win.

Zone of Exhaustion: Area where momentum fades and price is likely to reverse.

This glossary will evolve with your experience. Definitions become deeper as your eyes mature.

Indicator Settings Library

This appendix provides a practical reference for indicator settings used throughout the book. These settings are optimized for scalping across multiple instruments, including forex, indices, gold, and crypto. They serve as starting points; traders are encouraged to adapt based on volatility, session, and personal data.

.1 EMA Clusters

Short-Term Momentum (1M to 5M)

EMA Fast Cluster: 5, 8, 13

- Entry timing within micro pullbacks
- Visual trend confirmation
- Scalping trigger zone

Medium-Term Structure (1M to 15M)

EMA Structure Cluster: 9, 20

- Trend continuation detection
- Reversal confirmation
- Filter for chop vs trend

Macro Bias and Anchoring

EMA Macro Filter: 20, 200

- Define overall market bias
- Avoid counter-trend entries
- Act as dynamic support/resistance

.2 VWAP and Deviation Bands

$$\text{VWAP} \pm n\sigma$$

- $\text{VWAP} \pm 1\sigma$ — first deviation
- $\text{VWAP} \pm 2\sigma$ — extended move
- $\text{VWAP} \pm 3\sigma$ — extreme stretch

Usage:

- Mean reversion
- Institutional bias anchor
- Dynamic support/resistance

.3 RSI

$$\text{RSI: } 14$$

- Micro-reversal signal when price sweeps liquidity
- Divergence on 1M/5M
- Overbought/oversold filter

Micro-Timeframe Version

$$\text{RSI: } 7 \text{ or } 5$$

- Faster reaction
- Ideal for extreme short-term conditions

.4 MACD

Standard setting:

$$\text{MACD: } 12, 26, 9$$

Applications:

- Momentum shift detection
- Trend continuation confirmation
- Avoiding chop entries

.5 ATR (Stop Engineering)

ATR: 14

- Stop-loss calibration
- Volatility-based trailing stops

Recommended formula:

$$\text{Stop} = 1.5 \times \text{ATR}$$

.6 Volume Profile

Volume Profile: Session or Visible Range

Outputs:

- Point of Control (POC)
- Value Area High (VAH)
- Value Area Low (VAL)

Usage:

- Identify liquidity zones
- Trade from value to value
- Fade extremes

.7 Footprint / Order Flow Settings

- Bid/Ask imbalance: 3:1 or higher
- Delta divergence: exhaustion signal
- Cumulative delta: trend strength

Signal Types:

- Absorption
- Exhaustion
- Iceberg detection

.8 Trendline and Structure Tools

Min Requirements

- At least two anchor points
- Third touch = validity
- Avoid diagonal guessing

.9 Universal Filters

These filters reduce false signals:

- Trade only above/below VWAP in direction of bias
- Use ATR for stop-loss scaling
- Confirm structure with 5M timeframe
- Avoid low-volume sessions

.10 Example Combination Setups

Trend Scalping

- EMA 5/8/13 aligned
- Price above 20 EMA
- MACD histogram rising
- VWAP slope aligned

Mean Reversion

- Price stretched beyond 2σ
- RSI divergence
- Volume spike exhaustion

Breakout Failure

- Sweep of high/low
- Rejection wick
- Return below/above VWAP

.11 Summary

- Indicators are tools, not signals.
- Their job is to enhance context.
- Structure and price action come first.

The trader wins through clarity, precision, and discipline — not through indicator overload.

Sample Playbooks & Checklists

This appendix provides practical templates for execution. They ensure that every trade is aligned with structure, risk, and discipline. These playbooks should be printed, laminated, or placed on the desk for daily use.

.12 A+ Trade Playbook Template

Before entering a trade, confirm all components:

Market Context

- Trend direction confirmed (1M + 5M).
- Price relative to VWAP (above for longs, below for shorts).
- Liquidity sweep or structural break.
- No major news in next 5–10 minutes.

Setup Criteria

- Defined entry trigger.
- Stop-loss location based on structure or ATR.
- Minimum reward: $2R$ or more.

Execution Rules

- Enter only on confirmation candle.
- No chasing missed entries.

Exit Strategy

- Partial profit at $1R$ or $1.5R$.
- Stop moved to break-even when structure is confirmed.
- Full exit at $2R$ or trailing logic.

Emotional State

- Calm, focused, no urgency.
- No revenge or tilt.

If any item fails → No trade.

.13 Daily Pre-Market Checklist

1. Sleep: 7+ hours?
2. Mind clear? (No stress, alcohol, or emotional load)
3. News calendar reviewed?
4. Identify sessions:
    - Asian,
    - London,
    - New York.
5. Key levels marked:
    - Highs/Lows,
    - VWAP,
    - Value Areas,
    - Liquidity zones.
6. No-trade periods defined:
    - low volume,
    - lunch,
    - pre-news,
    - exhaustion zones.

Preparation precedes profit.

.14 Post-Trade Checklist

Immediately after trade exit:

- Did I follow the plan?
- Was the entry valid?
- Was stop-loss respected?
- Was sizing correct?
- Was the market environment supportive?
- Emotional notes:
  - calm, anxious, greedy, fearful?
- Screenshot saved?
- Journal entry created?

Improvement happens after trading, not during it.

.15 Weekly Review Template

- Total trades taken:
- Win rate:
- Average R:
- Net R:
- Best setup:
- Worst setup:

Patterns to Study

- Times I performed well:
- Times I performed poorly:
- Emotional triggers:
- Market conditions:

System Refinements

- Remove weak setups.
- Add clarity to rules.
- Adjust time sessions.
- Adjust sizing if stability is proven.

Every week, the edge becomes sharper.

.16 No-Trade Conditions Checklist

- Inside lunchtime chop.
- Low volatility.
- Spread widening.
- Pre-news conditions.
- Emotional turbulence.
- Lost more than:
    - $-2R$ in a day, or
    - $-5R$ in a week.

Not trading is a profitable decision.

.17 Micro Pullback Entry Checklist

1. Trend and bias confirmed on 5M.
2. Price pulls into EMA 5/8/13 zone.
3. Volume contraction during pullback.
4. Entry trigger:
    - rejection wick, or
    - engulfing candle.
5. Stop below last swing structure.
6. Target:
    - $1.5R$ partial,
    - $2R+$ full.

.18 Liquidity Sweep Reversal Checklist

1. Sweep of high/low.
2. Fast rejection wick.
3. Return inside prior range.
4. Volume spike at sweep.
5. Entry on confirmation.

$$\text{Sweep} \rightarrow \text{Rejection} \rightarrow \text{Return} \rightarrow \text{Entry}$$

.19 Emotional Circuit Breakers

If any of the following occur:

- frustration,
- tilt,
- excitement,
- FOMO,
- revenge impulse.

Then:

Stop trading for at least 20 minutes.

Walk. Hydrate. Breathe. Reset.

.20 Desk Setup Checklist

- Clean workspace.
- No distractions.
- Screens arranged:
  - execution chart,
  - higher timeframe chart,
  - news/calendar,
  - journal window.

- Headphones if needed.
- Phone in another room.

Environment shapes performance.

.21 Summary

Checklists turn chaos into clarity.

- A+ playbook ensures high-quality trades.
- Pre-market prep reduces surprises.
- Post-trade analysis improves edge.
- Weekly reviews accelerate mastery.

We do not rise to our goals — we fall to our checklists.

Risk Templates & Journals

This appendix provides practical templates for risk control and performance journaling. They help transform scalping from an emotional activity into a repeatable business process.

Professional traders manage risk first. Profits are a byproduct.

.22 Daily Risk Template

Before trading, complete this checklist. If any item fails, reduce size or do not trade.

Capital and Limits

- Current account balance: _______
- Risk per trade (R): ____ (% of account)
- Daily max loss: ____ (e.g. $-2R$ to $-3R$)
- Daily max number of trades: ____

Rule: Stop trading if daily limit is reached.

Conditions to Trade

- No emotional stress (sleep, health, etc.)
- Market session active (London / New York)
- No high-impact news in next few minutes
- Spreads normal, liquidity sufficient

If conditions fail → Walk away.

.23 Trade Risk Template

Use this template for every trade.

Setup Confirmation

- Setup name: _______
- Direction: Long / Short
- Entry trigger: _______
- Stop location:
  - Structure low/high
  - ATR multiple
  - Outside liquidity
- Target structure:
  - $1R$ partial
  - $2R+$ full

No entry without predefined exit.

Position Size Calculator

- Account: _____
- Risk per trade: ____ %
- Dollar risk: _____
- Stop size (points/pips): ____

$$\text{Size} = \frac{\text{Dollar Risk}}{\text{Stop Size}}$$

.24 Post-Trade Journal Entry

Immediately after exiting the trade:

Trade Details

- Date:
- Instrument:
- Session: Asian / London / NY
- Entry price:
- Exit price:
- Stop price:

Outcome

- Result: +__R / -__R
- Execution quality: Excellent / Good / Poor
- Emotional state: Calm / Anxious / Overconfident / Angry
- Notes:

Every trade teaches. Write it down.

.25 Weekly Risk Review

At the end of the week:

Performance Metrics

- Total trades:
- Winning trades:
- Losing trades:
- Win rate:
- Average R:
- Net R:

Risk Observations

- Did I follow max loss rules?
- Did I stop for the day after limits?
- Any revenge trading?
- Any emotional trading?

The biggest risk is yourself.

.26 Monthly Risk Audit

Key Questions

1. What caused the biggest drawdowns?
2. Were they technical or emotional?
3. Which setups were the most profitable?
4. Which should be removed?
5. Did I respect daily and weekly limits?
6. Do I need to reduce risk next month?

Eliminate errors. Reinforce strengths.

.27 Drawdown Protocol

When drawdown exceeds a threshold (e.g. $-8R$ or $-10R$):

Immediate Actions

- Stop trading for 24–48 hours.
- Resume at half size for 2 weeks.
- Journal emotional triggers.

Goal: recover psychology before capital.

.28 Circuit Breakers

If any of the following occur:

- $-2R$ day,
- $-5R$ week,
- tilt or revenge impulse,
- exhaustion or stress.

Then:

Stop trading. Walk away. Reset.

There is always another trade.

.29 End-of-Month Evaluation

Quantitative

- Monthly net R:
- Largest winner:
- Largest loser:
- Max drawdown:

Qualitative

- Best discipline habits:
- Biggest emotional mistakes:
- One thing to improve:

Mastery is iteration.

.30 Summary

These templates reinforce:

- discipline,
- clarity,

- consistency,
- emotional regulation.

Trading success is not about prediction. It is about process, review, and improvement.

Recommended Reading

The following books, papers, and resources provide deeper insight into market structure, psychology, risk management, and professional trading disciplines. They complement and expand the material in this book.

Foundational Trading Literature

- **Trading in the Zone** — Mark Douglas Psychology, discipline, emotional neutrality.
- **The Disciplined Trader** — Mark Douglas Mental models and belief systems of traders.
- **Reminiscences of a Stock Operator** — Edwin Lefèvre Classic narrative on speculation and market behavior.
- **Market Wizards** — Jack D. Schwager Interviews with top traders; timeless insights.

Price Action and Technical Structure

- **Technical Analysis of the Financial Markets** — John J. Murphy Comprehensive reference on market structure and indicators.
- **The Art and Science of Technical Analysis** — Adam Grimes Deep statistical approach to price behavior and setups.
- **Al Brooks Price Action Series** — Al Brooks Microstructure, scalping patterns, and price action logic.

Order Flow and Microstructure

- **Trading and Exchanges** — Larry Harris Institutional market microstructure, liquidity, and execution.

- **Market Microstructure Theory** — Maureen O'Hara Academic foundation for how markets function beneath price.
- **Order Flow Trading for Fun and Profit** — J. Crooks Practical order flow concepts for futures and indices.

Risk Management and Position Sizing

- **The Mathematics of Money Management** — Ralph Vince Position sizing, drawdown control, risk-of-ruin.
- **Expected Value and Position Sizing** — Van K. Tharp Statistical foundations for trading edge and expectancy.
- **Hedge Fund Market Wizards** — Jack D. Schwager Real-world risk discipline and portfolio behavior.

Psychology and Performance

- **The Inner Game of Tennis** — W. Timothy Gallwey Performance under pressure; flow state.
- **Peak Performance** — Brad Stulberg & Steve Magness Habits, systems, mindset for elite execution.
- **Thinking, Fast and Slow** — Daniel Kahneman Cognitive biases, decision heuristics, emotional traps.
- **Mindset** — Carol Dweck Fixed vs growth mindset — critical for mastery.

Options and Gamma Scalping

- **Option Volatility & Pricing** — Sheldon Natenberg Foundation for volatility, gamma, hedging.
- **The Volatility Surface** — Jim Gatheral Modern volatility models.
- **Dynamic Hedging** — Nassim Nicholas Taleb Professional risk management under uncertainty.

Quantitative and Algorithmic Trading

- **Algorithmic Trading** — Ernest Chan Practical building and testing of automated strategies.

- **Advances in Financial Machine Learning** — Marcos López de Prado Machine learning applied to market behavior.
- **Trading Systems and Methods** — Perry Kaufman Comprehensive reference for building systematic approaches.

Crypto, DeFi and On-Chain Markets

- **Mastering Bitcoin** — Andreas Antonopoulos Foundation of blockchain and crypto markets.
- **Mastering Ethereum** — Andreas Antonopoulos Smart contracts and decentralized markets.
- **MEV and Flashbots Research Papers** On-chain liquidity, arbitrage, and execution.

Suggested Study Approach

1. Begin with psychology and risk.
2. Study price action and structure.
3. Explore order flow and microstructure.
4. Add options, gamma, and volatility models.
5. Finally, study automation and algorithms.

Depth is more important than volume. Mastery is built through repeated study and application.

www.ingramcontent.com/pod-product-compliance
Lightning Source LLC
Chambersburg PA
CBHW050519240926
51846CB00003B/622
* 9 7 8 9 3 5 6 0 2 1 5 8 7 *